# Praise for *The C*
# *Margaret Lloy*

'Thanks to the archive of the Rev. J. T. Rhys, the author's grandfather and private secretary to Margaret Lloyd George, we can now understand rather better the remarkable work and words of this indefatigable woman whose influence has previously been underplayed.'

Angela V. John
President of Llafur, the Welsh People's History Society

'Dame Margaret Lloyd George, the first wife of the prime minister, is commonly thought of as either a fringe figure or else a victim. She had to endure her husband's prolonged relationship with his secretary, mistress and eventual second wife, Frances Stevenson. This fascinating book, largely based on the archive of her private secretary, Mr O'Brien's grandfather, the Rev. J. T. Rhys, gives her a far more substantial role in history. It was indeed a remarkable life for any woman in high politics then, only a year after women first gained the vote. While there is no hint of the undercurrent of personal scandal, Rhys's account, with lengthy quotations from his personal notes, illuminates Dame Margaret's very active role in defending Lloyd George's coalition government against its many critics, notably embittered Asquithian Liberals thrown into the wilderness by Lloyd George's opportunist coalition with the Unionists (Conservatives) between December 1918 and October 1922. Dame Margaret is shown as an indefatigable campaigner in national and by-elections across England and Wales, and notably the fierce contest in Cardiganshire in

February 1921, a Liberal civil war that shook the government to the core. And she became a Dame.

This book is therefore an important contribution to Welsh history as well as to the story of party politics in general after the First World War. It contains important documentation of considerable interest not only to scholars but to any reader seeking to understand Wales's only prime minister and the background to the politics of the British left in the present day.'

Kenneth O. Morgan
House of Lords


'This highly readable book is a meticulous and valuable contribution to our undestanding of the admirable Margaret Lloyd George, offering fascinating insights into her life and to the lives of the public figures around her.'

Ffion Hague
Biographer of Margaret Lloyd George in
*The Pain and the Privilege: The Women in Lloyd George's Life*


'Finally, a serious study of the life and work of this remarkable woman. Dame Margaret was a hugely influential campaigner, political operator and activist. In this authoritative work, her contribution is deftly explained, bringing her bright, shrewd personality to light.'

Huw Edwards
Broadcaster and journalist

The Campaigns of
# MARGARET LLOYD GEORGE
THE WIFE OF THE PRIME MINISTER 1916–1922

*'My main task was to restrain her
from overdoing herself in doing good.'*

*Rev. J.T. Rhys*

The Campaigns of

# MARGARET LLOYD GEORGE

## THE WIFE OF THE PRIME MINISTER 1916–1922

RICHARD RHYS O'BRIEN

First impression: 2022

© Copyright Richard Rhys O'Brien and Y Lolfa Cyf., 2022

The publishers wish to acknowledge the support of
Cyngor Llyfrau Cymru

Cover photograph: Dame Margaret speaking from her car at
Taunton, July 1922, My South Western Tour, NLW Album 1291 C
Cover design: Y Lolfa

ISBN: 978 1 80099 231 3

Published and printed in Wales
on paper from well-maintained forests by
Y Lolfa Cyf., Talybont, Ceredigion SY24 5HE
*website* www.ylolfa.com
*e-mail* ylolfa@ylolfa.com
*tel* 01970 832 304
*fax* 832 782

# Contents

# Foreword

'The authentic voice of Dame Margaret Lloyd George comes through loud and clear.'

'A real breakthrough in understanding and evaluating the immense contribution of Dame Margaret.'

THIS GENUINELY REVISIONIST, impressive study attempts to rehabilitate the traditional assessment of the life and career of Dame Margaret Lloyd George (1864–1941), wife of our last Liberal Prime Minister David Lloyd George, who held that office from December 1916 until he was toppled from power in October 1922. Lloyd George was the only Welshman ever to become Prime Minister of the United Kingdom. His political career was buttressed by the unfailing support of his devoted wife: herself a natural political animal and immensely talented. She was, together with Mrs Catherine Gladstone, another formidable figure, one of only two Welsh women ever to assume the status of the 'first lady' of the United Kingdom.

Part of the problem has been the nature of the surviving sources. There are a fair number of interesting letters penned by Dame Margaret, mainly to members of her immediate family, and several hundred addressed to her, notably the long series from her husband when they were apart, as they often were. Many of these have been published in Kenneth O. Morgan, *Lloyd George: Family Letters, 1885–1936* (Oxford and Aberystwyth, 1973). There are also some helpful outline speech notes in her hand. But Dame Margaret never published any memoirs of substance, and only a few short interviews given by her survive. Nor did she ever attempt to keep a diary of any kind, not even an engagement diary, which would have been of immense value to historians and biographers.

There is only one biography, namely Richard Lloyd George, *Dame Margaret: The Life Story of His Mother* (London: George Allen & Unwin Ltd, 1947), but this was a highly personal account, replete with an array of lively anecdotes, written by the author in the wake of his father's recent death. Thirteen years later he also published an unfailingly critical quasi-biography of his father entitled *Lloyd George* (London: Frederick Muller Limited, 1960).

There is a great deal of interesting information about Dame Margaret in the two books published by Lloyd George's devoted, long-suffering Principal Private Secretary A. J. Sylvester (1889–1989) who, bitterly antagonistic to Frances Stevenson throughout their close working relationship, was forever anxious 'to restore Dame Margaret to her rightful place in history'. These two volumes were *The Real Lloyd George* (1947) and *Life with Lloyd George* (1975), the latter tome comprising most illuminating extracts from the author's diaries now held by the National Library of Wales.

There is also much of interest and relevance in the accomplished four-volume biography by John Grigg who is also highly sympathetic to Dame Margaret throughout.

But by far the most significant, substantial scholarly work in this field, a real jewel in the crown, is Ffion Hague's *The Pain and the Privilege: The Women in Lloyd George's Life* (Harper Press, 2008), a brilliant analytical study that looks perceptively at Lloyd George's intricate relationship with both his wives and a host of other female associates.

Hence Richard O'Brien's volume is a real breakthrough in understanding and evaluating the immense contribution of Dame Margaret. It succeeds admirably in rescuing his heroine from the so-called 'shades of oblivion' which have hitherto tended to shroud her life. The traditional depiction of the dumpy, dowdy Welsh woman, tied to the kitchen sink and bringing up her brood of five demanding children at her native Cricieth has long been proven wholly misplaced and indeed erroneous. This key volume certainly helps to redress the balance even further.

The motivation for the present work was the recent inheritance by the author of a quite substantial archive, hitherto unused, of correspondence, speech notes and papers squirrelled away by his grandfather the Rev. J. T. Rhys who served as a highly trusted and dedicated private secretary to Dame Margaret during the key period when she was resident at No. 10 Downing Street as wife of the Prime Minister. During those frenzied years she was extremely active in the metropolis in several different spheres.

As the Rev. Rhys was clearly notably conscientious in collecting and carefully preserving the material which came his way during those years, it is probably fair to say that this is the most important archive which exists illuminating Dame Margaret's many activities during the period of the Great War and the immediate post-war coalition government. The correspondence and speech notes in the custody of the National Library of Wales are woefully thin for these years. Hence the vital importance of the Rev. Rhys's archive. In order to fill out the narrative, Richard O'Brien has undertaken an immense amount of detailed, painstaking research work scouring through countless issues of national and local newspapers and journals. The underlying research work is admirably complete, original and indeed enlightening.

This volume, comprising twenty-one chapters, covers the crucial years of Lloyd George's second premiership after the end of the Great War when the Liberal Party was sharply divided into two distinct, perpetually feuding camps. Much of the focus is on Dame Margaret's immense contribution to a long succession of crucial election campaigns which took place during those frenzied years, several of these in south Wales. By now there is some appreciation of her vital role during the key Cardiganshire by-election campaign of December 1921 when she undertook several series of speaking engagements throughout the county in a powerful attempt to drum up support for the Coalition Liberal candidate Captain Ernest Evans against the Asquithian Liberal aspirant W. Llewelyn Williams. Captain Evans's resounding success there was widely attributed to Dame Margaret's all-important contribution.

But she also travelled widely to other venues throughout the kingdom, from Yorkshire to the West Country, delivering powerful perorations in support of a succession of Coalition Liberal candidates at a crucial time when support was gradually slipping away from the concept of an ongoing coalition administration. She regularly attracted large audiences wherever she travelled and she was praised to the skies for her contribution in various press columns. On numerous occasions she was even asked to stand as a parliamentary candidate herself.

Given the fresh archival material used here, these papers certainly cast original light on Dame Margaret's unremitting efforts to rally support for the flagging post-war coalition government and in building up various councils scattered across the realm which supported her husband. Also striking are the efforts which the Rev. Rhys himself made to encourage the Nonconformist communities which by this time were certainly beginning to lose faith in the so-called 'Welsh wizard'. Some new light is also shed on these times by the correspondence which was exchanged between the Rev. Rhys and the Lloyd George children.

Especially commendable is Richard O'Brien's use of contemporary press columns and Dame Margaret's personal speech notes to convey the ethos of these years. As a result the authentic voice of Dame Margaret Lloyd George comes through loud and clear to the reader. I commend the volume most highly.

J. Graham Jones
Director Emeritus, The Welsh Political Archive
National Library of Wales, Aberystwyth
December 2021

# Acknowledgements

APART FROM MY thanks to my grandfather for his squirrelling tendencies, I owe a great deal to all those who have shared in my efforts to shed more light on the public contributions of Dame Margaret.

My thanks to Dr J. Graham Jones, Emeritus Director of the National Library of Wales, who has painstakingly reviewed and expertly critiqued all my research; to Rob Phillips, the Political Archivist at the NLW, for his enthusiastic support; to the Lloyd George family, notably to David Lloyd George, 4th Earl Lloyd-George of Dwyfor for his review and encouragement of my work and permission to publish, as well as to Benjy Carey-Evans and Elizabeth George; to Angela V. John for her friendly and professional advice; to Helen Palmer of Ceredigion Archives for her research support; to the Addison, Astor, Balfour, Bonar Law/Sykes, Cecil, Fitzalan-Howard and Gladstone families for their permission to publish from family correspondence; to my Cardiganshire cousin Yvonne Davies for her translations from her poetical yet to me still unfathomable language; to Barbara Jones and the Museum of Lampeter for publishing my first article on Mrs Lloyd George; to Robert Cadwalader of Cricieth for sharing the fruits of his research; to Liz Moyle, Marian Hirst and Jane Cherrett for their Menai Bridge welcome; to Lyn Davies and to Michael Prest for their detailed comments on my draft manuscript; and to Ffion Hague for her generous advice and experience.

Thanks also to my editors Dr Jen Llywelyn, Eirian Jones and Carolyn Hodges for their patience; to Alan Thomas for his design; to Lefi Gruffudd and Y Lolfa for supporting this venture; and most of all to my wife Christine for reading all my research and being unfailingly encouraging and critical at the right moments.

# The Inspiration

MARGARET LLOYD GEORGE, wife of the Liberal politician David Lloyd George (Prime Minister, 1916–1922) left neither a diary nor a memoir, though at times the latter was said to be well under way. This absence is one reason why, today, Mrs Lloyd George is relatively unknown. Yet in her time she was one of the best-known women in Britain, and in the words of her recent biographer, Ffion Hague, 'one of the most successful Prime Minister's wives of all time'. To the extent she is known today, it is largely for her charitable works; she was made a Dame in 1920 for raising more than £250,000 (approaching £15m today) for her First World War Troops Fund.

This book aims to fill the void, to draw attention to Mrs Lloyd George's major contribution to British public life, not least as the first, and perhaps the only wife of a British Prime Minister to campaign on the political hustings around the country. The role of a Prime Minister's partner is undefined, in theory allowing each holder of the 'office' to fashion it at will – but minefields as well as opportunities abound. Mrs Lloyd George seized the opportunities and avoided the minefields with great skill, and while she only too often exhausted herself, she never over-reached.

The inspiration for this work lies in an archive of unpublished papers collected by my grandfather, the Rev. J. T. Rhys – 'JTR', her private secretary: speeches by Mrs Lloyd George, and correspondence with her whilst she was at 10 Downing Street.[1]

For these momentous years of her life it is one of the largest collections of such papers, and through it, supplemented by contributions from contemporary newspapers, the remarkable public life of Mrs Lloyd George emerges. The archive also includes my grandfather's tantalisingly brief notes, under the working title 'Dame Margaret Lloyd George GBE JP., Recollections and Reflections', for what might have become her autobiography. I like to think I have made progress with what he began nearly a century ago.

Due to the sheer amount of material, and intensity of her public activities, this volume is confined to her time as the wife of the Prime Minister during peacetime, from the Armistice in November 1918, until the close of 1922, when David Lloyd George left No. 10.

Much of this book has been written by Mrs Lloyd George, journalists and eye-witnesses, allowing the reader to be immersed in events as they happened. Newspapers, like all observers, have their own point of view, which I have identified where appropriate. Her favourable press, with the exception of the suffrage journals, may be ascribed in part to the fact that, during the Lloyd George-led Coalition, the Tory papers had little incentive to be critical of her. She was a genuinely likeable force for good; 'the acceptable face of Lloyd George', one might say. The *Daily Mirror* society columnist reported in 1916:

> One of the distinguished foreigners at the wedding of Prince George of Battenburg and Countess Nada Torby asked. 'Who is that bonny little woman over there?' I could have told him. She was Mrs Lloyd George and his adjective applied admirably to her.[2]

The observation sums up one of Mrs Lloyd George's great attractions: a kindly friendly face that stood out in a society crowd who were all dressed to impress.

In reality, little would be gained from criticising a popular figure. The best policy for a critic might well have been silence, not giving her publicity. *The Sketch* prefaced a full-page profile of her in 1915, when wife of the Chancellor of the Exchequer, as follows:

The forty-second verse of the unpublished, and in parts unpublishable, rhymes that the flippant diner-out of last year used to chant below his breath to his neighbour, and ascribe to the genius of Max Beerbohm, went thus:

> And I shall write a book, For Mr Martin Secker,
> About the good lady of The Chancellor of the Exchequer.

But it avails nothing to go to the Adelphi for a copy of the promised volume. Max never did, and never could, write a book about Mrs Lloyd George: she gives the caricaturist no openings, and takes none.[3]

JTR's Notes suggest her putative autobiography might have begun thus:

> This book does not owe its existence to any ambition on my part to appear among the body of authors distinguished or otherwise but to the importunity of the publishers.
>
> I would have thought that the number of volumes already published in whose titles the name Lloyd George appear – some way or another ought to have satisfied the public but Publishers say no and they ought to know.
>
> All I can hope is that reading the book will afford the readers some of the pleasure it has given me to recall from the shades of oblivion memories over half a century.[4]

It is my objective to rescue the public achievements of Mrs Lloyd George from the 'shades of oblivion', so that at least no one will claim that she did not engage in politics. With many women finally getting the vote in 1918, the opportunity for her to break precedents was there, and she grasped it as no one has done before or since. That she repeatedly withstood the calls to run for Parliament – in the words of her son Richard, having 'no political aspirations' – has too often been interpreted as a disinterest in politics. As a political campaigner, no one in her office before or since has done so much.[5]

A remarkable woman.

CHAPTER 1

# Margaret Lloyd George: The Story So Far

IF MRS LLOYD George had not begun her autobiography in the manner expressed in this book's introduction, JTR's Notes suggest that she might have started as follows:

> This autobiography will begin with the note [on which] most books of the kind end – the note of gratitude.
>
> Those Mysterious Powers that determine the conditions under which we start our race in this life treated me with unusual indulgence for which I am duly thankful. Nothing could have been more fortunate for me than the place where and the class into which I was born and the parents chosen for me.[1]

Margaret 'Maggie' Owen was born on 4th November 1864 on the family farm, Mynydd Ednyfed Fawr, Cricieth, Caernarfonshire. She was the only child of Mary Jones (daughter of William Jones, of the nearby farm, Tyddyn Mawr) and Richard Owen, a prosperous tenant farmer and committed Calvinistic Methodist. She enjoyed a good education at the girls' boarding school, Dr Williams' School, Dolgellau, which she regarded as the equivalent in quality to Newnham, Cambridge or Somerville, Oxford.[2]

Margaret took pride in her paternal lineage from Owain Gwynedd, the twelfth-century prince of Gwynedd, and maternal lineage from the tenth-century king of south Wales, Hywel Dda, who first codified Wales' medieval laws.[3] She was destined, perhaps, to be one of the only two Welsh-born women to reign in Downing Street – the first being Catherine Gladstone.

It is clear that she emerged from her upbringing as someone of strong character, who understood her purpose and how to make a contribution to society. In his Notes, JTR made a little list, reflecting the strengths of Margaret Lloyd George:

1. Naturalness, upset no one – courage
2. Resourcefulness – lapping up Memoranda for Speeches
3. Steadfastness with principles CM [Calvinistic Methodist] TT [Teetotal] Sabbatarian.

On 24th January 1888 Maggie married young local solicitor David Lloyd George, the Manchester-born son of schoolmaster William George, who died when David was eighteen months old. The boy was subsequently brought up in Llanystumdwy, less than two miles from Cricieth, by his mother Elizabeth George (née Lloyd) and her brother, shoemaker Richard Lloyd. Both the Owen and Lloyd families were wary of the match, not least the Calvinistic Methodist Owens, concerned that their daughter would be marrying a Baptist. The determined Maggie obtained her parents' consent. Their first child, Richard, was born in 1889.

Shortly after their wedding, David took on the Llanfrothen legal case that would begin to make his name locally and nationally: he helped a local Nonconformist family defy the Anglican vicar, who was refusing, in defiance of a recent law change, to allow a deceased man to be buried besides his daughter in the church burial ground. Though the church defended the case successfully in the local court, the High Court in London ruled in the family's favour. The country solicitor began to be noticed wider afield.

A year later, in 1890, Maggie's future direction changed radically and unexpectedly when David was elected (his initial loss being overturned after a recount) as the Member of Parliament for the Carnarvon Boroughs. He retained the seat for virtually the rest of his life. In the same year, their first daughter, Mair, was born, followed by Olwen in 1892, Gwilym in 1894 and Megan in 1902. Margaret preferred to bring up her children in the healthier climes of Wales, as opposed to smoky London, whilst David pursued his London career.

In addition to raising her family, Maggie's life was dedicated to supporting her husband – the first cottage-bred and Welsh Prime Minister – the man who would lay the foundation of the country's welfare state (observed closely from the Commons Ladies' Gallery by his wife), before becoming the 'Man Who Won the War'.

Geography, and David's roving eye, put the marriage under strain. The family lived in various flats and houses in London. In November 1907 tragedy struck when Mair – the apple of her parents' eyes – died after an operation for appendicitis. Her brother Richard later wrote: 'She would have outshone us all in her accomplishments as well as in her saintliness'.

When Lloyd George became Chancellor of the Exchequer in April 1908, and they entered No. 11 Downing Street, Megan was only six and the other children were still at school. It was not easy.

Mrs Lloyd George had been increasingly playing a political role, supporting Lloyd George and the Liberals, helping in the Carnarvon Boroughs constituency, and being the political hostess. Lloyd George was very encouraging from an early date, writing to her in 1895:

> You have more brains than you give yourself credit for. Mrs Freeman was telling Towyn Jones on Monday that you were the very essence of commonsense. She never met anyone so thoroughly sensible. That is exactly my opinion. You have the most valuable intellectual facility – sound judgement & if you have transmitted it to the children I shall be more content than if they have inherited all the troublesome powers I may be endowed with.[4]

In a sad postscript, the perceptive Kate Freeman, wife of a

Mayor of Swansea, died in January 1915 after being knocked down by a bus on a damp foggy evening in Whitehall, after leaving a meeting with Mrs Lloyd George in Downing Street.[5]

From the onset of war in August 1914, when party politics was set aside, Mrs Lloyd George went into a wartime campaign mode. She established her Welsh Troops' Comforts Fund, one of many such funds designed to supply additional clothing and other 'comforts', such as cigarettes and chocolate, to the troops, supplementing their initial supply. She actively promoted recruitment for the new Welsh Army. She supported the women's food economy campaign and the opening of communal kitchens; and continued her temperance campaigning, not least to ensure the munitions workers and the troops were sober, and that women, now on their own looking after their children, did not resort to drink for their solace. She played her part alongside many others, as charity activities boomed throughout the war.

At the onset of war David Lloyd George was Chancellor of the Exchequer. In 1915 he had become Minister of Munitions (to shake up war production), and in December 1916, after a spell as Minister of War, he became Prime Minister. The family moved next door to No. 10.

The end of hostilities in 1918 changed everything. Charity giving (already facing some fatigue) slowed. The majority of the new kitchens and restaurants were soon closed (not least because the private sector disliked the subsidised competition). Now the economy and society had to be put back on its feet. Once peace was finally negotiated by mid 1919, troops would return, hoping to resume their previous occupations. Many returned with disabilities that would hamper them for the rest of their lives. Meanwhile, women, having become a significant part of the wartime workforce, did not want to surrender the progress made in achieving a degree of employment equality with the men.

Mrs Lloyd George's peacetime campaigning phase focused

on meeting urgent welfare needs, especially in health, education and training, better living conditions, and support for women, children and the disabled. Monies still unspent from her Troops Fund would contribute to the nascent Pensions Ministry's schemes for long-term training and care. Drink was still a major problem, not helped by a forever-divided temperance movement. Healthy homes had to be built, and she campaigned for continued access to allotments, which had been a great boon to people during the war.

At the same time, party politics was back on the agenda and, with 8.4 million women finally getting the vote in 1918, the opportunity to break precedents was there. Margaret Lloyd George grasped it with both hands.

An undercurrent to this book's story is the personal domain, in part shaped by David Lloyd George's infidelity and his long affair with his political secretary, Frances Stevenson. In this book it remains an undercurrent: I cannot add anything to Ffion Hague's impressive and sensitive work, *The Pain and the Privilege*, that weaves together the stories of 'the women who loved Lloyd George' through all their complexities. Both relationships played important parallel roles in the life of Lloyd George. There remained very strong bonds of love and respect between David and Margaret all their lives.

The story of this book is also part of the story of my grandfather, the Cardiganshire-born Rev. John Thomas Rhys. Just two to three years younger than the Lloyd Georges, JTR had been an admirer of Lloyd George for many years. In 1890, while in London training to be a draper, he first heard Lloyd George, then a new arrival at Westminster, capture the audience as the final speaker at the Spurgeon Tabernacle at Elephant and Castle. 'The audience began to scatter but he arrested their attention and revelled the audience.' In 1895, shortly before JTR returned to Wales to train for the ministry, they met at a temperance meeting chaired by the notable preacher, the Rev. Elvet Lewis, at the King's Cross Welsh Congregationalist

Chapel. JTR engaged Lloyd George to appear at a later meeting, but the future PM cancelled the engagement. They met again in 1906 at the Cardiff banquet of the Welsh cultural society, the Cymmrodorion, and then casually at other meetings.[6]

JTR was a prominent temperance campaigner. In 1912 he dedicated his much-referenced research book *Wales and its Drink Problem* to the Chancellor of the Exchequer, David Lloyd George. Shortly before JTR's appointment to the No. 10 secretariat, they renewed their acquaintance in April 1917 when JTR accompanied a Temperance delegation to Downing Street. In November 1913 Mrs Lloyd George had spoken at the unveiling of the foundation stone of the second of the churches JTR built in south Wales.

In November 1916, wanting to do more for the war effort, JTR resigned his Swansea pastorate and moved to London to become the Metropolitan Secretary of the British and Foreign Sailors' Society (BFSS), an inter-denominational society supported by the Free Churches, providing havens around the world for seamen. In London he worked closely with Lady Sybil Rhondda as she promoted the wartime food kitchens. 'His energy and enthusiasm so impressed Mr Lloyd George that in 1917 he joined the Premier's secretarial staff at No. 10.'[7]

Coincidentally, as JTR moved, so did the Lloyd Georges. On 5th December 1916, the day before Lloyd George replaced Asquith as Prime Minister, Mrs Lloyd George launched an appeal for funds for the BFSS, a cause she had long supported. The appeal greatly increased the number of postbags delivered daily to the Lloyd Georges' new home. The country's seamen were under pressure to keep the country's supply routes open – even more so when, in February 1917, Germany announced its U-boats would attack all shipping, merchant or naval.

It is highly likely that JTR would have met Mrs Lloyd George quite soon, almost certainly at the BFSS AGM in May 1917, when she presented an early contribution of over £37,000.[8]

JTR was appointed to Lloyd George's secretarial staff in

1917, and was invited (probably in May 1917) to work with Mrs Lloyd George, succeeding William Lewis (the Hon. Secretary of her Troops Fund) as her private secretary.

Thus, as the cessation of hostilities approached in November 1918, JTR had spent two years 'doing more for the war effort', and was well established at No. 10, ready to work with Mrs Lloyd George for the reconstruction of the country.

## CHAPTER 2

# Peace, and the 'Coupon Election'

## (November and December 1918)

WRITING IN 1927, Margaret Lloyd George recalled the moment the world had been waiting for:

> The most dramatic moment of our life at No. 10 happened one Sunday evening in November 1918. We were at Walton Heath for the week-end, and I had returned in the afternoon from a drive, when Mr Lloyd George said 'Don't take off your hat, we're going back to Downing Street.' When we got there we had a little dinner party, consisting of General Smuts, Mr Churchill, my husband and myself.
>
> I did not know what news was expected, but during dinner I sensed excitement in the air. Suddenly a message came for my husband: 'You're wanted on the telephone from the War Office,' and he went immediately. The three of us that were left never spoke a word. Mr Churchill paced restlessly up and down the room. General Smuts and I sat in silence. He was not gone many minutes, but to us sitting there it seemed an age. When he returned he was smiling and said only, 'They're going to sign.' Then he shook hands with us all, even with me.
>
> I felt proud at that moment that I had been able to help him even a little in bringing the war to a successful end and the country out of its darkest hour.[1]

All around the country there was celebration, mixed with sorrow and relief.

In his Notes, JTR recorded her words:

> When I looked down on the crowd on Armistice morning it seemed a road paved with humanity.[2]

Time to hope. And to act.

Although armed conflict was now drawing rapidly to a close, at home the wartime political truce was ending – but in an unconventional manner. The major parties, notably the Liberals and the Unionists (also termed Conservatives or Tories)[3] and the smaller, steadily growing Labour Party, could have returned to their pre-war positions, consigning to history the Coalition Government, first established in 1915 under the Liberal leader Asquith, and later headed by Lloyd George. But now Asquith, still the Liberal Party's leader, was in the shade of his former protégé Lloyd George, 'the Man Who Won the War', and their erstwhile friendship had probably crossed the Rubicon in May 1918 when Asquith and his supporters opposed Lloyd George, by then Prime Minister, in the so-called 'Maurice Debate', a vote of no confidence which LlG survived.[4]

As a result, the Liberal rift would harden, and during the summer of 1918 the wartime Coalition partners, Lloyd George's Liberal supporters and Andrew Bonar Law's Unionists, prepared an unusual electoral pact. For many reasons, it was by no means clear how the electorate might vote in the first election since 1910, but a Coalition headed by Lloyd George (who, Bonar Law quipped, could have been elected for life at the time if he had wanted) offered Lloyd George his best opportunity to stay at No. 10 and, at the same time, keep the Unionists in government. The relationship between the two men, in contrast to that between the rival Liberal champions, was a good one, Bonar Law happy to play the role of deputy.

Many thought the wartime Coalition should stand down, but the choice was put to the country by calling an immediate election, tagged derisively by Asquith 'the Coupon Election', alluding to wartime ration coupons and in reference to the letter written by Bonar Law or by Lloyd George to their chosen Coalition candidates. At this point the Unionists and the combined Liberals (of either camp) had an almost identical number of MPs. The LlG-Bonar Law electoral pact was to choose either a Coalition Liberal candidate (in other words a Lloyd George-supporting Liberal) or a Coalition Unionist to stand in each constituency, the party without the coupon standing aside. In some cases, those not chosen refused to stand aside.

Thus the Liberal split was now transferred into the open arena of a public election, not just within Westminster. The contest, at times also involving Labour candidates (a few of whom received the Coalition 'Coupon') might pit a Lloyd George Liberal against an Asquithian (or Independent) Liberal, with Unionist voters being asked to support the Lloyd George Liberal; or a Coalition Unionist fighting against an Asquithian Liberal, with Lloyd George Liberal voters being asked to vote Unionist.

It was into this unusual electoral campaign that Mrs Lloyd George became the first, and it seems the only, wife of a Prime Minister to campaign actively on the hustings outside the confines of her own husband's constituency. She might be calling on Liberals to prefer her husband's Liberal candidate over an Asquithian Liberal, a sensitive request especially when old friendships were being tested, and doubly sensitive when calling on Liberals to vote Unionist. Over the next four years she was frequently having to reassure her audience that she and her husband would always be Liberals.

It was complicated, and perhaps not an ideal way for a country to come together after war. As Mrs Lloyd George would later say, the peacetime Coalition would no longer have the unifying factor of the 'Mighty Leveller' of fighting a common enemy to make it work.[5]

On 12th November, the day after Armistice, rumours of a Liberal reunion circulated. Not only did Asquith praise a speech given by Lloyd George, but Margot Asquith called on Mrs Lloyd George:

> The fact that Mrs Asquith a few days ago called on Mrs Lloyd George at 10 Downing Street is seized upon by the politicals as an indisputable sign that the spirit of compromise is in the air, and that the two rival statesmen may after all be seen in the near future working in complete harmony.[6]

The *Edinburgh Evening News* headlined the same story: 'MRS ASQUITH UNBENDS.' But if there was any peace between Liberals, it was short-lived.

The Coupon Election was unique and unpredictable for many other reasons. Not only was it eight years since the previous poll – the 1915 election having been called off due to war – Parliamentary boundaries had been changed, altering the electoral mix within constituencies.

It was the first election where the vote was awarded to women over 30 – although a fifth of women over 30 were ruled out because they did not fit the property or other qualifications. It was the first time women could run for Parliament. Adding to the complexity, the votes of the troops still serving abroad – many being young men empowered with the vote for the first time – were to be canvassed, and their votes had to be counted, delaying the final tally until 28th December.

Meanwhile, the party landscape continued to shift, the Labour Party steadily gaining credibility, competing with Liberals for the socially conscious voter.

Two important factors encouraged Mrs Lloyd George to campaign. First, Lloyd George was fully occupied with organising the peace negotiations, with little time to campaign. But Mrs Lloyd George could fly the 'Man Who Won the War' banner on the hustings in support of her husband's Coalition candidates.

Secondly, the scene was set for women to be actively campaigning, including addressing the women voters. The suffrage movement, still campaigning for *all* adult women to have the vote on the same terms as men, did not want a low turnout. In 1918, when 8.4 million women over 30 obtained the vote, the voting age for men was simultaneously lowered from 30 to 21, adding another 7.4 million men – a sop to those against women's suffrage, and to get the Act through Parliament. Men who had turned 19 whilst in war service could also vote, though there was confusion as to whether this applied to men already discharged.

Given male wartime casualties, equal suffrage in 1918 would have seen women electors outnumbering the men. Women over 21 won the vote in 1928, finally equalising eligibility between the sexes.[7]

Mrs Lloyd George, with her ringside view, was now well versed in politics. She later recounted how she steadily increased her political work, while raising her young family:

> As soon as he began his political career I began to help him. I started by canvassing with him at election time in Criccieth. Then I began to address meetings, just occasionally at first because I was nervous – more often as my nervousness left me. The next step was to take a hand at organising during election time, but I still only worked in my husband's constituency.
>
> It was not until three elections had passed and my youngest son was six years old that I began to do political work in other parts of the country. Megan was not born then, and the other four children were old enough to be left... [in the care of grandparents].
>
> The beginning of the difficult years for us both came with our entry into Downing Street when my husband went to the Treasury. Megan was then only six years old and three of the other children were still at school... I had my own full share of social work, and at the same time I had always to be ready to help my husband, and even to be his deputy as often as possible at minor engagements when his presence was required more urgently elsewhere.[8]

She was also an experienced observer. In 1908, as Lloyd George argued the case for his welfare reforms in the House of Commons through the night, her solitary night-time vigils behind the Ladies' Grille had been noted:

> Up in the gallery one devoted woman kept the vigil... on the floor of the House a man after long years in Opposition was making the great fight of his life, and the lone woman, regardless of the approaching dawn, was watching the contest... It was not until the Chancellor of the Exchequer some time toward the morning vanished in the shadows behind the Speaker's chair that the silent watcher above broke her lonely vigil.[9]

Writing in 1922, Lloyd George's former private secretary, Ernest 'Ernie' Evans, the young man whose parliamentary career was launched by Dame Margaret's most notable political campaign, commented:

> Mrs Lloyd George takes a keen personal interest in the debates in the House of Commons, and many an hour have I seen her listening to speeches.
> There was sound method in Mrs Lloyd George's attendance in the Commons. To be made acquainted, second-hand, with speeches can never be as satisfactory as first-hand listening, so to speak.[10]

Thus, by December 1918, two years after her husband became Prime Minister of Great Britain, the motherly woman from Cricieth was well positioned to take the opportunity at hand, as her daughter Olwen would later observe:

> I think it was this election which really proved her worth, and showed the people of Wales and beyond that she was a forcible character in her own right.
> Olwen Carey Evans[11]

Mrs Lloyd George's electoral campaign started on 22nd November, accompanying her husband to Wolverhampton – the PM's visit was to accept the Freedom of the Borough.[12] At the Grand Theatre, Lloyd George launched the reconstruction campaign, to make Britain 'a fit country for heroes to live in', a phrase which later spawned slogans such as 'Homes Fit for Heroes'.

The *Aberdeen Daily Journal* noted the precedent being broken:

> I do not think that political history has so far recorded a Prime Minister's wife taking part in her husband's electoral campaign. But these are days when precedents are broken. ... A keen advocate of woman suffrage, she has developed greatly within recent years as a platform speaker, and now is quite the 'finished' orator. Her reason for going to Wales is that Mr Lloyd George may not be able to go there himself. His electioneering arrangements have been disorganised by the urgency of State business, particularly the visit to London of M. Clemenceau.[13]

This time Mrs Lloyd George was not going to campaign actively in the PM's safe seat, Carnarvon Boroughs, but in fourteen other constituencies across south and north Wales, adding Huddersfield and Crewe for good measure. On 5th December she took the train to south Wales to begin her 'whirlwind', two-week tour, on behalf of Coalition candidates.

## Week 1: South Wales, 5th to 7th December 1918

Mrs Lloyd George reviewed the first week in an interview with the Cardiff-based *Western Mail*, a Unionist/Tory paper, which would be supporting all Coalition candidates – in Wales, mostly Liberal:

> After her return to Cardiff from Blaenavon Mrs Lloyd George kindly gave a *Western Mail* representative some of her impressions. She was quite enthusiastic, and said: 'Yes, it has been a most gratifying experience. Everywhere I went large audiences met me, and convinced me that South Wales and Monmouthshire are sound for the Coalition. When the Prime Minister gets my report I know he will be pleased, for naturally he is anxious that

those candidates who are unqualified in their support of Coalition should be returned. I do not know how far my own personal appeals will carry weight but it is important that no risks should be run in constituencies where the Coalition is being attacked. However, my experiences during this remarkable tour have shown that the men fighting on the side of Mr Bonar Law and my husband are doing well.

'I started at Chepstow on Thursday in support of Mr Martineau, and then came to Cardiff to stay overnight with Col. and Mrs Lynn-Thomas [a pioneering surgeon with whom she worked a great deal]. Friday I was at Ammanford and Llanelly speaking for Mr Towyn Jones, at Swansea and Morriston for Sir Alfred Mond, at Neath for Mr Hugh Edwards, and at Aberavon for Major [Jack] Edwards. They were all splendid meetings, and the people made me feel quite at home amongst them.'[14]

In the Monmouth constituency, her Coalition Liberal candidate, Hubert Martineau, was defeated by a Coalition Unionist – an occasion where neither was awarded the Coupon.

Speaking for Major Edwards, she praised the Welsh Army and made the personal link: 'I was telling my eldest son I was coming to support Major Jack Edwards, and he told me, "Well, mother, tell them he is a thorough good sort, that he has done his bit in the trenches".'[15] Major Edwards and Dame Margaret's son Richard had served together in the 38th Division; in 1916 the Division had suffered appalling casualties at Mametz Wood, on the Somme, in their first major engagement. The battlefield is today marked by a dramatic Welsh dragon.

Major Jack Edwards won his seat, Aberavon, but not before an Independent Coalition candidate had been persuaded to stand down by the Coalition Chief Whip.

On Saturday I again started from Cardiff for Pontypridd, where I spoke for Lieut. Lewis, and afterwards, on the way to Merthyr, had to stay at Cilfynydd, Maesycwmer, Treharris (I believe I have given the places correctly), as well as other centres on the way, to address crowds that had gathered to watch us pass through. It was a most encouraging experience.

In Pontypridd, a Unionist candidate without the 'Coupon' refused to stand down, but came a distant third for his pains. In Merthyr the crowd was so large that her meeting had to be moved to the relatively new Olympic skating rink:

> After tea with Mr and Mrs Hankey [the Mayor and Mayoress], I spoke at the Rink at Merthyr in support of Sir Edgar Jones. That was a great and impressive meeting, and the indications given me of Sir Edgar's success were particularly pleasing to me. Looking back it is difficult to recall in sequence all the places I did speak at, but I think the next place was Blackwood, where I spoke for Capt. Williams, and afterwards I found splendid gatherings awaiting me at Pontypool, Abersychan, and Blaenavon, in Sir Leonard Llewelyn's division.
>
> At Pontypool and Blaenavon the meetings were for women only, and, without posing as a prophetess, I predict great support for Sir Leonard from the women, and from what I hear his popularity amongst the working men is proverbial.[16]

The proverbial popularity of Sir Leonard was not enough to win him the seat. He was contesting the seat against Reginald McKenna, the notable Asquithian Liberal and Lloyd George opponent (and one time ally), and Thomas Griffiths, a Labour trade unionist and early Ruskin College student. McKenna's North Monmouthshire seat had been abolished in the boundary changes.

Mrs McKenna went into battle on her husband's account, saying that 'for many years her husband had worked hand in hand with Mr Lloyd George. She had been a great friend of Mrs Lloyd George, and she therefore deeply regretted that the Premier had seen fit to send a letter of congratulation and good wishes to Sir Leonard Llewelyn, and was also sending his wife to speak on the Tory platform.'[17]

But neither Mrs McKenna nor Mrs Lloyd George was successful. The personal and Liberal civil war allowed the Labour candidate, Griffiths, to win the seat, with Llewelyn second, and McKenna third.

In Bedwellty, Coalition Liberal Capt. Williams lost in a straight contest with Labour. The industrialisation of the coalfields of south Wales made it one of the earliest regions to become Labour strongholds, as they largely remain today.

The *Daily Mirror* estimated that on the Saturday, Mrs Lloyd George travelled 95 miles, saw 20,000 people, addressed ten meetings – four in the open air – spoke in two languages, and in four different constituencies.[18]

In south Wales, seven of Mrs Lloyd George's candidates, all Coalition Liberals, won, whilst three candidates lost: Sir Leonard Llewelyn, in Pontypridd, where the Liberal vote split; Capt. Williams, in Bedwellty, in a straight fight with Labour; and Hubert Martineau, Coalition Liberal, in Monmouth, losing to the Coalition Unionist where the 'Coupon' had not been awarded.

There was more to come:

'And where next? Oh,' said Mrs Lloyd George, with a happy laugh, 'on Monday I go to Wrexham, and on Tuesday Caernarvonshire, then I shall be at Huddersfield and Crewe, and on Thursday back again in Caernarvonshire, and on Friday in Anglesey.'

'Phew!'

'Yes, you may well stare,' she remarked smilingly, 'but, really, although it is hard work it is work that I think is due as my quota in the election, and I am doing my best. All I hope is that little effort will have good effect amongst the electors, and especially amongst the women voters.'[19]

Mrs Lloyd George's typical stump speech, often short, was such as that reported from her first stop, in Ammanford:

Ladies and gentlemen, I am very sorry to be so late coming here this afternoon, and I am sure you will bear with me when I tell you that I can only give you about two minutes. Some have called this South Wales campaign of mine a whirlwind campaign, and I think it is so. You know that a whirlwind does not stop long in the same place. I am due in Llanelly now, but I wanted to put in a word for

Mr Towyn Jones. He has been a great supporter of the Coalition Government, and I am sure you will agree that he is the best man to represent you in Parliament. [Applause]

I hope there are many among the women present who have the vote. I have heard that some women are not very keen with their votes put in their hands by the Coalition Government – but I hope they will not be indifferent, because, when we come to reconstruction, the things that will be put forward – better housing, child welfare, &c. will touch every one of us; and I hope you will all go to the poll. I have heard of some men who were afraid they would not get home in time for the poll, but when asked about their wives, said: 'Oh, they are not going to the poll.' Mrs Lloyd George finished her speech in Welsh, and left amidst loud applause.[20]

A short list of policies, encouraging the women to vote, and partly delivered in Welsh. Not for the first time, running late, and a brief appearance. In most cases, she would be on a platform with the candidate, often addressing a friendly crowd, and if tricky questions came up, that was for the professional politicians to handle.

In Llanelli Mrs Lloyd George spelt out the Coalition's socio-economic priorities:

It was a fact that millions of people in this country had fared better during the war than ever before. During the past four years they feared the 'eagle' [Germany/war], but had no fear of the 'wolf' [hunger/poverty]. A London doctor said the other day that the children had the time of their life during the war. She wanted to say emphatically that there was something radically and criminally wrong with a social system under which people were better off in war than in peace. Such a system was not only unsatisfactory, but a scandal and a menace.

How could we alter that? By such a system that would make people better off in peace than in war. The land laws must be reformed. Allotment-holders should be allowed to retain the land they now held. That would be a small measure of reform, but it would make an immense difference to the happiness of thousands of homes. More and better homes must be within reach of the people. One man, one vote, one house, one family. The drink problem must be dealt with effectively; the men disabled in the war must be provided for. Nobody was so likely to secure these reforms for us as the Coalition Government. The men who were able to win the war were well qualified to lead us in time of peace. [Applause][21]

Speaking in Swansea for Sir Alfred Mond, she referred to the ongoing peace process:

No one liked war and we must prevent a recurrence by securing the best terms of peace from the enemy now, and they must make that quite clear. [Cheers] Germany must pay for the devastation and for the trouble and anxiety that nation had caused.[22]

'Germany Must Pay' would be one of the divisive issues in the campaign, and a serious faultline running through the Versailles Treaty and the post-war settlement. During the election the Coalition hardened its approach, concerned that being soft on Germany might worsen their chances. Here Mrs Lloyd George may have disagreed with her husband's tactics. Lord Riddell wrote in his diary, that Christmas, that she had said to him:

It is a pity that the PM accepted any assistance from Beaverbrook and Rothermere [owners of the *Daily Express*, and of the *Mirror* and *Daily Mail* respectively] at the election. I am sure he did not need it. I don't trust them or like their ways. The PM does best when he goes his own way and keeps clear of all those wire pullers and people who want nothing but to grind their own axe.[23]

In Merthyr the wife of the Prime Minister didn't pull any punches:

Mrs Lloyd George, at Merthyr yesterday, said there were three classes of people who hate war – men who have been to the war themselves, people who have conducted the war, and people who have done nothing to conduct the war and have done nothing to bring it to a successful conclusion.[24]

In some attention to detail Mrs Lloyd George did her best to capture all votes on offer, as an addendum to her interview shows:

'By the way,' added Mrs Lloyd George, 'the *Western Mail* will oblige me by explaining one little matter which, if it is not explained, may be misunderstood. At one of the places – I think it was Blackwood – a letter was handed to me. It was signed 'Democrat' and the opening sentence ran 'Dear Madame, – In my humble judgment your esteemed and distinguished husband and our worthy and tried Premier is the only available man capable and safe to lead the democracy of our country during the coming years.' Thinking it was just an eulogy of Mr Lloyd George, I did not in the excitement of the moment read any more of the letter.

But since the meeting I have read the letter through, and find that a question was asked in it in order that I might answer at the meeting. Unless I give an answer that voter's support may be lost, and that is where I now want the aid of the *Western Mail* in giving my explanation and apology. The writer wanted to be assured that, whatever the result of the election, Mr Lloyd George will never forsake democracy. My answer now is that my husband will never forsake the cause of democracy whatever happens. His whole life is a guarantee of that, and his wife goes bail for him in it.'[25]

On the Sunday, before leaving for north Wales, Mrs Lloyd George visited the Prince of Wales Hospital for the limbless and disabled in Cardiff. The hospital – one of Mrs Lloyd George's most important 'movements in which I have been interested' – was a new project led by the pioneering surgeon Sir John Lynn-Thomas,[26] who, with his wife, was hosting Mrs Lloyd George during the election.[27] The hospital was first opened in 1914 in a private house, and by then had grown, in larger premises, and was formally opened by the Prince in 1918. Mrs Lloyd George visited often, chairing the hospital council.

## Week 2: 9th to 13th December 1918: North Wales, Huddersfield and Crewe

The whirlwind sped on to north Wales, Mrs Lloyd George stressing the need for a just peace and better housing. She began on Monday, 9th December, in Wrexham, speaking for Sir Robert Thomas, one of the most generous donors to her wartime funding campaigns, including her Troops Fund and her British and Foreign Sailors' Society Appeal. Addressing an audience of women, she called for improvements for teachers' pay: 'It was not fair that the teachers did not receive as much as unskilled labourers. The profession must be made attractive so that the best men and women would adopt it.'[28]

On Tuesday, 10th December, after speaking in her husband's Carnarvon Boroughs (Lloyd George had one opponent, unlikely to depose him), she spoke in the more rural Carnarvonshire Division for Major Breese, the Coalition Liberal, who was in a three-way contest with an Independent Labour candidate and an Independent Liberal. The first job Lloyd George had had was with Charles Breese's father, in Porthmadog, so there was a long relationship, to which she referred in her remarks.

Wednesday, 11th December, was spent in Huddersfield and Crewe, first speaking for Sir Charles Sykes, with whom she and Lloyd George had stayed when he spoke there in 1914 – when police manned the vestry of the Congregational chapel where they worshipped, in case of suffragette disturbances. In Crewe, speaking to a women's audience in support of Sir Joseph Davies, a Coupon Liberal (the Unionist stood down), she delivered one of her familiar quips:

> They wanted more houses for the people, and women's influence might be advantageously used in house planning. Surely women could plan their own houses. [Hear, hear] They knew more about them than others. A woman at one of her (Mrs Lloyd George's) meetings had said that women lived in the house and men were only lodgers. [Laughter and cheers][29]

It was then back to Caernarvonshire and Anglesey for further speeches on Thursday and Friday, 12th and 13th December, as the whirlwind became a hustle:

> Mrs Lloyd George, continuing her whirlwind campaign in Caernarvonshire, addressed five crowded meetings yesterday, starting at Conway, then on to Llandudno Junction, Llandudno, Penrhyside, and finishing at Trefriw. At Llandudno she received a tremendous ovation in the Town Hall. She had addressed meetings in Wales from Holyhead to Cardiff, she said, and knew the people were with them. She had no fear in looking forward to December 28th and a great triumph for the Coalition.[30]

A planned stop in the new Denbighshire constituency may not have taken place, where David Saunders Davies (Conservative) won very comfortably.

Election day was spent in Pwllheli.

All-bar-one of her six second-week candidates were successful, Labour being less of a power in the more agricultural communities (as opposed to industrial, coal mining south Wales). The unexpected result, and one of the major surprises in the country, was in Anglesey, where the incumbent Sir Ellis Ellis-Griffith was defeated by Brigadier Sir Owen Thomas. The latter, standing for Independent Labour, was well known as a local farmer and had been a prime mover in establishing the Welsh Army. At the close of the war, the fund he had established for the troops was merged with Mrs Lloyd George's Troops Fund and both were integrated into the King's Fund for Disabled Officers and Men, run by the Pensions Ministry.

On her return from the fray, Mrs Lloyd George again reflected on the experience in an interview with *The Sketch*:

> Mrs Lloyd George returned from a most extensive tour very hoarse, and rather uncertain as to the sort of language she ought to use when she got to No. 10 Downing Street. I ventured to ask the Prime Minister's wife how her first electioneering campaign

had progressed. 'I hardly know in which language I have been speaking,' said Mrs Lloyd George. 'At some places I have talked in English, and at other places in Welsh. It has all been rather difficult and I am afraid at times my thoughts have become rather mixed – but at any rate I am sure that I have made my meaning clear. And my reception was lovely – yes, lovely everywhere.'[31]

The *Carmarthen Journal* noted the new precedent that had been set:

Has Mrs Lloyd George, in her Election tour in South Wales created a record, not only as a Premier's wife but as a public speaker? Those who know her best in her domestic sphere would have thought her better fitted for the role of Mrs Gladstone, whose one object in life was to look after the Grand Old Man's physical comfort and wellbeing. Lady Palmerston is said to have been as indefatigable a politician as her husband, but never addressed a public meeting! Lady Salisbury would have been aghast at the idea of stumping the country at election time. Mrs Lloyd George, as little of a politician as either, and naturally of a more retiring disposition than any, has taken the plunge they dreaded. And see what she has accomplished! Even a Nonconformist preacher deems himself hard worked to be called upon to preach three times of a Sunday. But last week Mrs Lloyd George thought nothing of addressing half-a-dozen different public meetings in a single day![32]

That said, Mrs Lloyd George was often well within her comfort zone, zipping from one chapel or mission hall to another, places where she would have experienced the power of public speaking from an early age.

With women voting, the logic for the wife of a Prime Minister to be out talking to the new electorate was faultless – and Mrs Lloyd George took the opportunity. There remains a puzzle as to why the other Prime Ministers' wives have not followed suit, though in 1918 a unique set of factors were at play that made it work. The right person, in the right place, at the right time? All Prime Ministers' wives have made their own contributions, according to their own abilities, interests, and in keeping with the times. But none have campaigned in the political arena as openly as did Mrs Lloyd George.

Overall, the whirlwind reaped a dozen wins and four losses. Did her presence make a difference? Where the contest was close, probably yes. She ensured that, in the wake of the war, 'the Man Who Won the War' was well represented, and by a popular figure, providing a focal draw for the crowds. Later, as the government's popularity declined, his absence from contests would be criticised (even though by convention Prime Ministers did not campaign at by-elections). But for now Lloyd George's Coalition Liberals had found a formidable campaigner to rally support and keep waverers onside.

Lloyd George was certainly happy with his wife's support:

> You have done brilliantly. Your tours have been the feature of the campaign. You have been flitting about though so much, I found it impossible to know where to write you.[33]

In February 1919 the winners – or 'those MPs I am responsible for', as she referred to them in a note to JTR – would also break precedent, entertaining Mrs Lloyd George to dinner at the House of Commons, as reported by the *Dundee Evening Telegraph*.

> The honour which is to be paid to-day to Mrs Lloyd George is unique in the history of Parliament. Never before has the wife of a British Prime Minister been entertained to dinner within the sacrosanct portals of the House of Commons in recognition of political services... Mrs Lloyd George's hosts are the various MPs on whose behalf she made election speeches in the recent general election. She is a fluent and very winning speaker, and her lightning dash through Wales – during which on one occasion she delivered as many as ten speeches in one day – was an achievement which very few women politicians could hope to excel.[34]

This list of dinner attendees survives on a sheet of No. 10 notepaper (on the back of which was part of a speech that was never given, in Derby, March 1919), under the heading, 'These are the names you wanted.' The list also includes Mr Herbert Lewis (for whom she did not campaign), who won the new University of Wales seat against Millicent Mackenzie, the first woman to run for a seat in Wales. Lewis was a major player amongst the London Welsh and JTR helped him in developing the Welsh Guild of Graduates. (illustration 8)

Also on the list was Richard Morris, the Denbighshire-born Coalition Liberal MP for Battersea, one of 23 MPs with Welsh associations who had won seats outside of Welsh constituencies.[35] As he was competing against the notable Mrs Despard it would be surprising if Mrs Lloyd George had campaigned in person for him. On 17th February, shortly before the dinner, Morris was asking questions in the Commons concerning the employment of disabled soldiers and sailors, an issue of interest to Mrs Lloyd George.

Olwen, Gwilym and several ladies were present at the dinner. Towyn Jones, although recovering from a severe attack of bronchitis, was determined to be there,[36] and Mrs Lloyd George herself shook off a cold to attend.

Nationally, the election was a triumph for Lloyd George, for his Coalition, and for the Unionists. With the support of many Tory/Unionist votes through the electoral pact, Lloyd George's Liberals won 127 seats, whilst his Coalition partner party, the Tories/Unionists, won 379 seats (up from 271), a majority of 81. Labour increased their tally from 36 seats to 57. For Asquith's Liberals it was a disaster, winning only 36 seats and Asquith suffering the personal humiliation of losing his own seat at East Fife. The Liberals, combined, won 163 seats, down from 272. Asquith himself would return to Parliament in a by-election in Paisley in 1919.

While Liberals divided, Labour continued to consolidate a power base, winning 20.8 per cent of the popular vote, against a combined 26.4 per cent for all Liberals (and 38.4 per cent for the Unionists). But Lloyd George, the minority head of the Coalition, was beholden to Tory support. The glory of winning the war would soon lose its gloss if recovery did not come apace.

In Ireland there was major change, heralding the conflict that would bedevil Lloyd George: Éamon de Valera's Sinn Féin, standing on an Independence manifesto, almost eliminated the Irish Parliamentary Party, winning 73 of the 80 seats. Constance Markievicz (née Gore Booth) was the sole winner from the 18 women standing for election across the British Isles, and became the first woman elected to Parliament. But Sinn Féiners did not take their seats in Westminster. Sinn Féin's absence in fact gave the Unionists a potential majority of well over 100 (save for any Unionists not favouring Coalition). Lloyd George's position was down to his reputation as a leader.

The final public duty of 1918 for Mrs Lloyd George was entertaining the visiting US President Woodrow Wilson and his wife. On 27th December she joined Mrs Wilson, Mrs J. W. Davis, the wife of the American Ambassador, and Mrs Asquith at a lunch hosted by Lady Reading, wife of the British Ambassador to the USA, Lord Reading – and long-time ally of Lloyd George.[37] The next day, 28th, it was off to the Guildhall where the President was honoured with an Address of Welcome. 'Clubman', the gossip columnist of the *Pall Mall Gazette*, having witnessed the President's processional drive through London, managed to create a personal story:

> The cheering for Wilson had died away; the guard had been dismissed, and the crowd had already scattered when a large motor-car carrying a white-haired gentleman and a quiet little lady, turned the corner. When the crowd realised that Mr and Mrs Lloyd George occupied the forgotten motor, an amazing scene took place. Never have I heard wilder cheering, and it was

with difficulty that the police were able to force their way to the Premier's side. I caught Mrs Lloyd George's eye, and her look as she nodded recognition told me this was one of the proudest moments of her life.[38]

Finally, on 30th December, Mrs Lloyd George entertained the ladies to tea at No. 10. Alice Balfour, the younger sister of Arthur Balfour (Prime Minister from 1902 to 1905, and Foreign Secretary under Lloyd George's Coalition), wrote a letter of apology:

Whittinghame, Preston Kirk, Scotland
Jan 2, 1919

Dear Mrs Lloyd George

I have just seen in the papers that you were so kind as to invite me to tea and meet the President of the U.S.A. and Mrs Wilson. I suppose as I was in Scotland my brother forgot to tell me, but I hope that at any rate he explained that it was impossible for me to have the pleasure of accepting. Having seen in the papers that you had been so kind as to ask me however, I feel that the least I can do is to thank you very much and express my great regret at my enforced absence.

May I congratulate Mr Lloyd George on the great Coalition success.

Believe me... yours sincerely Alice Balfour.[39]

Alice Blanche Balfour (1850–1936), one of the earliest female pioneers in genetics, and an accomplished water-colourist, lived much of her life with her brother in London, when she wasn't in her Scottish home.

On New Year's Eve, Mrs Lloyd George, Brigadier-General Sir Owen Thomas (now MP for Anglesey), William Lewis (Hon. Sec. of her Troops Fund, her former private secretary) and three others were appointed trustees of the King's Fund for Disabled Officers and Men, run by the Ministry of Pensions (incorporating her Troops Fund and Sir Owen Thomas' Fund). Mrs Lloyd George was the first woman trustee.[40] The Fund attracted controversy, however, when seeking charitable donations, it being suggested it was thereby seeking to reduce the State's existing obligation to support the disabled.

There was a long road ahead.

CHAPTER 3

# Settling the Peace
## (January to July 1919)

NINETEEN NINETEEN STARTED quietly for Mrs Lloyd George. She published an article on 'Mothers' Wages' and awarded Good Service ribbons to 55 Land Girls in Caernarfon. Her first priority was to ensure that Lloyd George was suitably accommodated in Paris for what would be six months of peace negotiations. She travelled to Paris in late January, accompanied by Megan, and after three weeks returned to London on a destroyer, possibly to avert any disruption from a threatened rail strike – which was called off. (illustration 3)

Megan returned shortly afterwards to Paris, chaperoned by Frances Stevenson, and was installed at a finishing school in Neuilly-sur-Seine, the well-to-do residential suburb of Paris, adjacent to the Bois de Boulogne. Megan had thrown herself into the party life at the British HQ, the Hotel Majestic (dubbed the 'Megantic' by some observers of her enthusiasm).[1] Some discipline was necessary. For a while she communicated with JTR a combination of requests spiced with short asides – 'I hope Downing Street is still keeping up the reputation of sobriety that it holds when I am there. It does need a steadying hand!! I hope you are not encouraging Mrs Lloyd George to overdo herself.'[2] (illustration 2)

In Paris Megan began two important friendships, with Thelma Cazalet, who became almost an 'adopted member' of the Lloyd George family (and later an MP), and Ursula Norton-Griffith. (In 1922 Ursula married J. H. Thorpe MP;

their son Jeremy becoming the future leader of the Liberal Party.)

In Mrs Lloyd George's absence, the Duchess of Marlborough wrote asking for support for her re-election bid to the London County Council.[3] JTR duly relayed a positive response to the Duchess, who retained her seat, albeit narrowly.

With hostilities over, concerts at No. 10 became a feature of 1919, often promoting Welsh artistes. On Monday, 10th February, two days after returning from Paris, Mrs Lloyd George presided over a concert at No. 10 at which Misses Blodwen and Irene Hopkin figured prominently: young musical sisters from Aberkenfig, a village near Bridgend, and most probably known to JTR.[4] Artistic people were important to Mrs Lloyd George: JTR's Notes for her putative autobiography recorded, 'People who have interested me: 1. Preachers (came first in order of time); 2. Politicians; 3. Artistic; 4. Miscellaneous.'

The next day Mrs Lloyd George travelled to north Wales for more public duties. In Bangor, she opened an exhibition of war trophies in aid of the local District Nurses' Institute. Later she would express her dislike for the display of such 'trophies', and when presented with a war gun, hid it behind bushes.

Also in Bangor, joined by her former secretary, William Lewis, now with the Ministry of Pensions, she formally opened a new training school for ex-servicemen, established by the Ministry. She said that 'it was a great help to north Wales to have such a gentleman so full of energy as Mr Wm Lewis, who had real sympathy with the disabled men'.[5] In three large shops side-by-side in Bangor's High-street, several rooms had been adapted for an electrical engineering class, a commercial class, a shoemaking class, and a tailoring class, each limited to 15 men.

The school had the most modern equipment and the pupils would 'be afforded the fullest opportunity of attending the laboratories of the University College' so that 'in six months no establishment in Great Britain will afford the training possible at the Bangor centre'.

The committee was also considering a hairdressing class: 'Major Mitchell, director of training, noted that already 5,000 to 6,000 alien hairdressers had been deported, together with 20,000 to 30,000 tailors, and men were wanted to fill their places.'[6]

After one speaker had recounted problems in coordinating responsibilities for treatment and for training between the Ministry of Pensions and of Labour, William Lewis recounted that when he went to the Ministry:

> the first packet of papers he opened was bound with white tape... an excellent omen; but [he] found out that owing to the number of new ministries formed they had run out of the stock of red tape. [Laughter] Apparently, most of the red tape used in this country had been made in Germany.[7]

More seriously, he warned that if disability claims were made on dubious grounds, this would undermine public support for such ventures.

The left-wing *Daily Herald* interestingly juxtaposed a remark made by Mrs Lloyd George in Bangor, 'that the chief aim of the centre was to make the men independent rather than that they should be mollycoddled and pampered by the country',[8] with a comment by a businessman in Blackburn:

> Out of work and pension fever is spreading like disease. The system is injurious to the masters, and more, the employees. Pensions to able-bodied men and women have a tendency to kill their ambition, progress and usefulness.[9]

Managing the diary and fulfilling all promises was a challenge – as Mrs Lloyd George reflected later:

> There were shoals of letters alone to be read and answered and the invitations to open bazaars and other charitable functions, all of which I accepted quite happily at first, became so numerous in the end that I had to limit them to three a week.

Had it not been for my secretary, I am afraid I would have forgotten many an appointment. One such occasion, when forgetting an appointment would have upset an important function, comes clearly to mind. I had been so busy from ten in the morning that I had not had time even to take off my hat, and at six thirty was feeling utterly done and grateful for the prospect of a little rest. Just to make sure, however, I went to my secretary and said, 'That's all for today, isn't it?' My heart sank when his answer came back promptly, 'Hospital dinner at seven and you've to receive the guests.' I said nothing only 'Order the Car', and went to my room to dress. But in twenty minutes I was down again and drove off to keep the appointment.[10]

Back in 1914, when missing a second engagement with the Croydon Women's Liberal Association (of which she was President), *The Times* reported her hosts' irritation:

Miss Morland, chairman of the meeting yesterday, said it was a pity Mrs Lloyd George had accepted the presidency. She seemed to undertake more than she could always fulfil; it was not treating the association fairly. When she received the letter [from Mrs Lloyd George] she felt too angry to be sorry, but was not going to move a vote of censure.

All the same, she thought they would do better to elect a president in a less exalted position instead of one whose face they, as an association, had not yet seen. The executive were not recommending her re-election, preferring to leave the matter with the meeting.

A member suggested that Mrs Lloyd George should first be consulted before a new president was elected, but the other members dismissed the idea with some scorn. Ultimately, it was referred to the executive to make an appointment, apparently of a new president.[11]

But then she was merely wife of the Chancellor of the Exchequer.

While in north Wales, Mrs Lloyd George had been due to deliver a speech to the Free Church men and women of Derby.

But it was not to be. On the evening of 12th February, in Derby, her abandoned host, the Rev. Stephen, unburdened himself to his audience:

> Announcing the disappointment, the Rev. W. Stephen said the greatest blow of all came since Sunday, when he got a telegram from Downing street that Mrs Lloyd George could not come. He considered that after he had announced that she was coming, he ought to give the grounds for his statement, and then they would know as much about it as he did. This was an age in which they were told there should be no secret treaties.

In July 1918, six months ago, he received a letter stating:

> 'I am directed by Mrs Lloyd George to acknowledge the receipt of your interesting letter, and to say that it will give her great pleasure to visit Derby for your annual meetings in February. ["This is February," interjected Mr Stephen.] Mrs Lloyd George will be glad if you will select either Feb. 5 or Feb. 12 ["This is Feb. 12th," he added], but regrets it impossible for her to spare time for two meetings. Will you please therefore decide whether you wish her to preside in the afternoon or in the evening. Wishing you every success in your work.'
>
> Mr Stephen suggested the evening because he thought the larger audience could have a look at the Prime Minister's wife and hear a few words from her lips. He had been to London three times since. The last time was on Friday last, and each time he called to see if was still all right. [Laughter] Besides that he had written a letter every now and then. [Laughter] On Friday he called Mrs George's secretary for the last time to see if everything was in apple pie order, and he was assured she would attend, the secretary knowing nothing whatever to prevent her. He arranged for a special carriage from St Pancras to Derby, and he saw the stationmaster at both ends.
>
> When he got back to Derby he said to his wife, 'It is all right', and there he was now saying it was all wrong. He was disappointed, and felt he was entitled to their sympathies. [Hear, Hear][12]

A letter from Paris, from Mrs Lloyd George to JTR, now explains it all:

> Dear Mr Rhys
> I want you to find out if you will from the Women's Free Church Council whether the Derby meeting is the annual meeting or are they going to have a meeting afterwards in London. If the annual meeting is going to be in London I must attend that one to give up the chair to the next President. They asked me something about it. I want to know so I can arrange my next visit to Wales. Find out at once will you and put a note in the pouch. Mind I do not want to attend 2 Free Church Council meetings. MLG[13]

The Council meeting was, in fact, to be in Sheffield, so Derby was cut.

JTR preserved his handwritten draft of her speech, and in reading it you would think it had truly been delivered.[14] (illustration 27) The speech is a good example of her survey of the challenges ahead: helping unwanted babies even if 'There are phases of the problem we may deplore and may not care to discuss'; that after sending comforts to the fighting troops, they needed support now, having returned with their injuries; and that there were things the State could not do but still needed to be done. The deletions, underlinings (here italicised) and annotations retained below reflect a speech in its final preparations:

> Fellow members of the Free Churches
> It is a great relief to find myself here tonight. The strikes and the rumours of strikes ~~have~~ made me fear more than once that I might be unable to redeem my promise to be here this evening. It is true that ~~we have now~~ I had the alternative of an aeroplane, but the British *weather* ~~might be unfavourable~~ is not dependable.
> I fancy it is ~~a relief~~ an equally great relief to your excellent Secretary, Mr Stevens [*sic*]. One wonders sometimes why some men have even been appointed to the positions they occupy. I do not wonder why Mr Stevens [*sic*] is Secretary of the Derby Free Church Council. He seems to have a rooted objection to taking 'no'

from people like myself; and once he has had a promise of a visit he takes care that the visit is paid.

Then, after further friendly compliments to Derby...

It is a pleasure also because this is a meeting of Free Churchmen. The Prime Minister and I are Free Churchmen by tradition, connection and association and it is always a ~~privilege~~ pleasing duty to assist in such work as you are doing.

Well, Ladies & Gentlemen, we are living in eventful and even critical times. Happily, the war is over. Let us hope we shall soon be able to say that *all* war is over for *ever*. Still, though the war is over, all our troubles and tasks are not over. The work of the soldier ~~is over~~ has ended, but our work as ~~citizens~~ civilians and Christians is ~~only beginning~~ far from ended. There are today gigantic, delicate, intricate, and urgent problems awaiting solution. The Army is being demobilised; but that only means that the time has arrived for the Churches to mobilise their forces.

What services can the Churches render to the nation and to humanity today? I have not come here to unfold a programme. I would like, however, to suggest a few things arising out of my own experience and in connection with various movements with which I am associated. As some of you may be aware ~~Lady Henry~~ I have lately sent out an appeal for Lady Henry Somerset's scheme for unwanted babies. It is a very noble work. There are phases of the problem we may deplore and may not care to discuss. But it cannot be denied that to care for a helpless babe is a patriotic, humane ~~itarian~~ and Christian task. With all ~~our~~ her efforts Lady Henry cannot provide for one child in every 20! I venture to suggest that the Free Church Council would do well to ~~try and~~ take a share in this work. Adoptions & Institutes. [A pencilled annotation.]

Think again of the *women* who are War Victims. There are tens of thousands of these outside all churches bearing ~~their~~ heavy burdens of ~~grief~~ sorrow in loneliness and almost despair. Thousands are fighting a bitter & hopeless battle with poverty; and a still more bitter and hopeless battle with grief. They need and deserve all the support and sympathy we can give them. To ~~cheer and~~ diligently seek these out in order to cheer and help them is another task not unworthy of the very best people in our churches. Visit 'at homes' wd be a real, kindly & worthy service to make these brave women feel neither forgotten nor broken.

Think again of the *men* who have been in the war and to whom the world can never be the same again. I am thinking of the men who have come home ~~broken in~~ whose careers have been wrecked, and those who because they fought so ~~valiantly~~ valorously for us cannot now fight for themselves. We *owe* them a debt we may *own* but which we shall never be able to discharge. We ~~provided for them~~ made provision for their cheer and comfort while we needed them to fight for us. We owe it to ourselves to provide honourably for them now that the fighting is over. If the excellent temporary arrangements of the YMCA can be made permanent by the Free Church Council they will render the State in general & the soldier in particular a great service. This is another task I ~~commit to you~~ commend to you.

These are not all. These are only samples. They are things State cannot do at all: or certainly (?) not solved as State. State kind. Church kindly.

How far the Churches should take part in politics is a question that has often been discussed. I am not going to attempt to decide it. I venture however to make one or two suggestions. There are now millions of women voters. They have now political power. But political power does not always mean political wisdom. I think if the Churches helped to spread political knowledge among women voters they would be rendering the ~~women~~ State very great service. Besides, that, I think the Free Churches might exert their great influence to ~~secure~~ protect our statesmen against unfair methods often attempted to harass them in their work. Fair ~~think~~ play is a distinctively British virtue but I sometimes think it a rare plant in the political garden.

The draft speech survives on the obverse of two letters, also of some interest, in that one is from William Lewis to JTR (the only known remaining correspondence between the two private secretaries) on the stationery of the Troops Fund, and the other to Mrs Lloyd George from G. A. Sawyer, the silversmith who did frequent tasks for the Lloyd Georges, notably in fund-raising and other financial matters. On the obverse of the third page is JTR's handwritten list of her victorious MPs at the House of Commons dinner held in her honour on 26th February. (illustration 8)

JTR, a Free Church man himself, doubtless was sorry to have let down the Derby audience. The speech also draws on a powerful address Mrs Lloyd George gave on 6th November 1918, shortly before the Armistice was declared, to the Welsh Temperance Association at the Welsh chapel in King's Cross.

> Power is one thing to possess, political wisdom is quite another thing. Women have won the right to vote. We must now see that they vote right. Political power without political wisdom is a great danger. (Bolshevism is a case in point.) As women will have such a large a share of political power in Britain, it is of the utmost importance to take all the means in our power not simply to organise but also to educate them.
>
> I hope also that women will not only study how to vote but study the problems which have to be solved so as to bring an original & fresh contribution to the discussion on such questions as housing, health & above all Temperance. Women ought to be able to make invaluable suggestions, although we cannot exactly see the end of the War, still we all feel *'Mwy sydd eisioes wedi ei dreulio nag sy'n ôl o'r anial dir'*. [Literally, 'More has already been spent than is left of the desolate ground.'] The end of the War will be the beginning of a new era in the history of the world. What kind of a world is that.[15]

During wartime, on St David's Day Mrs Lloyd George, Olwen and an army of ladies would have been focused on selling flags for the Troops Fund, buttonholing financiers in the City, traders in Covent Garden and the public on the London streets.

In peacetime, the London Welsh community reverted to more conventional practices – in 1919 attending the Welsh National Festival dinner at the West End's Café Monico. Mrs Lloyd George and Olwen joined the Prime Minister, the principal guest. Sir Vincent Evans, leader of the Welsh cultural revival and Treasurer of the Troops Fund, presided over nearly 400 guests. The Lord Chancellor, the newly appointed Lord Birkenhead (F. E. Smith, a strong ally of Lloyd George but an opponent of Welsh Disestablishment and of women's suffrage), proposed the toast of 'Wales, the Prime Minister, and the coming Peace.'[16] Rev. Elvet Lewis proposed a toast in Welsh to the PM.[17]

The magazine *The Landswoman* celebrated St David's Day by publishing an amusing imaginary dialogue, in Welsh, taking place when Mrs Lloyd George had been awarding good service ribbons in Bangor in January, wherein one winner explains all to a bemused visitor. Here is a translated extract:

'Oh, so you say; you understand things better than I do – this war has turned the world upside-down, I'm afraid to talk to anyone these days, – everything is so different to when I was young. I would never consider wearing the type of clothing you have – I would have shocked the world back then.'

'Quite possible, but the present crisis has created the need for Landgirls, and you know it would not be appropriate for a girl to go to the fields to tend the soil in flimsy shoes, and long skirts that would drag in the soil and get very dirty. See how dry my feet are, and my joints are supple, and after all it's our well-being that's important.'

'Yes, quite true – have you worked on the land for long?'

'Yes, I have faced the seasons of sowing and reaping, Summer and Winter more than once, and I truly believe that my work and that of the girls here in Caernarvon today have stood us in good stead to win the war.'

'You surprise me! So you have been fighting for your country?'

'Yes, fighting the worst enemy – that of starvation. You know how close we came to starvation, but with the help of the Landgirls, enough food was produced to turn things against the enemy.'

'Wonderful, my girl – thank you so much for helping me to understand things in these days. And every blessing on you all. I did feel rather upset on seeing girls trying to look like men, but I'll remember from now on that you are all helping your country. Good day, my girl.'[18]

In early March Mrs Lloyd George travelled to Sheffield and York, delivering her speech 'How to Utilise Women's Growing Influence in National Life', on the 'Homes Fit for Heroes' theme. She drew on her homemaker's perspective, sensitive to the post-war social challenges, and championing the advancement of women, and urging that advances made in wartime were not lost.

> In these houses that they were going to build they must see that they've got plenty of fresh air, plenty of room, plenty of water, and plenty of light, both natural and artificial.
>
> Then again [she said], she believed that they ought to get gardens and allotments with their houses. Perhaps they did not agree with her, but she believed it was very essential. She thought that they would all agree that during the war the gardens and allotments were a great boon to the people, and she could prophesy that they would still be a great boon to the people in peace time.[19]

The trip was to close her year as President of the Women's Council of the Free Churches, in Sheffield, and to call on the Free Church community in York. Keeping the Nonconformists onside with Lloyd George was important. The York visit closed with a breakfast at the Royal Station Hotel, attended by more than 30 Free Church guests, followed by a tour of the city with her hosts, after which she was able to slip unnoticed, with a friend, onto the 12.19 train for London.[20]

Back in London, after addressing a Mansion House meeting in support of a proposed nurses' club for London,[21] Mrs Lloyd George addressed the Conference of the Royal Sanitary Institute, London (today The Royal Society for Public Health), linking child welfare with the quality of the buildings they lived in:

> There may be a great deal of infant mortality due to palpable negligence... but I really think much more of it is due to want

of knowledge and want of resources, bad housing, lack of
ventilation, and lack of fresh air. The poor mother has no less
love for her child than those who are better off. What we have
to do is to try and help those poor mothers. We must make it
possible for them to bring up their children in good health as a
first step. [Applause][22]

Her remarks were published in the Journal *Unity* and in
the *Journal of The Royal Sanitary Institute* (retained in the JTR
Collection), with a further typed version of her speech in the
NLW collection.[23]

On Tuesday, 18th March, she again addressed the welfare
of women and children, at a League of Roses meeting, at
Islington Town Hall.[24]

There were official events for the Prime Minister's wife
to attend. Victory was still being celebrated: on 29th March,
accompanied by Olwen and Megan, she joined the Lord
Mayor and Lady Mayoress of London on the Mansion House
balcony to watch the Victory March of the Horse Guards from
Buckingham Palace to the Lord Mayor's residence.[25]

There were other causes to support: The Children's Jewel
Fund – which sold donated jewellery and the like in aid of
the welfare of mothers and children, and of which she was
Vice President – held a sale in London's Regent's Street, at the
Marshall and Snelgrove department store. After presenting
some prizes she took the opportunity to buy an ostrich feather
fan for Olwen's birthday.[26]

She and Olwen had recently been taken by Alfred T. Davies,
MP for Lincoln, to visit a south London chocolate factory – a
birthday treat before Olwen travelled to India?[27]

While Mrs Lloyd George's national political contribution
has been overlooked, her contribution to local governance
in north Wales has not been ignored. Indeed it is often cited
as the exception, misinterpreting the fact that she never ran
for Parliament as reflecting disinterest in politics. It would

be fairer to say that she, like JTR, was wary of the world of Westminster politics.

At the beginning of April she was amongst the first three women to stand for the Cricieth Urban District Council, two of whom were successful: Leah Thomas, a Liberal activist and suffragist, second in the poll, and Mrs Lloyd George, third equal with the headmaster of the county school. The third woman candidate missed out by three votes. This was a public position she would hold for the rest of her life, chairing the Council for three years, 1931 to 1934. (illustration 9)

While she was hopeful of success in the Cricieth polls, Mrs Lloyd George was no longer favoured in the eye of Asquithian women:

> Yesterday the National Liberal Women's Federation met – 600 [?] delegates from all parts of the country. Mrs Lloyd George and Mrs Fred Guest stood, among others, for a place on the committee. Hitherto Mrs Lloyd George had always headed the poll. Yesterday, they – the wife of the 'Liberal' Prime Minister and the wife of the 'Liberal' Chief Whip – were at the bottom, while the wives of the 'Old Gang' were high up in the list. Of course, things cannot and will not rest where they are. I suppose Mrs Lloyd George will soon proceed to start a Coalition Liberal Women's Federation. We shall see the result.[28]

Which, in effect, is what transpired. Mrs Lloyd George had long been an active member of the Federation. In Wales her defeat was certainly noticed:

> With Mrs Lloyd George off the committee, the Women's Liberal Association in Swansea noted that there was no Welsh representative on the national committee, which they hoped could be remedied at some time.[29]

In May Lady Stafford Howard from the Llanelly branch of the Women's Liberal Federation resigned in protest at Mrs Lloyd George's expulsion.[30]

The *Labour Leader* observed: 'the sins of the husband are visited upon the wife'.[31]

Coincidentally, at the time when Parliament was affirming the right of women to sit in the House of Commons, the March issue of *The Millgate Monthly* ran a character sketch and interview with Mrs Lloyd George, by Mr George A. Greenwood. When informed of this 'she said she had not had time to look at the papers', but 'the wife of the Prime Minister proclaimed the news most interesting', but adding, 'I doubt personally whether many women will go in for such a political career as membership of the House entails, but those who do ought to be of great service to the country, and particularly to women. Their influence upon legislation ought to be very useful indeed when questions affecting the welfare of women and children are being considered.' Mr Greenwood said that he considered it 'a true sign of the sure coming of British democracy that such a woman, from such a home, so simple and so profound, should be the wife of our first statesman'.[32]

She would later write in her 1927 article 'Petticoats behind Politics' (when no longer 'wife of the Prime Minister') 'I shall doubtless call down vials of wrath on my defenceless head if I divulge a private inclination of my own, and say that I do not believe in young married women having political careers! I am even so old-fashioned as to unabashedly declare that I consider that they have a more important "career" to hand, in the bringing up of their children!'[33]

On 31st March, Mrs Lloyd George attended a dinner with the men of the advertising world, who showed their ability to talk up a product by claiming to be 'one of the civilising forces of the world':

When Mrs Lloyd George responded to the toast of 'The Ladies' last night at the festival banquet of the National Advertising Society, she remarked that she appreciated and felt the honour, which was 'a compensation for being the wife of the Prime Minister'.

Lord Leverhulme [the soap manufacturer, Liberal, and

philanthropist] presiding, said that if the Kaiser had been a
member of the society and had learned the true art of advertising,
there would have been no war. The advertising man was one of
the civilising forces in the world. A special fund had been set up
to help advertising men who had suffered from the war, and the
widows and orphans of those who had been killed.[34]

Mrs Lloyd George then signed 50 menu cards, given to the
attendees, who despite having been given her autograph for
nothing, then auctioned them repeatedly to each other to raise
a further £200. To paraphrase the motto, as they say, 'sell it,
sell it and sell it again'.[35]

Mrs Lloyd George, social observer and commentator, returned
to print with a front page article in the Paris daily newspaper
*Le Journal* entitled *'Aprés La Guerre: Au Secours des isolés'*, or
'Help for the Lonely', calling for a return to the camaraderie
experienced during wartime.[36] British papers ran the article on
the same day: here are some extracts:

> Why should this horrible war have been needed to teach us
> cordiality and solidarity? In any case, we have now learned the
> truth, and ought not to return to the old system of a hermetically-
> sealed society, a society separated into water-tight compartments.
> We must no longer be lonely as before the war. We must not
> cultivate the reserve and timidity which existed at a time when
> the separation of the classes was a dogma which we fervently
> worshipped and when it unfortunately often happened that we
> lived for years in a neighbourhood without knowing our own
> neighbours.[37]

As a practical solution she suggested that unused wartime
huts should be donated to communities to facilitate social
interaction, more useful and appropriate than displaying
cannon in public parks:

> It appears that certain municipalities have categorically refused

the gift of a cannon. I am not at all surprised. If I had lost a son
in the war I would not look to see a German cannon every time I
visited the public park or sauntered across the village green.[38]

The enterprising and growing cinematic industry saw an
opportunity, recommending that such huts should be equipped
with the latest film equipment, for teaching the young.[39]

She also favoured the American example of mixed-sex
schools.

The Tory, Church of England supporting *Carmarthen
Journal* took the opportunity to suggest that the Free Church
community, with its multiple sects and chapels, might show
greater openness and camaraderie:

> Let us be a nation of chums! To-day religion, as practised, militates
> against this chumminess by making the nation narrow, prejudiced
> and bitter. Each place of worship endeavours to prevent its
> worshippers from wandering outside the fold.[40]

May 1919 began with a sprained ankle, though that didn't
stop her from venturing out of her Downing Street door on
the 6th to ensure the tins were rattled for the Royal National
Lifeboat Institution, another favourite cause, before she
travelled to Harrogate, Yorkshire, for a further Jewel Fund sale.
In this pre-television world she was well known by reputation
but perhaps less by sight, as her reception in Harrogate
suggests:

> The quietly dressed lady who walked into the Winter Gardens
> at Harrogate yesterday was not instantly recognised as Mrs
> Lloyd George by those who were gathered to receive her. The
> photographers, however, were in no doubt as to her identity. She
> was immediately taken in charge by them, as if she were a film
> actress attending a rehearsal. For several minutes she submitted
> with great good humour to their importunities, and the first act
> ended with a pretty picture of a little girl in a white frock selling
> the Prime Minister's wife a bunch of daffodils.[41]

Back in London there was another Welsh artiste to support, the young Megan Foster – tagged 'the young Melba' – on her London debut at the Aeolian Hall, New Bond Street. Megan (the daughter of Welsh baritone Ivor Foster) would have a lifelong singing career, including on the radio.[42] At the close of the concert Megan, presented with many bouquets, gave some daffodils to Mrs Lloyd George (in the front row), who pinned them to her dress.[43]

On 15th May Mrs Lloyd George was 'at home' to delegates of the British Women's Temperance Association.[44] On 20th May she was stationed in Trafalgar Square organising street collections in aid of St Dunstan's, the charity for blind veterans.[45] Although charity work subsided after the war, many initiatives established then survive today: St Dunstan's, for example, continues as Blind Veterans.

On 22nd May No. 10 was packed for a reception for the Ivory Cross (National Dental Aid) Fund. Improving the appalling state of the country's teeth was another favourite cause:

> What is undoubtedly one of the biggest things in the way of receptions was held at 10 Downing-street to-day, when Mrs Lloyd George received several hundred guests on behalf of the Ivory Cross. The guests overflowed into three rooms in which meetings had to be held. Mrs Lloyd George made one of her charming speeches. Over £1,000 was collected for the fund in the room.[46]

The same day, she was also down to attend a National Baby Week fancy dress ball at Piccadilly's Prince's Galleries but may have been too busy to attend.

The busy 22nd May closed at the Royal Opera House, to hear the up-and-coming Welsh mezzo-soprano Leila Mégane (born Megan Jones, in Bethesda) making her Covent Garden debut.[47]

The month was rounded off at the London Guildhall (29th May), when the Prince of Wales was admitted to the Freedom of the City of London. Before the arrival of the royal party, 'The wife of the Prime Minister was cheered, and very graciously acknowledged the greeting as she passed on her way to the dais'.[48]

# CHAPTER 4

# The 'Lampeter Incident' and Peace Day

## (June 1919)

MEANWHILE, ALL WAS 'serene' at No. 10 on May 22nd, according to the *Cambrian News*:

> The atmosphere of 10, Downing-street, was never more serene.
> What a world of difference the personnel of the private secretary
> makes. The character of Captain Ernest Evans permits of no
> pretentiousness and make-believe. Mr J. T. Rhys who has replaced
> Mr W. Lewis as private secretary to Mrs Lloyd George, brings
> Mrs Lloyd George into a nearer relation with Cardiganshire.
> Mrs Lloyd George has the sense, capability, and tact to use her
> great position to the highest ends of life. There was never yet
> anything so wonderful as this. Princesses and duchesses are glad
> to adapt themselves to her outlook and to help her in her myriad
> enterprises for benefitting the race. Never had a great minister a
> greater or nobler wife.[1]

This is the only written acknowledgment of William Lewis as having been Mrs Lloyd George's private secretary.

The reference to Ernest 'Ernie' Evans, and that JTR was bringing her closer to Cardiganshire, suggests the pro-Lloyd George *Cambrian News* was warming up for Mrs Lloyd George's forthcoming tour through Cardiganshire in June. After recharging her batteries with a short yachting cruise, in mid-month Mrs Lloyd George would traverse Wales pursuing her welfare and political campaigns, from the extreme north-west, Anglesey's Holyhead, down through Aberystwyth and Lampeter, and on to Cardiff in the south-east.

In Holyhead, she opened the new Lady Thomas Convalescent Home, financed and built to a very high standard by the ever-generous Sir Robert Thomas, on his Garreglwyd estate, to care for discharged and demobilised soldiers and sailors.[2]

The political tour from Aberystwyth to Lampeter via Aberaeron was designed to be low-key. But in Cardiganshire, politics was anything but low-key. The sitting MP, Matthew Vaughan-Davies, was unpopular with the Asquithian 'Wee Free' members of the Cardiganshire Liberal Party, and it was expected that this former Tory would soon retire. ('Wee Free' was the label sported by the Asquithians as being proudly 'independent' Liberals. The epithet was first used for the Scottish Free Kirk after 1900.) It was no real secret that Lloyd George was planning, at the time of his own choosing, to force a by-election and replace Vaughan-Davies with his own man, Ernest 'Ernie' Evans – as noted above, a member of his 'serene' secretariat at No. 10, and himself Cardiganshire-born.

As the *Cambrian News* pointed out, Mrs Lloyd George's own private secretary, JTR, was also from Cardiganshire, born in the Lampeter district. He was well connected, in that the secretary of the Cardiganshire Liberal Association was one of his younger brothers, Harry Rees (JTR had switched from the anglicised spelling 'Rees' to 'Rhys', in the 1890s).

But politics ran deep in Cardiganshire, and when it came to the Lloyd George/Asquithian rift, the Rees family was divided. Harry was an Asquithian, which put the two brothers on opposite sides of the Liberal divide. Harry had been discussing for some time with W. Llewelyn Williams, the former MP for Carmarthen Boroughs, the latter's possible candidature for Cardiganshire, Williams' own seat having been abolished in 1918 as a result of the Parliamentary boundary changes.

Harry Rees, anticipating Mrs Lloyd George's visit in April,

had been planning to use it to incentivise women to take more interest in politics.

> At a meeting of the Aberystwyth branch of Women Liberals, Mr Harry Rees, Lampeter, Liberal agent, urged women to further effort and interest in the work of the branch, and also to watch their interests with regard to the vote, which was not being utilised by every woman. Mr J. R. Griffiths said the organisation of the branch was not good. The members had not met for some time. Women had come up to scratch in the elections on Saturday, 75 per cent of the votes being cast by women. Most women had a strong resolve to exercise their rights. Mr Harry Rees said Mrs Lloyd George would visit Lampeter on June 17th. Mr J. R. Griffiths suggested a small emergency committee to organise the branch. It was decided to appoint women to canvass for additional members. Mrs T. J. Samuel thought Mrs Lloyd George's visit would be an incentive to women to take greater interest in political work. After appointing six people to reorganise the branch, it was suggested that a public meeting should be held, and Mr Rees said he could find speakers.[3]

Also in the Rees family, an elder brother, George Rees, was the founder/editor of the pro-Asquithian, bilingual *Welsh Gazette*, and their sister Margaret was married to the deputy editor, whose mentor as a journalist was W. Llewelyn Williams, who was the future 'Wee Free' candidate. Furthermore, Liberal radicalism in the family went back at least two generations.

In 1868, when male suffrage was extended significantly in Britain, there was a notable 'rebellion' in Cardiganshire: the newly-enfranchised tenant farmers voted Liberal against the express wishes of their Tory landlords. The success of the Liberals in that election saw reprisals against tenants, including evictions – among them the Rees brothers' father, nurseryman George Rees, and their maternal grandfather, blacksmith Joshua Thomas. The Liberal press published a list of some 50 tenants who had suffered. The Tory press responded by seeking to debunk the claims.

A study published in 1998 noted that there has been no systematic appraisal of the validity of the claims/accusations on either side.[4] However, the suggestion that my great-grandfather had not been evicted by his landlord, but by a Mrs Griffiths, who was subletting land to him, misses the fact that she was his aunt, who had brought him up since his father had died when he was young. Her landlord's agent was making it clear she was not permitted to sublet the land. However, his 'native heath getting too warm for him', George Rees moved his growing family up the road from Llanybydder to Lampeter, establishing a prosperous nursery between the university and the new railway, on land rented from the Lampeter Tory, J. C. Harford. From there he supplied the grand houses of south and west Wales with thousands of trees and plants.[5]

The Liberal conflict came to a head in February 1921, at the Lloyd George-engineered by-election, where Mrs Lloyd George would play a starring role.

The June 1919 political tour started in Aberystwyth, and already even the simplest issues caused problems, as the Aberystwyth Town Council minutes show:

> The Secretary of the Liberal Club wrote asking for the services of the Town Band to take part at a social on Monday evening in welcoming Mrs Lloyd George.
>
> Mr Morrison: On behalf of the Conservative Party, I would like to apply for the service of the Band at a fête to be given by Lord Lisburne.
>
> Captain B. Taylor Lloyd: I understood we were now under a Coalition Government, but as the political question has been raised I ask that the application be withdrawn.
>
> Alderman Samuel opposed the application. If the town knew of Mrs Lloyd George's coming, he would be in favour of welcoming her as the wife of the Welsh Prime Minister. The Council, however, ought to be clear of any political suspicion.
>
> The application was withdrawn.[6]

So the town was allowed to welcome the wife of the Prime

Minister, but not if this was politics. A reminder why wives of Prime Ministers often keep a low profile.

Ernie Evans attended the Aberystwyth evening welcome event on 16th June, hosted by the Liberal Club. Mrs Lloyd George claimed that she came to Aberystwyth to spend the night quietly on her way to Lampeter. She said she must blame Mr Ernest Evans for having to speak in public, which was a thing she disliked doing.[7] She spoke up for the Government, saluted the fighting men, the brave Welshmen and the Welsh Army, and the success of her Welsh Troops campaign (which still had £30,000 to distribute, funds which were ultimately contributed to the King's Fund set up by the Ministry of Pensions), looked forward to the establishment of a lasting peace (the Versailles Treaty, soon to be finalised), and ended by giving a pat on the back to their long-serving MP, Matthew Vaughan-Davies.

After more speeches there was music, the Town Band not being the only musicians in Aberystwyth.

The next day, Mrs Lloyd George, driven by Sir John and Lady Lynn-Thomas, her Cardiff hosts, set off for Lampeter. On the way, the incoming Chair of the Cardiganshire Liberal Association, J. M. Howell (a Lloyd George supporter) organised a large welcoming party for Mrs Lloyd George at his coastal home town of Aberaeron, with speeches and presentations. (illustration 17)

In contrast, in Lampeter there was no civic welcome, though Matthew Vaughan-Davies hosted a private luncheon for her with a few guests at Walter's Temperance Hotel. The main event was the AGM of the Cardiganshire Liberal Association (organised by JTR's Asquithian brother Harry). Mrs Lloyd George spoke to a packed audience of almost 500, with admission by ticket only from the secretaries of local Liberal Party branches. The local girls' school pupils were given the day off to attend. Given the sensitivities, her comments might not have pleased everyone:

Cardiganshire has been so magnificently loyal to Liberalism that I sometimes think 'Cardiganshire' and 'Liberalism' are almost synonymous terms.

Numerous efforts have been made during the past 50 years to break your allegiance to Liberalism. The efforts have only served to show how deep-rooted is your faith. Your forefathers, and perhaps some of you, were severely tried in 1868, but you stood the test. It is perhaps because you *were* so severely tried that you have been so splendidly true ever since.

She went on to praise their sitting MP, adding: 'May he long live to enjoy your confidence and to represent you in Parliament.'[8] Not a sentiment they all shared.

Shortly after speaking, Mrs Lloyd George left the meeting (which continued with its formal business), and was driven to Cardiff, in the pouring rain, by Sir John and Lady Lynn-Thomas. While there, Mrs Lloyd George and the Thomases visited the Prince of Wales Hospital, for limbless soldiers and sailors. She attended the AGM, and viewed the gardens that had been adapted to help the patients develop skills with their new artificial limbs:

Having ascended the balcony, the party viewed the parade of the patients who had been recently fitted with artificial limbs, and later visited the gardens.[9] (illustration 22)

In the afternoon Mrs Lloyd George opened another new hospital, Rookwood, again for disabled soldiers, in Llandaff, Cardiff. Rookwood, like Garreglwyd in Holyhead and many other wartime hospitals, also began in an existing building. Unlike Garreglwyd (later a maternity hospital, birthplace of Dawn French, amongst others), Rookwood remains a hospital today, within the NHS.

Whilst the Welsh tour had seemingly gone to plan, complaints were made later. These resulted in a letter being sent to Mrs Lloyd George, and published, jointly signed by the Mayor of Lampeter, by the Vicar of St Peter's Church, and by the Deputy Principal of the University, apologising for the lack of a civic reception in Lampeter. In contrast, the Lloyd Georgian J. M. Howell, by then Chairman of the Cardiganshire Liberal Association, defended his enthusiastic efforts in Aberaeron in a private letter to Harry Rees, rubbing a little salt in the wound by reminding Harry that it was his brother JTR who had suggested it in the first place.

Whilst the tour was clearly part of the long game being played by Lloyd George, the idea that this was a well-choreographed campaign might be an exaggeration. Not long before the visit Mrs Lloyd George wrote in an undated note to JTR: 'What is the meeting at Lampeter? I have no idea. Let me know here at Criccieth during [the] week.'[10]

The 'Lampeter Incident', as it was dubbed, was a minor affair but reflected the increasingly bitter rift opening in Welsh Liberalism, and Liberalism nationally. Harry Rees immediately started to plan, with the Independent Liberal party HQ in London, for Asquith to visit Wales later in the year, with a big splash in Aberystwyth – suggesting that J. M. Howell be kept out of the planning as far as possible.[11]

Cardiganshire was inexorably moving toward the bitter confrontation of the two Liberal camps in 1921.

On 26th and 27th June there were successive concerts at No. 10. The first was in aid of the Welsh Industries Association, with significant involvement by JTR – the engraved silver salver presented to him now graces the desk of his grandson. It was the first concert at No. 10 where the paying public, at 23 shillings a ticket, were invited. (illustration 50)

> Wales is much before the public just now, and small wonder
> that the Welsh Industries Concert at 10, Downing-street on
> Wednesday was a great success. The Hon. Elaine Jenkins showed
> me (writes a lady correspondent) her gold bag full of money for the
> programmes. It was a superb concert, with Miss Carrie Tubb and
> Mr Ben Davies among the singers. ...

The decorator has been busy since the armistice, and I liked the dead white staircase and bright red velvet carpets, which are new.[12]

Amongst the performers were Mr Ivor Foster (the father of Miss Megan Foster); Mr Ben Davies, Miss Nanette Evans, Mr Lyn Harding (a leading Welsh actor); Gwendolen Mason (harpist); Mlle Leila Megane (Miss Megan Jones) and Mr J. Watcyn Watcyns (Welsh Guards).[13]

The Welsh Industries Association at the time had a London shop near Victoria Station selling Welsh-made products.

Concert arrangement had its own politics and sensitivities. On returning from Cardiff Mrs Lloyd George received a strong letter from the best-selling author Marie Corelli. Ms Corelli protested that Miss Nanette Evans (formerly using her first name, 'Laura'), an up-and-coming performer, was calling herself a protégée of the Lloyd Georges – without acknowledging that Marie Corelli was the one who had 'found her', and paid for her expensive violin and her studies abroad. While careful not to make accusations against Mrs Lloyd George, Marie Corelli published her letter of protest in the press soon afterwards.[14]

The concert might have had a completely different programme: Dame Clara Butt, the popular contralto, had also written to Mrs Lloyd George offering her services. She would have wanted to arrange all the programme herself, as she did for most of her charity events. However, the plans for the Welsh Industries Concert were probably too well under way to accept her offer.[15] Dame Clara would shortly be singing to thousands, in Trafalgar Square, in the imminent Women's Victory celebrations.

The second No. 10 concert was in aid of the Children's Jewel Fund, tickets at three guineas, treble the price from the day before, and organised by Dame Nellie Melba, who was also a lead performer.[16]

The long negotiated Versailles Peace Treaty was finally signed on 28th June, with a Peace Day planned for 19th July. On Sunday evening, 29th June, Mrs Lloyd George joined the

King in welcoming her husband back from Paris, as London celebrated:

> A popular welcome was given to Mr Lloyd George on his return from the Peace Conference. For considerably more than an hour before the special train was due, the platform had been barricaded off and the body of the station rapidly filled by the general public.
>
> The King arrived at the station at 6.30, the Prime Minister's train steaming in six minutes later. As it drew up, his Majesty, with Mrs Lloyd George, crossed the platform to the Prime Minister's saloon, and when Mr Lloyd George alighted, greeted him with a cordial handshake. Mrs Lloyd George had for these few moments stood a little apart, and the Prime Minister, suddenly becoming aware of her presence, clasped her round the waist and kissed her. The Prime Minister then shook hands with the Prince of Wales.
>
> The party then went to the Palace. A few minutes after 7, the Royal carriage, in which the Premier and Mrs Lloyd George, both looking radiant, were now seated side by side, drove out of the gate to the accompaniment of cheers, which grew in volume as the peace celebrants of Trafalgar-square and Whitehall joined more uproariously in the welcome. Shortly after entering No. 10 Mr Lloyd George appeared at the window overlooking the porch.
>
> Speaking slowly and distinctly, he said 'Yesterday at Versailles a just Peace was concluded by the labours and sacrifices of men of all classes and of all races in this great Empire. A peace charged with hope has been won for the world. [Cries of "You helped to do it!"] I hope we have all helped to do it, and it is because everybody helped it has been won. I now sincerely trust that unity, the spirit of concord and co-operation which won this great Peace will continue until we have established on a firm foundation the new world which has been won by the sacrifices of millions of valiant men. The hideous slaughter of brave men has come to an end – it has come to an end in a righteous Peace, let us thank God for that. Let us rejoice in this great victory, not in the spirit of boastfulness which was the downfall of Germany, but in a spirit of reverence which is worthy of the noble sacrifices which have been made.' [Cheers.]
>
> Mr Lloyd George then withdrew, and the crowds quickly melted away after a final cheer for Mrs Lloyd George.[17]

Alongside the celebrations, a new Victory Loan was launched to finance reconstruction. Mrs Lloyd George, the President of the Women's Advisory Committee of the Victory Loan Campaign, wrote to the papers urging women to contribute:

> Mrs Lloyd George asks how can women best show their thankfulness to the men who have fought and died to make our hearths and homes secure. Perhaps (she says) our thoughts fly to poetic visions. To something great and sublime that shall enshrine their memories for ever. But a country such as ours is today burdened with the weight of years of the greatest war history has ever known, and needs more than flights of fancy, however lofty – our practical help. Is it prosaic, sacrilegious even, to repay a moral and spiritual debt in hard cash? To immortalise the dead by means of pounds, shilling, and pence? No: for they, our dead and our living, gave their all for England. Cannot we, too, give ours? They gave finer things than money – things we cannot give; it is our money that is asked of us women, and today is the moment.[18]

There was a three-day Victory Loan fête in Trafalgar Square, Mrs Lloyd George leading the raft of women speakers, and selling Bonds in the Square.[19]

*Common Cause*, the newspaper of the National Union of Women's Suffrage Societies, took the opportunity to highlight the role of women in celebrating the Peace in London:

> Many great processions of women have passed through the streets of London. In the days of the Suffrage agitation we had every variety, from the Mud March in 1907 to the Great Pilgrimage in 1913. We have had elaborate processions, with beautiful banners and careful decorations, and we have had monster processions, with eager crowds; we have seen men and women marching for the sake of every cause they love: for religions, for freedom, for protests, for work or for play, for good and for evil, but never among them all has there been a more wonderful moment than when, after the great Women's Victory Loan Procession of Saturday last, it fell to the lot of Mrs Lloyd George to announce to the people of London that Peace had at last been signed. That

she should have beside her on the plinth of the Nelson Column the well-known leaders of the Suffrage Cause seems now a most natural and fitting thing. For did we not always struggle to become part of our own country?[20]

Mrs Lloyd George again went into print, with an article in the *Liverpool Post* on 'Women and Peace'.

Women have at least two substantial reasons for rejoicing in the establishment of peace on earth.

War is absolutely alien to women's nature and does violence to everything that she cherishes in life. Women's thoughts are thoughts of peace, and to her war is an unspeakable torture, an indescribable agony. Woman is so constituted that peace is essential to her wellbeing and the return of peace she therefore hails with joy unfeigned.

She can rejoice, too, because she has contributed so magnificently by her endeavours and by her endurance to the great victory which has made peace possible. Though she loves peace and loathes war, yet she laboured with unexampled devotion to end the war.

If every woman in Britain had received due 'recognition' at the hands of the state, the Honours List would be almost as long as the Directory.

Nor must we forget the women whose part in the tragic struggle was to suffer in silence, and today are longing for 'the touch of the vanished hand' and for 'the sound of the voice that is still'; 'They also serve who only stand and wait'.[21]

During the first week of July Mrs Lloyd George made her first by-election contribution, sending a message to the women in Swansea, in support of the Coalition Liberal candidate.[22] By-elections were steadily taking place due to resignations, elevations to the Lords, deaths, or promotions to the Cabinet or other senior posts.

The latter convention, since discontinued, was that a by-election might be triggered when an MP was promoted to a senior position, including to the Cabinet. Thus a new Minister might have to seek re-election, and one or two careers foundered as a result – though an initial loss was often followed by a tilt at another seat when available. Where ministers had to seek re-election, Mrs Lloyd George generally campaigned for them.

One hundred and seven by-elections were held during the Coalition Government. Mrs Lloyd George actively participated in 18: campaigning on the spot in ten, and in eight by sending supporting messages to the electorate. In reality she campaigned in as many as made sense.

She campaigned primarily in seats where a Coalition Liberal was standing (25 of the by-elections), and my analysis suggests she campaigned in all of these unless there was a good reason not to: for health reasons; when the candidate was unopposed; when she was on tour elsewhere; or during periods of intense social/economic tension. During the 1921 coal strike, Mrs Lloyd George participated in only two by-elections, in the largely rural constituencies of Taunton and Bedford.

On 7th July the *Western Mail* reported: 'London (says the *Spectator*) has come to regard Mrs Lloyd George with steadily increasing admiration and respect.'[23]

During a brief respite in Cricieth the Lloyd Georges entertained Winston Churchill, General Sir Henry Wilson (the British Permanent Military Representative at the Supreme War Council at Versailles) and Sir Maurice Hankey (the Cabinet Secretary) to dinner.[24]

On Peace Day, 19th July, Mr and Mrs Lloyd George joined the King and Queen on the stand at the foot of the Victoria Memorial at the head of The Mall to witness the Victory March of the British and Allied troops.[25]

It was then back to Cricieth, for a concert in aid of the planned Memorial Hall, joined by Olwen and Tom Carey Evans, and by fellow Councillor Leah Thomas, President of the Memorial Hall Committee.[26]

She then returned to London, again joining their Majesties for a further peace celebration, at the Guildhall, on 29th

July, returning the next day to the same venue when Marshal Ferdinand Foch of France became a Freeman of the City.[27] One of JTR's obituaries recalled:

> During the visit to No. 10 of a French military delegation, with Marshal Foch at the head, one of the delegates was struck by Mr Rhys's likeness to Foch. He borrowed Marshal Foch's hat and put it on Mr Rhys's head to prove what an effective double he was for the famous French soldier.[28]

JTR, 'with his flowing white hair, ruddy complexion, white moustache, and similar build' was one of a number of 'Lloyd George doubles' of the time.

July, like May, ended at the Royal Opera House, for a gala performance, attended by the King and Queen and other Royal Family members, in aid of the Housing Associations for Officers' Families.[29]

Another glass ceiling was soon to be broken: the Welsh Methodists appointed their first deaconesses, including Mrs Lloyd George, Lady Clwyd, Mrs Herbert Lewis, and Mrs Peter Hughes Griffiths.[30] The Rev. John Thickens, the progressive Welsh Calvinistic Methodist pastor of William Lewis's church in Willesden, north London, was a leader of this reform.

It was now five years since the First World War had started with the invasion of Serbia on 28th July 1914. A delegation of Serbian women sent a letter of thanks, via Mrs Lloyd George, to British women for aiding their men during the war:

> An expression of the gratitude of Serbian ladies towards their British sisters for the noble assistance rendered them during the war has been forwarded to Mrs Lloyd George by Fratt Telsiava Borota, president of the Committee of Serbian Women, through Captain G. Tomas, RTO, Trieste.
>
> The communication, addressed to 'Dear sisters, noble British women,' states that the hearts of Serb women are full of gratitude to the great and noble friends of the Serb nation, the glorious British nation, who mothered the Serbian soldiers when their own

women could do nothing for them. Serb women will never forget this kindness, and desire to be kept for ever in the hearts of their British sisters.[31]

During the war there had been a natural empathy between the people of Wales and those of the other small nations, Belgium and Serbia, caught in the war between the Great Powers.

CHAPTER 5

# From the Normandy Coast to the Spen Valley
## (August to December 1919)

IN THE FIRST week of the holiday month of August, Mrs Lloyd George and Megan attended the annual National Eisteddfod, that year at Corwen.[1] After opening a sale of work in Bangor,[2] it was time for a foreign holiday.

On 20th August Mrs Lloyd George and the PM, accompanied by an entourage of secretaries and ministers, visited the Normandy coast for their first holiday since before the war. There was some confusion, possibly deliberate, as to whether they were bound for Normandy or Brittany, but the paparazzi still photographed her with the party on the beach, and as she watched GB defeat France in the finals of the Lawn Tennis Davis Cup. She stayed in Normandy for a week, Lloyd George staying on longer to work. (illustration 11)

In September Mrs Lloyd George became vice-president of the new Save the Children Fund, formed to help starving children throughout the famine areas in Europe.[3] Britain was being blamed for causing child starvation by keeping up their blockade of supplies.

At home, a 'Mother of Ten' from Hull, citing Mrs Lloyd George, complained about the increasing level of state 'interference' in child welfare:

If you have a baby now an official comes to weigh it and leaves you a book of information on how to feed and wash it. And this, after you have brought children up to manhood and womanhood. Then when the baby grows up and goes to school, the least fault they can find means that you are pestered to attend the clinic.

Why a school clinic was ever opened, I have never understood, since there are three good charitable institutions in Hull where I have always had my children well attended to whenever I could not afford to take them to a doctor. No wonder the girls of today will not marry young. What used to be a pride and pleasure in bringing up children is now being made a worrying task by officialdom. Instead of interfering so much with home life, I think a bit of help in getting rid of the ration cards and in reducing the cost of living would be a great deal more sensible than harassing mothers.

The Premier's wife said, 'Our British women are not a whit worse than any other Women.' Yet America does not inspect its mothers and children. I should like to emphasise this – that the maternal instinct in every normal mother is sufficient to protect and help her children, and she should not be needlessly interfered with. The percentage of cases where supervision is essential is really very small. l am, Sir, etc., A MOTHER OF TEN, Hull, September 19th, 1919.[4]

Before the welfare state, such services depended on private funding and generosity – hence the endless number of bazaars opened by Mrs Lloyd George. But she was acutely aware of the limits of private generosity, which was now on the wane after the wartime campaigning. The wife of the man who is largely credited with starting our welfare state was also backing the calls for more state support for health, albeit being careful not to interfere with government policy-making (one reason why Prime Ministers' wives are often seen but not heard). Did our 'Mother of Ten' perhaps take somewhat for granted the private support services available, and was she understandably happier if they asked fewer questions? Changing times.

On 20th September Mrs Lloyd George opened a new cottage hospital in Porthmadog, a war memorial funded by the Red Cross and by private support.[5]

In October Mrs Lloyd George travelled to Glasgow and Edinburgh for a major temperance conference. Presiding at a large meeting in St Andrew's Hall, Glasgow, she proffered three alternatives to the divided movement:

> They had arrived at a most critical period in the long and strenuous history of the cause and she hoped that the success of the campaign now being inaugurated would exceed the hopes of the most ardent temperance men and women in the country. She would very much like to see the day dawn in Wales, and she had even told her Welsh friends it was their own fault that they had not a similar measure there.
>
> The Temperance (Scotland) Act provided three alternatives. The first was no change in the existing conditions, but she thought that, with the knowledge they had, her hearers would agree that drastic change was necessary. [Applause]
>
> The second alternative was to reduce the public houses by 25 per cent. She thought the fewer public houses they had the better. One of Scotland's greatest sons, Mr Gladstone, said that the mere reduction in the number of public houses was no solution of the drink evil. A reduction in public houses would be a very good thing, but it was not enough. [Applause] They had an old proverb in Wales, 'It is not good where there is a better.'
>
> The third alternative was no licence at all. She herself would vote for that. [Applause] The arguments in favour of no licences were weighty. No harm would ever befall anyone who could not get hold of intoxicating liquor. She advised them all to vote for no licences, and to tell everyone else the same.
>
> She wanted the women to use the vote and she was sure the women of Wales would follow suit.[6]

The 1913 Temperance (Scotland) Act allowed voters in small local areas in Scotland to hold a poll to vote on whether their area remained 'wet' or 'dry'.

Another speaker was the noted Prohibition campaigner W. E. 'Pussyfoot' Johnson, of Ohio, of the American Anti-Saloon League, a former law enforcement officer known for his 'cat-like stealth' in pursuit of suspects.

From Scotland Mrs Lloyd George travelled south to join her husband for the annual (but the first since before the war) Cutlers' Feast, in Sheffield, where he also received the Freedom of the City. It was then to north Wales to open new accommodation at the Bangor Normal College.

At Bangor, the former St George's Hotel, overlooking the Menai Strait, was being turned into teacher training accommodation. Mrs Lloyd George expressed satisfaction that whilst the new facilities were for men, it meant that accommodation for women, made available during the war, could be retained. Both a typewritten copy and a version of the speech in Mrs Lloyd George's hand are in the JTR archive.

> The whole country might very well learn from the experience of the Normal College that it is possible to provide for the men, and at the same time to protect the interests of the women. It would never do for this country to fail in its patriotic duty to its roll of fighting men by withdrawing from them opportunities, whether for training or for services, but it is equally important to ensure that women who have acquired a taste for honest service during the war, should not be compelled to return to the ranks of those who wile away their time in semi-idleness.

She was pleased that more women could be trained in domestic science, favouring home cooking over tinned food from the corner shop:

> I rejoice to know that the Normal College is providing special courses for women students in domestic science which will enable them to train the young girls of the nation in domestic arts. These have been too long neglected. We hear a great deal nowadays about economy and extravagance.
>
> One of the worst forms of extravagance is that of mothers and others in charge of homes who, instead of providing for the needs of the family by cooking meals at home, run to the shop round the corner for tinned food which is dearer and less wholesome than what they could easily prepare with their own hands. There is far too much tendency to resort to the shop for wearing apparel which

mothers and daughters could easily make for themselves and their families.

Mrs Lloyd George continued on her theme that women must be allowed to continue to widen their horizons, after their major wartime contributions had begun to alter perceptions of their role in the economy – Bangor would be training women in rural sciences just as 'the women of the Land Army have shown how capable they can be made with suitable and efficient training to work on the land'.

Finally she praised their attention to the needs of mothers and their children. 'I see you have libraries too & observation nurseries & nursery schools. You do things thoroughly in Wales when you take a thing in hand.'[7]

(Perhaps the other JT at No. 10, J. T. Davies, the PM's principal private secretary, was aware of her visit to his alma mater.)

There followed a trip to Manchester to speak on child welfare, to London, hosting a meeting at No. 10 for the Adoption Society, and then to Birmingham to open a bazaar and speak to Free Church women. She may have noticed the Birmingham papers' coverage of the Asquiths' high-profile visit to Aberystwyth, organised by Harry Rees, in response to her Lampeter visit. The pressure was building ahead of the 1921 Cardiganshire by-election.

Whilst her travels prevented her from attending a banquet for the visit of Queen Ena of Spain,[8] she was present at the end-of-month banquet at Buckingham Palace in honour of the Shah of Persia.[9]

The appalling state of the nation's teeth, revealed in the medical examinations of the men signing up for war, was one of Mrs Lloyd George's great concerns. On 5th November she visited the Royal Dental Hospital in Leicester Square to perform 'the melancholy task' of unveiling the Roll of Honour for the 29 alumni of the dental school, students and practising dentists, who fell in the war – in the Middle East, on the Somme, in Flanders, in hospital from wounds, of scarlet fever when still training at home, and perhaps most tragically, of influenza when treating patients in Ireland, the day after Armistice had been declared. The Roll of Honour disappeared in the 1980s when the School/Hospital became a hotel, though I was able to reconstruct it in time for the annual alumni luncheon in 2019, the centenary of her visit.[10]

After the unveiling, Mrs Lloyd George presented the annual prizes to the students, delighted that, for the first time, the most prestigious award was won by a woman, Miss Doris Grose – the shortage of dentists during the war had forced the school to accept women students. It was a moment she frequently recalled, when encouraging women to join the professions, many now open to them for the first time. (illustration 34)

She would not have been impressed when a few years later the Royal Dental School stopped training women… a retrograde move, rescinded after protests were made.

On 13th November it was off to the East End for some traditional fare, witnessing the ceremony of 'stripping the gold and silver tree'.[11]

The next day, 14th November, was the eve of a by-election that marked an important moment in British political history, when Mrs Lloyd George travelled to Plymouth to speak twice for the candidacy of Nancy Astor, on the way to becoming the first woman to take her seat in the House of Commons as the Member for Plymouth Sutton. Mrs Lloyd George had 'never seen a more enthusiastic crowd except in our Carnarvon Boroughs'.[12] In fact, the numbers seeking to hear her were such that many were unable to gain admittance. Other dimensions of the crowd's 'enthusiasm' resonated elsewhere in the Empire, as referenced by Ontario's *Hamilton Daily Times*:

> One of the meetings addressed by Mrs Lloyd George in the election campaign here is characterised as having developed the worst attempt by hecklers to silence speakers in the whole campaign.

Mrs Lloyd George, when she obtained a hearing, warmly endorsed the candidacy of Lady Astor; first, she said, because a few women in Parliament nowadays was most advisable, and, second, because she was convinced that nobody could discharge such duties more thoroughly than Lady Astor.[13]

Her speech is one of the few handwritten electioneering speeches (albeit in JTR's hand) that still exist.

Speaking in the afternoon to a large audience of women, Mrs Lloyd George went through all the reasons why electing a woman was a good thing, confronting the charge that she was campaigning for a Unionist with her typical humour:

I think there cannot be a greater compliment paid to her than the very trivial objections that are urged against her. She is charged with being an 'American'. Well, that is neither her blame nor her shame. Besides, Americans and ourselves are one race.

Others charge her with being 'rich'. Well, I don't know many people who would object to being rich. Most people, I know, are making very big efforts to grow richer.

Others say she is a Tory. Well if she is, then all I can say is that I wish all were such Tories as she is.[14]

Great knockabout stump material, perhaps a deliberate echo of an earlier Nancy Astor exchange when visiting a military base: 'People say you are a Pussyfoot,' declared a servant. To which Lady Astor responded, 'They say also I am one of the idle rich, but I'll bet I have done more work in the last five years than the ILP orators.'[15]

Mrs Lloyd George, whilst reminding women this was a critical fight for their own future, skilfully avoided comment on the other candidates (one being a friend and a respected Liberal, Isaac Foot, father of Michael Foot, a future leader of the Labour Party):

Tomorrow you will be asked to give your vote. There are three candidates. I am not going to say a word against or about the

others. One may be good, the other may be better. I know Lady
Astor is the best of all.[16]

Before the result was known (it took two weeks), Lady
Astor wrote to Mrs Lloyd George, thanking her for coming
to Plymouth with the homely phrase: 'The West Country folk
were *so* glad to have you'.

Lady Astor also reflected on the pleasure of being at home
at Cliveden, 'riding with the children and having a real 2 days
holiday before I begin again', and saying 'I *still* feel that I would
rather have another baby than go to the HofC!!'.[17]

A typical Nancy Astor quip, or reflecting on the size of the
task ahead of her. Or she meant it! The result had yet to be
announced.

There was another by-election on the horizon, in Yorkshire's
Spen Valley. Shortly after Plymouth, Lord Astor wrote to Mrs
Lloyd George:

My wife would really like to go to Spen Valley or anywhere
else to help you but I hope you won't press her. The election
was a tremendous strain upon her. She has been inundated
with hundreds of letters of congratulation but every woman
with a grievance looks upon her as her MP and every Woman's
association has bombarded her.[18]

In the event, in December Nancy Astor did travel to Spen
Valley. Again this was a seminal moment in British electoral
history, but a triumph for neither the Tories nor for Liberals of
any persuasion. Women were out in force, though not pleasing
everyone:

The Lady Orator of Today: In the course of a short talk with a
political friend who has visited the Spen Valley Division during
the electioneering, I ascertained that one of the features of the
campaign that disappointed him was the nature and tone of the
platform addresses by women speakers. He was not referring
to Lady Astor or Mrs Lloyd George, but to the army of women

speakers who, day by day, addressed indoor and outdoor audiences on behalf of the three candidates.

My friend's complaint was that these speakers talked sex politics and class politics; their language was the same language they used before they obtained the franchise. There was no evidence that they recognised that they are now with the men. When this criticism was put to a very experienced lady organiser, she endorsed it, but thought that the defect could be eradicated in the course of time. Probably it was because Lady Astor talked ordinary politics that her addresses were so popular, people who came the first time to hear her out of curiosity returning to hear her a second time because of their interest in what she said.[19]

The last week of November was busy. On 18th November, at the big political social event at Londonderry House, the favourite question from the many who had queued seemed to be, 'How long did it take you to get upstairs?'

It was noted by 'Damaris' of the *Pall Mall Gazette*, that Mrs Lloyd George's progress through the packed room was most dexterous. She was wearing black satin, with panels of jet and paillettes of blue.[20]

But as she, doubtless also dexterously, avoided the champagne on offer, not all her good causes met with universal approval: as sights were being set on the Festive Season, 'Eve' of *The Tatler* bemoaned:

Oh dear, oh dear, when are we going to be free men and free women again? And when you dine at 7, to get to the opera by 8 or thereabouts, and sit through two hours of it, and then, going on to dance, are offered lemonade or pink grenadine.

Nobody (indeed) knows
On how many toes
A pussyfoot goes.
But I do wish, don't you, that
Mrs Lloyd George wasn't a pussyfoot, too.[21]

On Wednesday 19th Mrs Lloyd George opened a Japanese garden fair at the Wesleyan Hall, Forest Gate, London (perhaps a little more exotic than some events), and later presided at the annual meeting of the Queen Mary's Hospital Linen League held at the Conference Hall, Stratford, and visited the hospital and the adjacent new maternity home.[22]

On Thursday 20th she chaired a meeting at No. 10 for the promotion of the medical training of women at the National School for Medicine for Wales – a cause which brought together Wales, women, health and education 'under one roof'.[23]

The postbag included a letter from Helena, Princess Christian (daughter of Queen Victoria), asking Mrs Lloyd George to review a draft letter to be sent out to raise funds for a club for nurses: 'a really homelike place at which they can stay when in town and at which they can arrange to have their social gathering and lectures.' The idea was to ask the nurses to start the fund.[24]

Friday 21st was particularly busy, attending a lunch for the Ivory Cross, the dental fund, a meeting of the Widows' Friend Society – at both of which 'she delivered happy little speeches' – before presiding at a committee meeting in connection with the National Fund for Welsh troops, 'with a night engagement to follow'.[25]

The latter was an 'at home' at the Caxton Hall, Westminster, hosted by Herbert Lewis, MP for the University of Wales, and Mrs Lewis, and attended by JTR and his wife Jane, to meet the Old Students' Associations of Aberystwyth, Bangor, and Cardiff. JTR himself was a Cardiff Exhibitioner, and in 1915 the Chairman of Bala-Bangor Congregationalist Theological College.[26]

After opening a sale of work for the Women's Missionary Association at Croydon's Baptist Church – saying that 'she knew of no human service so notable as that of missionary work' – Mrs Lloyd George ended November with her regular winter cold and a partial loss of voice.[27] She recovered enough to open the YWCA bazaar at Central Hall, Westminster, on 4th December.

> The YWCA is not going to rest on its oars. There are far-reaching schemes for developing its work among young women. I am very glad to notice that in addition to providing clubs & Hostels it is proposing to provide Educational facilities, organise Holiday Camps & help girls to get a new start in life. They are not only going to provide for the body but for the soul of our young women.[28]

The same day she was speaking in her own drawing room at an event to raise funds for the Church Army, attended by its founder, Prebendary Carlile.[29]

The Spen Valley by-election, dubbed by *The Times* as 'a political event of great significance', marked when Labour could be seen as a real contender for political power.

The by-election was held due to the death of the Coalition Liberal incumbent Thomas Whittaker, a noted temperance campaigner. Lloyd George deliberately put up his own Coalition Liberal candidate, Col. B. C. Fairfax, to combat his arch foe, the distinguished Asquithian 'Wee Free' Liberal, Sir John Simon, and the Labour candidate, Tom Myers.

An observer of her speech to a women's audience at the Town Hall remarked on Mrs Lloyd George's contrasting styles of address:

> Essentially homely touches like these gave way to a talk about serious politics. Mrs Lloyd George has not the gift of oratory of her distinguished husband, and, quoting from notes, said the test was whether the Government was worthy of women's support. Sir John Simon opposed conscription, which, however repugnant to our national traditions, was the only means by which we had won the war. 'If all Liberals had voted as he did,' she said truly, 'Germany would have won.'[30]

Whilst the Liberals fought their private war, Labour's Tom Myers, who had lost in a straight fight with Whittaker in 1918, stole a march on them both and captured the seat.

Sir John perhaps had the last laugh, capturing Spen Valley in 1923 and retaining it until he went to the House of Lords in 1940.

On 6th December Mrs Lloyd George accompanied her husband, who was addressing the Manchester Reform Club.[31] After returning to London, on Saturday 13th December she met the Aberystwyth College alumni at No. 10, preparing for their 1922 jubilee, a meeting postponed from earlier in the month when she had been laid low.

On 11th December, at a special meeting of the Welsh Troops Fund at No. 10, a canteen of cutlery was presented to JTR's predecessor William Lewis. At one point an aspiring politician as the prospective Liberal candidate for Brecon and Radnor, Lewis had helped steer the Fund's merger with the nascent pensions system, becoming Deputy-Inspector for England and Wales in the Ministry of Pensions, before returning to the shipping business, where he had started his career.[32]

On 18th December, there was another concert and auction at No. 10, in aid of the Middlesex Hospital. JTR, a Governor of the Hospital, kept one of the silk-covered programmes.[33] The actor Sir John Martin-Harvey, with whom JTR would have future contacts, ran the auction. (illustration 49)

Just before Christmas, Mrs Lloyd George spoke in Wrexham at the tercentenary celebration for Morgan Llwyd o Wynedd, poet, missionary and a founder of Welsh Nonconformity, and presented prizes to students at Wrexham Girls' School, congratulating the school headmistress, Miss Jones, on her success.

There would be two postscripts: in February 1920 Miss Jones successfully opposed the plan to have dancing lessons between her charges and pupils of the boys' school with the opinion that:

Boys and girls should learn to associate with each other, but it was the work of the home to promote this, and not the school. It was better for the parents to be responsible for the boy friends of their girls.'[34]

Had she heard Mrs Lloyd George's call for camaraderie between the young?

Then in April 1920 Miss Jones visited London, JTR being charged with getting her tickets for the House of Commons. There were no major debates, but perhaps it was for the experience. It was the day Charles McCurdy, future Coalition Liberal Chief Whip (JTR's employer following Mrs Lloyd George), was sworn in as the Member for Northampton.[35]

The 'business' side of 1919 closed with Mrs Lloyd George's appointment as one of the first seven women as Justices of the Peace.

Christmas was spent at Cricieth with the family, including Richard, Gwilym, Olwen and Megan. Gwilym chaired a Boxing Day Eisteddfod in the town, with the Prime Minister making a speech. Ernest Evans, his private secretary, also attended.[36]

A busy first year of 'peace'.

CHAPTER 6

# Campaigning from North to South

## (January to March 1920)

IN JANUARY, MRS Lloyd George chaired a women's meeting in Cricieth Town Hall, addressed by the distinguished feminist campaigner Eleanor Rathbone, from Liverpool, who spoke on 'The Future of the Women's Movement'.[1]

On 8th January Mrs Lloyd George took her seat on the Magistrates' Bench in Caernarfon, becoming, chronologically, the second woman to take her seat, and the first Welsh woman. She took her seat beside the Chairman, but left half an hour later in the middle of a case – the first formalities over, we may assume.[2]

Mrs Lloyd George and the other women JPs – the Marchioness of Crewe (the first woman to take her seat), Elizabeth Haldane, Gertrude Tuckwell, Mrs Humphry Ward, and Mrs Sidney Webb – were also appointed to a Commission to advise on the appointment of more women JPs around the country. Under the Chairmanship of Lady Crewe, during the year they would select new women JPs, Mrs Lloyd George taking responsibility for Wales.

The suffragette community, as expressed through *The Vote*, the journal of the WFL (Women's Freedom League), while pleased to see women on the Bench, pointed out that the Commission was composed entirely of women of distinction and that there were many other women who should be considered.[3] *The Women's Leader*, in their lead story, approving the list as featuring many of the talented women in the country, also hoped there would soon come a second list to include people not known outside their locality, but who had the time and local knowledge to be effective JPs.[4]

Mrs Lloyd George's qualifications were not specifically questioned on this occasion, but at other times they would be:

> At a meeting of the Middlesex War Pensions Committee last evening it was stated that a deputation was to be appointed to wait on Mrs Lloyd George to elicit her sympathy in the movement to induce the Government to grant gratuities or pensions to women discharged from the army in consequence of wounds, injury, or disease attributable to war service.
>
> The Finchley Labour representative asked, 'Why Mrs Lloyd George? She holds no official position. Why not Lady Astor?' It was explained that it was desired to ask the help of a prominent lady, and Mrs Lloyd George had been chosen.[5]

Mrs Lloyd George did have some experience here, having merged her Troops Fund into the pension system. And while Nancy Astor was the only woman MP, she needed all the help she could get, with 'every woman's association bombarding her', as Lord Astor had written to Mrs Lloyd George in 1919.[6] But whether Mrs Lloyd George would have any influence over the Government might be a valid question for debate.

On 16th January Mrs Lloyd George and Megan were back in London, in time to serve tea:

> Six hundred children of fallen and disabled service men are to be entertained in London to-day, and among those helping to serve the tea, &c., are Mrs Lloyd George and her daughter, Miss Megan, Lady Astor, Miss Isabel Bonar Law, and Lady Islington.[7]

Mrs Lloyd George's role as 'hostess' was going to become more integrated into her increasingly political activities, alongside her use of No. 10 to promote her charitable campaigns. This was both serious and fashionable, as the London correspondent for the *Devon and Exeter Gazette* observed:

> The expectations are that the London season that starts practically with the opening of Parliament will be exceptionally full and brilliant. Now that the war is over, politics becomes the burning question of the day, the soldier retires into the background, and the politician becomes the important, and arresting figure. There are far more women of high position and wealth who are anxious to get into the House of Commons, and share with Lady Astor the prestige and the cachet of these magic letters, 'MP,' after their names, than many people imagine. This is one reason why political entertaining will be in such great swing and on such lavish lines immediately Parliament is opened by the King.
>
> I hear that Mrs Lloyd George intends to do a great deal of special entertaining at 10. Downing-street for charitable purposes. The Premier's helpmate realises what a great help to anything of this kind the fact of it being held in Downing-street is, and the accommodation for such entertainments could hardly be improved on elsewhere. One remarkable feature of the moment in fashionable and usually quite frivolous London is the big vogue of the drawing-room lecture. It almost rivals the jazz. Is London Society becoming high-brow now?[8]

The society gossip columns observed, somewhat approvingly, the changes in style at No. 10:

> Until now Mrs Lloyd George has had no opportunity of giving what a young damsel of my acquaintance, aged ten, calls 'really pompy parties'. Prime Ministers' wives positively can't have 'squashes' during War-time, and practically ever since the Armistice Mr Lloyd George has either been in Paris or in Parliament.
>
> Mrs Lloyd George has begun with two tea-fights for the Coalition Members and their wives. At her first party she broke away from the Downing Street tradition. In the old days you just drank your tea and talked, but Mrs Lloyd George had a little concert, chiefly of Welsh and Irish songs, so you didn't have to

talk unless you wanted to – a kindly dispensation of which nobody seemed to take advantage.

It was all extremely well done, and, personally, I liked the ermine trimming on Mrs Lloyd George's dress. Heavens! can you call ermine 'trimming'? Well, if you can't you know what I mean. And it certainly looked most 'pompy,' and absolutely the right thing.

Margot Asquith had also innovated, albeit in a different way:

Other Days, Other Manners: Mrs Lloyd George is not the first wife of a Prime Minister to introduce innovations at No. 10 Downing Street. Her immediate predecessor brought the flush of envy and annoyance to the cheek of every *couturière* in London by an exhibition, in those politically sacred rooms, of Paris dresses paraded before a vast tea-party on Paris *mannequins*. Some of the dressmakers wrote winged words to the newspapers about it.[9]

On 20th January the Downing Street hostess toured her husband's constituency to encourage women to interest themselves in public affairs. In Deganwy, Conway, Penmaenmawr and Llanfairfechan, she addressed mainly women's audiences, on housing, education, the increasing ability for women to join the professions, and encouraging women to play a greater role now they had won the vote.

The family meanwhile dispersed: 'Miss Megan, Major Richard, Major Gwilym have left London for Paris, New York and Wales respectively. Miss Carey Evans will shortly take a trip to Egypt.'[10] In fact Megan failed to return as promised to her Paris finishing school, making her father 'exceedingly annoyed'.[11] Lloyd George himself returned to Paris for Turkish treaty negotiations.

On 4th February the *Daily Herald* relayed some *Daily Mirror* speculation as to where suffrage was taking the country:

I see that a writer in the *Daily Mirror* has essayed the difficult task of selecting a women's government. Some the selections are good, for instance, Mary Macarthur has a portfolio, Mrs Philip Snowden is to look after our food, and the Lady President of the Council is Maud Royden. But other choices make one rather anxious. Mrs H. B. Irving can be charming on the stage, but she might shine less as a Minister of Reconstruction. Mrs Churchill is to be Chief Secretary for Ireland, Mrs Lloyd George is down as Chancellor of the Exchequer, and Miss Stevenson is the Secretary for India. (Miss Stevenson is secretary to Mr Lloyd George.) Such selections as the last indicate a possibly new evil – instead of petticoat government, coat-tail rule![12]

In the first quarter of 1920 there were nine by-elections, and Mrs Lloyd George campaigned in three: in February at The Wrekin, in Shropshire, and in March, in Stockport, Lancashire, and in Camberwell North West, south London.

In The Wrekin, on 5th February, Mrs Lloyd George spoke at two large meetings for the Coalition Liberal John Bayley. The by-election was lost, surprisingly, to Charles Palmer, standing for the jingoistic Independent MP Horatio Bottomley's Independent Parliamentary Group. Bayley came a rather distant third behind Labour. Palmer was the deputy editor of Bottomley's *John Bull* magazine, but died in October after catching a chill on a visit to his newly-won constituency.

Her speech was very similar to those delivered given in the Carnarvon Boroughs, the former trip perhaps a good warm-up for meeting the electorate of Shropshire.

Speaking at Wellington, Salop, yesterday, Mrs Lloyd George said we were living in times of great changes. The health of the country was now under one authority. We wanted one house, one family, and housing should be carried out promptly. There must be something radically wrong with a State that could not find work for the people. Now women had the franchise, they should help each other to carry out their civic duties. It was the Coalition

Government that gave them the vote and the Sex Disqualification (Removal) Act, by which many of the professions were now open to women.[13]

The responsibility for housing was now under the relatively new Ministry for Health: medical doctor Christopher Addison MP was the first to hold the post.

The next day, 6th February, it was sad farewells as Olwen left for India, creating extended duties for a private secretary and his wife:

Mrs Carey Evans, the older daughter of the Prime Minister, left Euston by the special boat train today for Liverpool to embark on the *Patricia* for India, where she will join her husband, who is there in connection with his military duties. Mrs Carey Evans was particularly anxious that her family farewells should not take place at the station. Only a few intimate friends saw her off. These included Mr Rees [*sic*], private secretary to Mrs Lloyd George, whose wife will have charge of Mrs Carey Evans' child during her absence.[14]

Olwen's three-week voyage to India took twice the expected time, including a stop for ship repairs in Marseilles (during which she took the chance to go to the Monte Carlo casino), a short trip to Malta for more repairs, before making their way via Aden to Bombay (today, Mumbai).[15]

JTR wrote weekly to Olwen, sending family news, Downing Street gossip, British news, and the newspapers. Surviving letters reflect Olwen's gratitude. (illustration 19) Secretarial duties also at times meant trying to track down personal packages that went missing en route to and from India – not the most secure of delivery routes. In October 1920, one Miss Sophie Ries, then 25, went out to India to be with Olwen (then 28). Later, Sophie would take over secretarial duties for Mrs Lloyd George in 1922 when JTR moved to work with the Chief Whip, Charles McCurdy.

My grandparents would have been sympathetic to Olwen in

her separation from her daughter: their own children spent the last year of war living in Pontycymer with their grandmother and aunt, when JTR and his wife came to London – albeit not as distant as India.

A week later Mrs Lloyd George was entertaining the Welsh Division of the YWCA (Young Women's Christian Association) at Downing Street:

> The Cymric At Home: Wonderful as was the result of the YWCA At Home at No. 10 Downing-street, it was by no means a record. One matinée given by Mrs Lloyd George produced £25,000. In the white and gold room, panelled with famous pictures of celebrated statesmen, Mrs Lloyd George invited her guests to take tea with her, as she says in her own Celtic way, but there was something more important before tea. Wales had to do her duty, and, as Miss E. Picton-Turbervill pointed out, Wales always had done her duty since the days of St Patrick, who was a Welsh missionary. Lady Llangattock and Lord Aberdare were among the early arrivals, while Sir John Lynn-Thomas and his wife held a court of their own and chatted in Welsh with many guests.[16]

Edith Picton-Turbervill was a social reformer and campaigned for women to be accepted as priests, and soon after the war was the first woman to be allowed to preach at a statutory Church of England service.[17] She was the Labour MP for The Wrekin from 1929–31.

On 26th February, arriving a little late, Mrs Lloyd George made it to the Edgware Congregational Church bazaar, an event postponed from before Christmas to suit her diary:

> Mrs Lloyd George, first apologised for her late arrival, stating that she had left Downing Street as soon she had seen the Prime Minister off to the House. She was glad the Edgware Church was cosmopolitan, different denominations forming one big family. Her household was the same, some members being Baptists and others Methodists, but for 32 years they had lived very happily together, and she trusted this was the same in their Church life.[18]

Did she have in mind the Carmarthenshire paper's criticism of the churches' lack of 'camaraderie'?

On the first of March 1920, London's Welsh celebrated St David's Day at the Connaught Rooms, the Prince of Wales in attendance (prior to his own trip to south Wales). 'The Prince was seated between the Premier and Mrs Lloyd George, Bonar Law to the left of Lloyd George and Miss Isabel Bonar Law being near Mrs Lloyd George.'[19] Lloyd George and the Prince were well-acquainted. In 1911 the then Chancellor of the Exchequer had given Prince Edward Welsh lessons ahead of his ceremonial Investiture at Caernarfon Castle. The formal invitation to the Investiture to Jane Rhys's father, Thomas Jones, a Pontycymer bootmaker, still adorns our family walls.

The next day Mrs Lloyd George entertained for tea at No. 10 the committee planning a charity matinée scheduled for 19th March at the Palladium, in aid of the National Adoption Association.[20]

The appeal for items for sale triggered a charming response from Princess Alice, Countess of Athlone (granddaughter of Queen Victoria):

> Henry III Tower, Windsor Castle. 8.III.1920
>
> My dear Mrs Lloyd George
>
> I shall be very pleased to send you something to sell at the auction on the 18th, but I am afraid it won't be very wonderful; perhaps some old Dutch silver toys I have had since a child would do? I have rather come to the end of possessions I can part with after all the different Red X sales and others during the War. I am afraid I cannot come to the Entertainment as I am already engaged down here that day, but gladly give my patronage if you want it.
>
> I hope your matinée will be as great a success in its way, as the concert you kindly gave for the Middlesex Hospital.
>
> Yours sincerely, Alice[21]

The letter reflects not only the charity fatigue that had

built up by the end of the war, but also the strong network of philanthropists supporting each other's ventures. The Countess' husband, the Earl of Athlone, Chairman of the Middlesex Hospital since 1910, had chaired the Committee for the 18th December concert at No. 10, which had been organised by JTR, himself a Governor of the hospital.

Later in the year Princess Alice would write to invite Mrs Lloyd George to be a patron of a Christmas fair at the Albert Hall in aid of the Barnardo's Homes jubilee, and to give her name in support of the Welsh Stall (stressing there was no need to attend, as Lady Rhondda and other Welsh ladies would be manning the stall). In the event, Mrs Lloyd George was *hors de combat*, in bed with a cold.[22]

> What I want is Temperance. I am not very
> particular by what method I obtain it.
>
> Mrs Lloyd George, Southampton

In early March Mrs Lloyd George made two trips to the south coast, first speaking at a temperance meeting in Southampton, and later addressing women electors in Poole, the constituency of Capt. 'Freddie' Guest, MP for East Dorset and also the Coalition Liberal Chief Whip. Her handwritten notes for Southampton were on the notepaper of Melchet Court, near Romsey, the home of her friend Lady Mond and Sir Alfred, chemicals industrialist and Swansea MP (later Baron Melchett), which suggests she stayed with the Monds. Lady Mond attended the Southampton speech.[23]

Her speech notes include a wealth of data on the effect of drink, most likely supplied by her temperance campaigning private secretary. She called on her audience of politically empowered women to join the campaign, and praised Nancy Astor's recent maiden speech in the House of Commons which had focused on temperance. The printed version of the latter speech was introduced by Mrs Lloyd George. Lady Astor, a teetotaller who favoured prohibition, backed more modest reform to get at least some legislation on the books.

A standard paragraph from Southampton, stressing Mrs Lloyd George's pragmatic approach to temperance legislation, was published widely around the country:

> Speaking on the temperance question at Southampton yesterday, Mrs Lloyd George said she never shared the faith of many people that the war would end the drink evil, though she shared the wish that that would happen. She did not advocate State purchase, but desired to impress upon women the duty of studying the facts. It was temperance she wanted, and she was not particular how she got it.[24]

The ultimate failure of the temperance movement to achieve anything substantive can be ascribed in part to the inability of the movement to unite around a common strategy. It was divided between die-hard prohibitionists (encouraged by prohibition legislation during the war in the US and in Canada) and those willing to accept more limited legislation, such as Local Option (allowing local communities to decide how hard to clamp down), and/or State Purchase, which would have seen the state purchasing the liquor enterprises. With a very powerful liquor industry it was hard to get anything through Parliament.

Perhaps the suffrage sequence (i.e. step-by-step action – votes for women over 30 in 1918, followed by complete equality in 1928) might have achieved more. Mrs Lloyd George, and JTR, both prohibitionists, were supportive of Lloyd George's more pragmatic, step-by-step approach. Both would be disappointed with the eventual lack of action and the failure of their life-long campaigns. In 1933 the US began to unwind Prohibition.

A week later, 'W.R.H.', a regular contributor to the *Bournemouth Guardian*, who frequently wrote with literary fervour, pulled out all the stops in introducing the arrival of

Mrs Lloyd George at the Amity Hall, Poole, before working his (or her) way towards covering a classic Mrs Lloyd George honest-to-goodness talk, albeit amongst friends. W.R.H.'s efforts to entertain make for a good read:

> The Amity Hall at Poole last Friday [12th March] had such an audience as the 'starriest' of its star film productions could never have drawn. Had the management piled the romantic Pelion of a Mary Pickford on the heroic Ossa of a Fairbanks, and had topped the dazzling structure by the magnetic peak of a Charlie Chaplin there would, at the last resort, have been at least 'standing room only'. That crucial stage of popularity had, however, been passed, for, as unearly comers discovered to their no little dismay on their arrival at the hour for the event, there was actually no room left to stand in! The whole disposable floor and gallery accommodation was filled to straining point by the women electors of East Dorset!
>
> Ponder the significance of such a scene. Construct, alternatively, a mental image of a meeting of mere men voters on any possible Friday afternoon drawn to hear any possible mere male expositor of masculine politics, and note the staggering contrast. Let the organisers of such a meeting perspire as they might their partisan zeal to fill the house, we know how unimposing the result would be, how distressingly prominent the bare gaps of bench. There was apparent a difference in the whole atmosphere. Somehow, in a meeting of men, you are conscious of a specific levity that seems inherent in the breed. Here, however, all was high strung and keen attention, a settled determination that no word that fell from the platform should be lost. Women, in short, have turned politicians! They have 'got the vote', and the pride and enthusiasm with which they regard the possession of that questionable privilege is a present-day portent that should give every political candidate furiously to think.
>
> Tensely they waited, while the orchestra, with the inconsequential perversity of males, filled the lagging moments with snippets from light opera. Suddenly, the conductor tapped with his ferule, and the fiddles leaped and swayed with the provocative, if unfamiliar strains of the Welsh National Anthem. The audience rises to its feet. A slight stir on the platform and there emerges before the footlights a little group of people, whom

the Mayor of Poole, who has come to preside, has risen to welcome
with his accustomed urbanity. Familiar figures in the group are
Lady Wimborne and Captain, the Hon. F. E. Guest, the member
for the division. The eyes of the audience, however, are chiefly
riveted on a little homely faced woman, who, after smilingly
bowing her acknowledgments to the rousing round of applause
which greets her appearance, quietly takes her seat next the Mayor
at the little table in front of the platform. It is Mrs Lloyd George.

The Mayor is brief. He explains that this is not a political
meeting – that is, in so far as it had nothing to do with parties
or groups of parties. Not a political meeting! – but his audience
of women politicians had their own opinion as to that, and
he would see! Theirs was the distinguished privilege, he said,
of having a visit from the wife of their most respected and
honoured Prime Minister, and in welcoming her they also
paid a tribute to the inestimable services rendered to this very
country during the war by her distinguished husband. [Cheers]
He believed that that this was the first visit paid to Poole by Mrs
Lloyd George – an error which was immediately corrected by
the members of the audience who recalled an earlier visit in the
far-off pre-war days! He hoped the women of East Dorset would
use their votes wisely and well – an injunction which, in the face
of those serried ranks of unfranchised femininity, was obviously
superfluous.

Another burst of applause and Mrs Lloyd George is on her
feet. With feminine intuition she has accurately grasped the spirit
of that first meeting of the women electors of Poole. She was not
used, she said, to appearing before the footlight. (The signal was
quietly given, and the offending illuminations were promptly
extinguished.) That was not the first occasion she had visited
Poole. She had been there once with Lady Wimborne [the mother
of MP Freddie Guest] before the war. At that time the women were
calling loudly for the vote, but soon after came the war, and the
women of the country had thrown themselves into the fight so
splendidly that when the time came to ask for it again they had got
the vote easily and without any trouble at all. Now they had got
it they were going make the best of it. [Cheers] She wished to call
their attention that evening to some of the measures that had been
lately passed which more directly affected them as women. The
result of the Sex Disqualification (Removal) Act had thrown open

most of the professions which previously had been closed to them by either law or custom.

Among these was architecture, and 'I am sure,' said Mrs Lloyd George, 'that we women could give the men many tips in building houses – especially in regard to the inside of the houses. [Hear, hear] Also they now had a woman member of Parliament. Lady Astor was a splendid woman, and had the courage, in the first speech ever made by a woman in the House of Commons, to champion the cause of temperance. They wanted to see more women of that kind in Parliament.

All these challenges were opening new and fresh possibilities to our girls, and were a stimulus to parents to give the very best education they could afford to their girls. The aim of the Health Bill, she said, was National fitness, and that would be more easily secured when they had a final single authority rather than divided up into various local bodies.

Then there was the urgent need for houses; she believed they wanted about half a million new homes in order to meet the requirements of the people. These it was hoped to put in hand with the least loss of time. The high cost of living and profiteering were two other problems which would have to be dealt with. There was nothing, she thought, which the world needed more today than to be made secure against war. War may perhaps pay individuals, but never humanity. Only slightly less disastrous than war were industrial strikes.

They ought to be able to establish justice by reason. They had as remedies against these two evils the League of Nations and industrial courts. If we wanted these great measures made effective, however, we must see that they were properly carried out – and here was the great opportunity for the women of the country. After all, the women were the chancellors of the exchequer of their own homes, so it was to their interests to see that they did not pay more than they need for their food and clothing.

Then they must try in some way to deal with the liquor traffic, which was perhaps the greatest handicap to the happiness and prosperity of the nation. The evolution of it had been greatly hampered by the quarrels among temperance people themselves, who did not see eye to eye with each other. Some wanted prohibition and others State purchase. 'The best thing,' she concluded, 'is to take what we can get and be thankful for it.'

The words were spoken with a single-minded sincerity which went to the hearts of her hearers. The enthusiastic burst of applause which she was accorded on resuming her seat made one feel that, if ever the women of East Dorset should be called upon to choose a representative of the constituency for Parliament, and if by any possibility Mrs Lloyd George should become a candidate for that honour, there would be no question as to how their votes would be recorded. W.R.H.[25]

The *Western Gazette* played it straight:

Mrs Lloyd George addressed a largely-attended meeting, chiefly of women of the East Dorset Parliamentary Division, on Friday afternoon at Poole. Captain F. E. Guest, the MP for the Division, was the other chief speaker, and he was subjected to repeated interruption, principally from members of the fair sex.

And, during this period of industrial unrest, Mrs Lloyd George wisely passed questions on to the MP:

A woman in the audience handed in a list of questions addressed to Mrs Lloyd George, and which were answered at the latter's request by Capt. Guest.

It was perhaps a tribute to the importance of the visit that there was any media coverage at all, given the seating arrangements:

At a meeting of the Bournemouth and Dorset branch of the National Union of Journalists, Bournemouth, on Saturday, pressmen who attended Mrs Lloyd George's meeting drew attention to the wretched accommodation provided for them – what appeared to be a dirty box about 2½ ft. square in a corner of the hall, which not only necessitated one journalist using the corner of the stage, but placed the others in a cramped position, and prevented them writing up. It was unanimously decided to call the attention of those responsible for the organisation of the gathering to the complaint, which, it was agreed, was more than justified.[26]

Perhaps the creative W.R.H. had a comfortable seat.

In her speech, Mrs Lloyd George had run briskly through the Coalition's reconstruction manifesto. As Lloyd George wrote in 1938:

> She rarely speaks for more than five minutes; but what a rich store of commonsense she compresses into those five minutes.[27]

In 1913, when he introduced Mrs Lloyd George to the audience at the unveiling of the foundation stone of his church in Swansea, JTR revealed that 'Mrs Lloyd George had just whispered in his ear that she wished the speeches were equally as short in the House of Commons, because then they would be able to do their work with greater expedition than at present.'[28]

Back in London, on 15th and 16th March she hosted afternoon parties at No. 10 for Coalition supporters, their wives and daughters. On the second day there was a programme of music given by Lady Brittain, herself playing the harp, with songs from Welsh and other performers.[29] The next day, Mrs Lloyd George opened the Northwood War Memorial Hospital in Middlesex.[30] The Lloyd Georges were well known in West London, having in earlier times lived there. Furthermore it was the constituency of Dr Christopher Addison MP, the new Minister of Health (also responsible for housing). He later fell from grace, however, in part due to the amount of money being spent. He moved towards Labour, becoming a Labour MP in 1924, serving in various Labour governments until 1951.

As always, Mrs Lloyd George was pleased to see a memorial having a useful purpose, and that four dental officers and five dental nurses were being appointed by the Middlesex County Council Maternity and Child Welfare Centre.

The next day she opened a floral bazaar at the Congregational church in Barnsbury, Islington, north London.[31] (The building still stands but its colour now comes from the paint sold there, not flowers.)

Mrs Lloyd George's next by-election engagements continued

to feed speculation that she might run for Parliament one day, which she continued to deny:

> In spite of the widely circulated rumours to the contrary, it is understood that Mrs Lloyd George has no intention of becoming a Parliamentary candidate at the next General Election. She has, it is true, been approached on the matter, but, although she is a keen politician and takes an active interest in the political problems of the day, she is of the opinion that her greatest sphere of usefulness to the nation is outside and not inside the House of Commons.[32]

On 19th March it was time for her matinée for the National Adoption Association at the London Palladium. As it clashed with another at the Palace, attended by royalty, for the Blinded Soldiers' Children's Fund, the press suggested helpfully that 'you can still buy tickets for both and give the spare ones away.'[33]

It was then back to the political campaign trail, to Stockport, Lancashire, to support the two Coalition candidates, Walter Greenwood, Coalition Unionist, and Henry Fildes, Coalition Liberal. Stockport was one of the last remaining two-seat constituencies. After speaking in three Stockport locations,[34] Mrs Lloyd George had little time to lose in travelling back to London to speak for Tom Macnamara, the newly-promoted Cabinet member seeking to retain his Camberwell seat.

Over these two elections, her three Coalition candidates all won.

In Stockport, her speech notes show that she gave a robust defence of the Government at three women's meetings, and, this being an election, delivered a comprehensive run-through of policy issues. In 1921 and 1922, rallying-the-troops speeches would often be lighter on policy and more focused on loyalty and support for the Coalition:

> In late war poison gas played a large part. Not an honourable

method even for warfare. Reading papers giving account of this election, I find very desperate efforts being made to poison the minds of electors against the Government.

In a biography of Walpole it is said: 'no assertion was too wild, no insinuation too incredible, no lie too glaring' to be used against that great and patriotic statesman. I think almost the same may be said of the enemies of the present Government.

I think it may be of some service, especially to the women electors of Stockport if I deal very briefly with some of the criticism levelled against the Government.

There are some speakers and writers who talk as if all the troubles now upon us were due to the Government. Judging by the speeches of some, one would imagine that the very *existence* of such troubles as the *food*-trouble & the *Irish*-trouble were due to the Government now in power.

I think it is wicked to make suggestions of that kind.

The *food*-trouble is due to the *war*. We did not have it before the war. If we had not had the war we would not today be troubled at all by the shortage of food. Those of you who read Mr Asquith's speeches and the *Daily Herald* know that both admit that fact. Whatever Government was in power would be confronted by the same food shortage & high cost of living. When about 20 million men are engaged in destroying instead of producing it is bound to result in a shortage of food and other materials.

The blame for the shortage and consequent high prices must not be laid at the door of the British Government but at the door of the Prussian Junkers.

When you are inconvenienced by the food shortage, never forget two facts: we have more food in this country than in almost any country in the world. Then, food is cheaper here today than in any country in Europe. That very satisfactory state of things is due to two parties. First to our sailors, and secondly to our statesmen, particularly to the Food Controllers.

Take again the vexed Irish Problem. The existence of this very grave problem is not due to the Coalition Government. The Irish Problem was in existence long before any of us were born. It baffled men like Pitt, Disraeli, Gladstone and many others. It ill becomes some critics to find fault with the Government's treatment of Ireland. Some of them had a far better chance of settling the Irish Problem than this Government has.

There are other critics who find fault with the efforts made by the Government to *solve* some of the problems.

Take *Housing*. I regard decent houses as the first need of the nation. A homeless people can never be a contented people. We should never rest in Britain until we can find a house for each family.

To solve the Housing Problem you need three things: land, money, and labour. The Government has found the land, and is willing to help to find the money. But the Government cannot find labour. You cannot in a free country compel people to work. That is slavery. I believe they have compulsory labour in Russia. But I don't want that in Britain. We have done with slavery for ever. It is hard enough to have conscription in war. We must not think of it in peace. The *will to victory* helped us to win the war. The *will to work* will enable us to get all the houses we need.

Take *prices*. This, like housing, is of supreme importance to women. She is the Chancellor of the Exchequer in the Home. The high cost of living is due to very many causes. But it is not due to anything the Government *has* done, or has *not* done. There may be many remedies, but you cannot remedy it by passing any number of Acts of Parliament.

I have no respect for the *Profiteer*. The Government has none. Much has been done to check profiteering, but no man has wisdom enough to devise a scheme by which you can deal equitably and effectively with the evil.[35]

The *Yorkshire Post* added more of her robust defence of her husband's Liberalism:

They say Mr Lloyd George is not Liberal. I saw the other day that the Northcliffe Press was saying so. I was rather amused to see *The Times* talking about Liberalism. I have lived with Mr Lloyd George for thirty years and I think I ought know whether he is a Liberal better than the Northcliffe Press, and I can assure you that he is a Liberal by birth, training, and conviction – as good a Liberal as any living man. These criticisms are very unfair and unjust, and I sure that the women of Stockport will take that sort of criticism with a pinch of salt.[36]

*The Times* owner Lord Northcliffe's media stable also included the *Daily Mail* and the *Daily Mirror*.

*The Daily Telegraph* noted that hundreds of women were unable to gain admission (there were 26,000 women voters in Stockport) and that they were 'quite as ready with questions', many being 'on the reform of Divorce Laws and on temperance'.[37]

A day later, on 26th March, in south London's Camberwell, Tom Macnamara, the newly appointed Minister of Labour, was seeking re-election under the 'ministerial' rule. Mrs Lloyd George's draft speech notes make no reference to women, probably because Macnamara was running against Labour's Susan Lawrence, the first woman to contest a by-election since the election of Nancy Astor – and the second of only four women to contest a by-election in these four years. Instead, Mrs Lloyd George called for the voters to 'stick with Macnamara', suggesting the tide had turned (albeit not by much) with respect to unemployment (relevant as Macnamara was now Minister of Labour) and again emphasising the achievements of the Coalition Government, 'formed of the best brains of all the parties':

> There is, however, one thing that can be said for this Government without fear of contradiction. It has passed more legislation than any Government in this or any other Country in this or any other age. The legislation has made Britain among the most advanced countries in the whole world. Bad as are the conditions here in many ways, they are better than in almost any country in the world.
>
> There is much yet to be done. There are many difficult problems to solve; many reforms need to be carried. I think a Government formed of the best brains of all the parties will do more for us than the best brains of one party.[38]

In her 1927 article 'Petticoats behind Politics', which included reflections on some of the women in Parliament, Mrs Lloyd George was particularly complimentary about Miss

Lawrence (defeated by Macnamara but elected to Parliament in 1922):

> Of the Socialist women MPs at present in Parliament, the outstanding feature that impresses one concerning Miss Susan Lawrence is her genuineness. One is convinced from hearing her speak that she has never been, and never will be, animated by any desire to play to the gallery, but solely by an ardent wish to carve another niche in the Rock of woman's progress.[39]

Honesty and integrity were important virtues for Mrs Lloyd George.

The welfare state was continuing to add its resources to charity care. It was reported on the 26th, during a visit by the Queen, that a North Kensington baby centre that Mrs Lloyd George had opened in November 1918, was now going to get half of its funds from the Ministry of Health. Continued royal attention no doubt also helped.[40]

In the first half of 1920 there were three more by-elections in England involving Coalition Liberal candidates.

In Northampton Mrs Lloyd George did not campaign: it might have been awkward with another woman in the field, and Charles McCurdy, the newly appointed Food Controller, well-known, and the incumbent, could probably look after himself in a sensitive Liberal atmosphere, albeit not a safe seat (the result was 55/45 per cent). The local Liberal Association had decided to support him, despite being more in favour of sustaining an independent Liberal Party, and the Unionists agreed to support McCurdy. It was a straight fight, which McCurdy won, against Labour's Margaret Bondfield, later the first woman to take her seat in the Cabinet.

In her 1927 reflections on women politicians, Mrs Lloyd George showed she was not all sweetness and light: 'Miss Bondfield may be dismissed as negligible as far as any oratorical influence in the House of Commons is concerned.'[41]

In Sunderland, on 24th April, Coalition Liberal Hamar

Greenwood was seeking re-election, having been appointed Chief Secretary of Ireland. Mrs Lloyd George sent a message to the women of Sunderland by contributing to a special edition of the *Sunderland Pictorial*.[42]

In Louth, Lincolnshire, Coalition Liberal Thomas Wintringham was seeking to retain the seat (after the death of the incumbent), again against an Independent Liberal. Mrs Lloyd George sent a message of support. When Thomas died prematurely in 1921, his widow, Margaret, successfully defended the seat, becoming the second woman to take her seat in the Commons, and the first English-born woman MP.[43]

Aside from these English by-elections, in April, Mrs Lloyd George sent a message to the women electors of Edinburgh South and Edinburgh North, where two Coalition Unionists successfully defended their seats against Asquithian Liberals (and also against Labour in Edinburgh North): sensitive conflicts that Mrs Lloyd George tended to avoid. Distance may also have been a factor: Penistone in Yorkshire was the furthest north she travelled for a by-election whilst at No. 10, although she visited Newcastle when rallying Coalition members. Her visits to Scotland were either accompanying the PM, or addressing temperance audiences, or cruising on the yacht of Richard Lloyd George's father-in-law, Sir Robert McAlpine.[44]

She was now in need of a serious break. Her condition was later described as a 'breakdown in health', which required her to cut back her programme through the summer months, though typically she was not inactive.

# CHAPTER 7

# Mid-year Miscellany
## (April to July 1920)

ASIDE FROM THE by-elections, April, starting with Easter, was spent in Cricieth, with some engagements.

On Good Friday, 2nd April, Mrs Lloyd George presided over a concert in Caernarfon, accompanied by the Prime Minister, who also said a few words, as was his custom, 'expressing his pleasure in being able to enjoy a brief respite after the strenuous times of the last few years'.[1] On Easter Sunday they attended the Ffestiniog annual preaching meeting,[2] and visited Olwen's father-in-law, Dr R. D. Evans, the father of Tom Carey Evans.

On 10th April, the sister of one Lieutenant Frederick Holt, condemned to death for murder, handed in a petition for mercy at Downing Street, for the attention of Mrs Lloyd George – an unusual request, perhaps a reflection on her visible public standing.[3] The case had attracted much attention, but Holt's family's appeal to the Home Secretary failed. Lt. Holt was executed at Strangeways Prison on 13th April.[4]

Downing Street was getting a spring clean in her absence.[5]

A note to her private secretary listed a few errands:

Brynawelon, Criccieth, 21st April 1920

Dear Mr Rhys

Will you send out invitations to the ladies whose names and addresses I enclose. I have promised to give the Welsh delegates a reception at 8 o'clock on May 14th. A few more *may* be sent later on. Will you ask Sarah to send me a slate coloured hat with purple feathers down her [*sic*], also my black and blue cloak. Ask her to send also small mauve feathers, and a black aigrette. I am feeling better these days.

Yours sincerely M Lloyd George.

Sarah Jones was the long-serving family housekeeper; an aigrette, a feather worn in a headdress.

In Scotland the libertarian *Montrose Standard* wasn't for any more 'pussyfooting' around:

> There is still evidence that Mrs Lloyd George, Lady Astor and others are determined to thrust their temperance views down the parched throat of the people, and the Premier himself is supporting the Welsh Veto Bill. Now this Bill allows a minority of the people to deprive their neighbours of legitimate refreshment, and although I, for one, cannot see why even a majority should interfere with the liberties of a minority, we cannot allow the few to dictate to the many, for this is the end of freedom. So let us be on our guard against the 'Killjoys'.[6]

On 26th April she attended a council meeting in Caernarfon of the King Edward VII Welsh National Memorial Association for the Abolition of Tuberculosis. The debate was enlivened by frustration at the preferential treatment given to England over the distribution of grants for treating tuberculosis. Over lunch Mrs Lloyd George apologised for her infrequent attendance and thanked them for not striking her off their rolls.[7]

By the last week of April, Mrs Lloyd George was 'indisposed':

> It was hoped that Mrs Lloyd George would be in town to welcome the Premier on his return [from San Remo]. Unfortunately, however, Mrs Lloyd George has not quite recovered from her indisposition and she is thus prevented from returning for a few days. The League of Nations Bazaar, which Mrs Lloyd George intended to open tomorrow at Acton, will be opened by Lady Mond.[8]

Lady Mond would often help by taking her place when

plans had to change. She was also well known to JTR from his time in Swansea, when Sir Alfred Mond was the MP – not least, supporting the *Lady Mond Cookery Book*, sold by JTR's church, with several recipes supplied by the Rhys family.

However, 'the first Welsh lady JP' was able to take her seat 114 on the bench, at Porthmadog, where her husband had first appeared as an advocate.[9]

On 4th May Mrs Lloyd George returned to Downing Street and then on to The Firs, Cobham,[10] a house the Lloyd Georges took in 1919 as an out-of-London retreat, larger and more comfortable than Walton Heath, though surrounded by trees and without a view.[11]

'Pusseyfoots' [*sic*] were still in the sights of the *Framlingham Weekly News*:

> What is the influence which puts a still greater burden on the beer drinker of the country and allows the drinker of gaseous fluids, such as lemonade and ginger ale, to go scot free? A penny on a bottle of minerals would be the most remunerative tax and would, although to a very small extent, tend to equalize the burden which falls especially on the working man who chooses beer as his normal drink. Has Mrs Lloyd George, who is declared a Pusseyfoot, or the Premier, who is half-way there, managed to persuade the Chancellor to increase this already very heavy burden for 'Pussey' reasons? And is it not time that this victimization was stopped?[12]

The small Suffolk town of Framlingham had a good selection of pubs and a brewery. This may be just coincidental.

On 7th May the Liberal civil war intensified, at Leamington, when a group of Coalition Liberals stormed out of the annual Liberal conference after being shouted down by the Asquithians, ending any remaining pretence that unity might be established in the foreseeable future, certainly under Coalition.

Over the next two years Mrs Lloyd George's campaign message was increasingly aimed at sustaining support for the

Coalition, and engaging with constituency Liberals to rally support around the Lloyd George standard.

On Monday, 17th May, although restricted to a few words due to her cold, Mrs Lloyd George opened the Women's Institute (WI) exhibition of village handicrafts at the Royal Horticultural Hall, Vincent Square, Westminster, with her sister-in-law Mrs William George, and Megan. A quartet of girls in Welsh national costume greeted her, in recognition of the importance of Wales in WI history.[13] Mrs Lloyd George bought a marketing basket, some eggs, butter, and beeswax at the Welsh stall.[14] The Institute was important to her: in August 1917 she had opened the first WI Hall in Britain, at Penrhyndeudraeth, Caernarfonshire.

On 29th May, Mary Drew, Gladstone's daughter, wrote, hoping to come and watch the Trooping of the Colour from No. 10: watching from the windows as they did in her day would be fine, as opposed to sitting on the wall. My grandmother, Jane Rhys, recalled watching the Trooping of the Colour from the windows of No.10.[15]

June 1920 began with the Welsh Anglican Church becoming Disestablished, i.e. independent from the Church of England, an important moment. The formal handover was marked by the enthronement of the new Archbishop of Wales at St Asaph Cathedral in Denbighshire, attended by the Premier and Mrs Lloyd George. The ceremony was performed by the Archbishop of Canterbury, who deplored the severance of the newly-named 'Church in Wales' from the nation's official life, but bore no recriminations. The new Archbishop of Wales, A. G. Edwards, Bishop of St Asaph, who had close links with Lloyd George, rejoiced in the sense of unity in Wales.[16]

All agreeing to disagree, perhaps. But perhaps all was not as it should be, as this clipping more than two months later suggested, under the headline 'Alleged Breach of Discipline':

The Secretary's notes in the *Church Union Gazette* include the following: 'It is more than unfortunate that the occasion of the enthronement of the Archbishop of Wales should, from the point of view all good Churchmen, have been marred by a gross and serious breach of the Discipline and Order of the Church.'[17]

The 'serious breach' related to the dissenters, Mr and Mrs Lloyd George, receiving Communion that day:

... either by the Archbishop of Wales himself or by the Archbishop of Canterbury. If the Prime Minister and Mrs Lloyd George presented themselves quite unexpectedly for Communion, then the celebrant had no choice in the matter. But if it is the case that arrangements were made for the Prime Minister's Communion overnight, with the knowledge and consent of either of the English Archbishops or of the Archbishop of Wales, then, of course, the matter is extremely serious.[18]

The matter was raised before the Council of the English Church Union and letters were written, twice, to the Archbishop of Wales, receiving no response. With no further mention in the *Church Union Gazette*, we may assume the matter was diplomatically resolved.

On 4th June Mrs Lloyd George attended the wedding of Isabel Law, her next-door neighbour, daughter of Bonar Law, to Frederick Sykes, the Controller General of Civil Aviation. The couple flew from Croydon Airport to Newcastle, en route to Lindisfarne, Holy Island. Like Olwen, the couple eschewed St Margaret's Westminster, the customary marriage venue for the political world, the occasion being celebrated more privately (nonetheless attracting great crowds) at the Scottish Presbyterian Church of St Columba, in Chelsea.[19]

Mrs Lloyd George then went down to Lympne, Kent, for some rest at the house of Sir Philip Sassoon MP, Parliamentary Private Secretary to the PM. From there she wrote to JTR checking that her 'ladies' were being presented at the upcoming 'Court' at Buckingham Palace – the first 'Court' to be held since war broke out – adding the warning 'Miss Megan is coming up on Tuesday & if you are not there she breathes slaughter.'[20] It would be the first presentation at Court for Megan.

On the morning of 8th June, Mrs Lloyd George and Megan accompanied the Premier to Euston where he caught the train for Pwllheli, for the Congregational Union conference.[21] For once, it was Mrs Lloyd George who was not returning to north Wales. That evening she was the guest of honour in Portland Place, London, meeting Liberal ladies, accompanied by Megan.

On 10th June it was off to Buckingham Palace for the 'Court'. On Friday, as the guests made their way to the Palace, the *Western Gazette* writer noted, at what sounds like a fashion show on wheels, the difference in the attire of Mrs Lloyd George and Lady Asquith, probably reflecting their difference in character:

Friday night's Court held at Buckingham Palace was the first evening function of the kind since the guns began their demoniac overture to the great war. Remarkable popular interest was shown in the event. Big crowds assembled round the Palace and its approaches, which needed sedulous chaperoning by the foot and mounted police, though for the most composed of women and girls.

The critical unblinking survey to which the Royal guests in their carriages and motors were submitted by the multitude as they passed slowly into the Palace Courtyard must have been disconcerting. Nor, a London correspondent remarks, was the criticism by any means silent. One heard on all sides in tones transcending a stage whisper every manner of openly-expressed expert sartorial verdict. 'That's a rather nice effect – that one here in the green motor – the fair girl with the fichu, etc, etc.' The Prime Minister came in for his customary ovation when he sailed past with Mrs Lloyd George and Miss Megan, who looked quite nice. Mrs Asquith was among the dress sensations of the evening in her tight-fitting black sequin costume, silver lace halo, and shoes with high silver heels – a strange contrast with the comely simplicity of Mrs Lloyd George.

But the impression one gathered generally at the Court was how extravagantly many elderly and quite hopelessly passé women lavish their thought and money on wonderful costume effects that serve in reality only to accentuate the brutal sincerities of Anno Domini. It is a great gift in a lady to know how to dress herself on all occasions and at all epochs in her life.[22]

Hmmm...

*The Daily Telegraph* devoted four columns to the list of guests, alphabetically from Miss Abernathy to Baroness Zouche, with full details of their individual dress.[23]

On 11th June Christopher Addison, Minister of Health, responsible for housing, sent a memento, or 'momento':[24]

Ministry of Health, 11th June 1920

Dear Mrs Lloyd George,

I think perhaps you would be interested to have this little momento [*sic*] of the Ruislip-Northwood Housing Schemes, in which I was specially interested as it was my own district. Four different schemes are in active progress, with, I believe, houses completed and occupied in every one of them. To a great extent, we owe it to the energy of Dr Abbott.

With kind regards, yours sincerely, Christopher Addison

The 'momento' might have been the drawings of the housing projects in Ruislip-Northwood.

On Sunday, 12th June, the family attended the wedding of Sir Robert McAlpine's daughter Margaret – the sister of Roberta, the wife of Richard Lloyd George – at Oakshott, Surrey.[25] Mrs Lloyd George, accompanied by her sons Richard and Gwilym, followed this by a cruise in Scotland aboard Sir Robert's yacht *Naida*.[26]

With serious news in short supply, this was a good time for more friendly features on the leading lady of Downing Street, albeit underplaying her increasing political activities:

The Prime Minister's wife does not take a prominent part in politics; she leaves that to her brilliant husband, but in her quiet, firm, almost motherly way tackles problems of immense importance to the national weal. One of the busiest of our women leaders, she is a 'home' woman too, and with all her gentle dignity is motherliness personified.

The Premier's wife is greatly interested in temperance. 'I hope every woman will do something for the temperance cause,' was her conclusion to a fine speech on this subject given in Southampton early in the year. Her essentially practical point of view is noticeable when she draws attention to the fact that as a nation we are spending about four hundred millions on drink in this country during the year. 'That money is needed urgently for building houses for people and for other necessary things,' she declares. 'We really cannot afford to waste money on drink as we do now.'

Mrs Lloyd George is an idealist, but her ideals, aided by her sound common sense, bid fair to become realities. To provide fit homes for the people is, in her opinion, the most insistent of the strong after-war impulses making for a new world. There is a homeliness and charm in her idea that homeliness, so long as it does not mean pokiness, is a real virtue in a house. Our best architects have shown that smallness is compatible with convenience and comfort, whilst every woman knows that size and work grow together like Siamese twins!

'I think the great essential is a big living-room with space not only to turn round but to let the children play on a rainy day without being too much in the way, and where a father can stretch out his feet without putting them out of the room.

'I would have wide windows, too, looking several ways, and in country cottages, at least, I would adopt Sir Edwin Lutyens' idea of 'crawling windows ' – little thick glass windows close to the floor through which baby can look and see the birds without being lifted up.

'Behind this large living-room I would have a kitchen-scullery, well arranged, well fitted with a convenient slab and sink, hot and cold water, crockery shelves, a meat safe, and a good cupboard.

'I would like,' Mrs Lloyd George adds, 'to see all cottages built to face east and west, so to catch all the sunshine that may be about', and she finishes with the typically sound remark: 'But when we have built our ideal cottages the greater part of their comfort and utility and beauty will still depend upon the women.'[27]

Attention to detail – even if Lutyens' 'crawling windows' were unlikely to be installed in the new 'homes fit for heroes'.

On Monday, 21st June, Mrs Lloyd George took a stall at a sale at 18 Hill Street, off Berkeley Square, London, in aid of the Bowmont Centre, Inverness, a home to benefit child welfare in the Highlands.[28]

On 27th June the Premier, Mrs Lloyd George and Megan attended the annual flower show at the Castle Street Welsh chapel, near Oxford Circus, where the PM spoke in Welsh and in English.[29] The flower show was an annual event in the London Welsh calendar that the Lloyd Georges seldom missed. Breaking, like Isabel Law, from political tradition, Olwen was married in this Baptist chapel, rather than St Margaret's, Westminster.

On 1st July Mrs Lloyd George hosted a No. 10 garden party for maimed soldiers from four London military hospitals (Millbank, Roehampton, Shepherd's Bush and Tooting).[30] The next day she opened a fête in Acton, West London, accompanied by Lady Rhondda and Lady Brittain, in aid of a hospital extension.[31] That evening, she chaperoned Megan to a jazz dance at the Hyde Park Hotel – for Megan, having being presented at Court, this was her first 'season':

> Mrs Lloyd George, in black, was shepherding Miss Megan Lloyd George in a white frilled dress of tulle. Lord St Oswald provided the musical portion of the dance, and while he played the drum, a few of his friends were hard at producing jazz sounds from weird instruments they brought with them.[32]

On 14th July a dance for the debutante Miss Megan was given at Downing Street, the Bastille Day date perhaps to honour her time in Paris. The menu at least was in French, a card autographed by Megan being in the JTR Collection, the final menu item *Petit Fours Parisienne*:

> An interesting and brilliant social function was given at No. 10

Downing-street, to-night when Mrs Lloyd George gave a dance for her daughter, Miss Megan Lloyd George, one of the season's debutantes. The Prime Minister, still detained with the Germans at Spa, was disappointed to have to miss this occasion. Mrs Lloyd George received her guests in a grey satin dress with gold embroidery and gold lace, while Miss Megan Lloyd George was radiant in a silver lace dress over a foundation of georgette of shell pink ninon, caught at the waist with a band of silver tissue. The white and gold reception room was decorated with choice summer flowers, and supper was served in the dining room.[33]

Among those who attended were Prince Paul of Serbia, Lord and Lady Birkenhead, Sir Alfred and Lady Mond, Sir Frederick and Lady Sykes, Bonar Law, and Megan's 'special girl friends', Miss Murchison, Miss Shaw, Miss de Worms, and Miss Roberts. (illustration 48)

On 17th July Mrs Lloyd George was back in Wales, in Denbigh, where a war memorial sanatorium was being opened by the King and Queen and Princess Mary.[34]

On 22nd July she hosted a concert at No. 10 for St Bartholomew's Hospital.[35] This concert was run by Alfred T. Davies, the MP for Lincoln, probably aided by JTR. The response letters in the postbag from Lord Crewe, Lord St Davids, Sir Arthur Griffith-Boscawen, David Brynmor Jones, and W. Burdett-Coutts suggests that invitees unable to attend might nonetheless send money for their tickets, at times with the ticket for resale. All tickets were sold, raising £1,400, with 1,000 guineas raised by an auction.[36]

In Suffolk, the Coalition Unionist Sir Arthur Churchman, of the tobacco family, was defending the Woodbridge seat in a by-election. Both the PM and Mrs Lloyd George sent messages of support. Addressing the women voters, Mrs Lloyd George repeated her familiar litany on the record number of acts passed by the Coalition, noting that 'the Health and Housing Acts are red-letter marks of social progress'. Lloyd George's message attacked the Labour contender: 'an avowed supporter of nationalisation – to take the land, the mines, the means of transport right out of private hands... and being ominously silent about compensation.' The Coalition retained the seat, the vote dividing 53/47 per cent.

Next on the social calendar, Mrs Lloyd George and Megan attended a Buckingham Palace garden party on 26th July.[37] That day Lord Sandhurst invited JTR to become a Governor of St Bartholomew's Hospital, reassuring him that 'the duties are practically nothing'. JTR accepted, later becoming a member of the house committee and chairman of the finance committee. His gubernatorial staff (rod of office) remains in the family's possession. JTR was a good fund-raiser, a keen stock-picker (his accounts books survive), a man of the material cloth turned Man of the Cloth – and he would also share market tips with Olwen's husband, Tom Carey Evans.

On 2nd August Mrs Lloyd George hosted a garden fête at Brynawelon, raising funds for the Cricieth war memorial. It was opened by Lady Astor, who auctioned sheep and pigs at the event.[38]

Mrs Lloyd George then travelled to Cardiff, to the Prince of Wales Hospital. She inspected, with Sir John and Lady Lynn-Thomas and others, new buildings built to replace those damaged by a fire in January.[39] Whilst in south Wales she and the PM were due to attend the Welsh Eisteddfod at Barry, and to stay with Sir Rhys Williams, MP at Miskin Manor, Pontyclun, but Lloyd George's work kept him away and Mrs Lloyd George's car broke down.[40] The Eisteddfod nonetheless had record takings.

CHAPTER 8

# Dame Margaret

## (August to December 1920)

ON 26TH AUGUST King George V announced that Councillor and JP Margaret Lloyd George was to become a Dame Grand Cross of the Order of the British Empire (GBE) in recognition for her wartime fundraising for 'charities, hospitals and other public-spirited movements', raising £250,000 (£10 million today).

> No one has received a war honour which has been more thoroughly deserved than Mrs Lloyd George, who has become the Dame of the British Empire in recognition of her work for charities during the war. This is the highest degree of the Order, and is a fitting acknowledgment of the success of the Premier's wife in organising assistance to various funds to the extent of a quarter of a million. What she did for the Welsh troops is well known in the Principality, but it only represents a small portion of her achievements.
>
> Since the armistice she has continued to labour for charities, always without ostentation: indeed, her breakdown in health was due largely to the way in which she overworked herself in the good causes to which she lent her aid. She is now much better, and hopes to join her husband at Lucerne shortly. In all her work for charity she has been greatly helped by her secretary, Mr J. T. Rhys, formerly minister at Swansea and Pontycymmer.[1]

For once she took a whole month off in Wales, and did not go to Lucerne. But even a little travelling had its risks:

When Mrs Lloyd George opened Merioneth Red Cross Cottage Hospital yesterday the chairman explained that she had been delayed by a motor car in front meeting with an accident, and only by the merest luck the Premier's wife was not involved.[2]

In late August it had been expected that she and family members would act in the Harlech Historical Pageant, but Gwilym, Megan and Lloyd George were all in Switzerland. Mrs Lloyd George did go to Harlech, and the family would participate more actively in 1922.[3]

From Cricieth Mrs Lloyd George worked with JTR on her selection of women JPs for Wales: 'What can you do to reduce the number of JPs to 20. You must not leave a county out. I think you must reduce Glamorgan in some way or other.'[4]

In the event 21 JPs were appointed in Wales, in addition to Mrs Lloyd George, the only Welsh woman amongst the original seven. On her list was Winifred Coombe Tennant, suffragist, arts philanthropist and spiritualist, then seeking a political career. Winifred wrote in her diary:

19 July, Monday. *Western Mail* telegraphed for my photograph – I wonder what this portends?
20 July, Tuesday. Heard from the Lord Chancellor I had been appointed a magistrate for the County of Glamorgan. It is one of the very few honours I ever desired.[5]

Later, in March 1921, Winifred was to meet Mrs Lloyd George, Megan and JTR at No. 10:

15 March, Tuesday. Lunched with Megan at 10 Downing Street, Mr Rees [sic] (Mrs Lloyd George's secretary) present. Much interesting political talk. He told me that every effort was made to down me in favour of another woman when the women justices list was being made, and the Lord Chancellor's Department returned it eight times to Mrs Lloyd George with my name crossed out and she put it back each time, and finally said that unless it was passed with my name as she had placed it she would cancel

the whole list. He is going to tell me the whole story next time we meet.

Her diary editor Peter Lord added: 'The "whole story" was not recorded in the diary. It may be that Winifred was considered a loose cannon by the Lord Chancellor's Department, given her association with socialists and pacifists.'

Later, Winifred was selected as the Lloyd George Liberal candidate for the Gloucestershire constituency of the Forest of Dean, honing her campaign skills with Mrs Lloyd George in 1922 on the latter's West Country tour.

Mrs Lloyd George's note to JTR also included another interesting comment to her Cardiganshire-born private secretary:

> I have heard from a lady who had been asked to speak at various towns in Cardiganshire that her meetings are cancelled because she has declared herself a Coalition.

On Wednesday, 29th September, Mrs Lloyd George and Megan opened a bazaar at Swansea, in fine weather, in support of local nurses. Attending was Mrs M. B. Williams (Killay House), one of the newly appointed JPs on Mrs Lloyd George's list.

After the break, October began with a bazaar in Fenland's Wisbech, Cambridgeshire (accompanying the local MP), and then laying the first stone at a new housing scheme in Llandudno, where she also addressed the local Liberal Association. There is *Pathé News* coverage of this visit. Lloyd George joined her in the Welsh seaside resort, addressing the Welsh National Liberal Council. The busy east-west schedule squeezed out a visit to Lincoln (the constituency of the supportive Coalition Unionist Alfred T. Davies), due to take place the day after Wisbech.

On 19th October she attended a luncheon of 100 women and their male guests in aid of the London Royal Free Hospital

School of Medicine for Women. Sir George Newman, the Ministry's Chief Medical Officer, was her guest. It was an early outing for 'Dame Margaret', although she had yet to be formally invested by the King. The attendees made for distinguished company:

> The New Chivalry: Famous Women Entertain Male Guests: The hostesses, headed by Princess Louise, Duchess of Argyll, included women distinguished in science, art, literature, the learned professions, and every walk of political, industrial, and social life. The chief guest of honour, the Premier, was unable to attend, and, in the absence owing to illness of Dr Addison (who was to have taken his place), Sir George Newman, Ministry of Health, was yesterday chosen as the guest of Dame Margaret Lloyd George.
>
> A note of plainness and simplicity was struck as regards dress – the Countess of Minto representing the women of the Court of Queen Mary, Lady Gosford – the Court; Lady Northcote – the Dominions; Lady Crewe – women JPs; Mrs Lloyd George – the Ministry; Lady Rhondda – women in business; the Lady Mayoress – City women; Lady Aberconway – women's suffrage; Lady Ampthill – VAD's; Miss Aldrich Blake – women singers; Miss Louisa Garrett Anderson – women in medicine; Dame Clara Butt (who led the National Anthem at the function) – singers; Lt.-Col. Miriam Castle – Salvation Army; Viscountess Burnham – women in journalism, Countess Curzon of Kedleston – the Ministry; Lady Hulton – women in the daily press; Miss Lilian Braithwaite – actresses; Miss Lena Ashwell – Drama.[6]

On 21st October Mrs Lloyd George presided over a meeting of some 400 members of the London Welsh community, now regarded as the foundation date of the Young Wales Association. She became its first President.[7]

> Proposals are afoot to organise in London a young women's association, and its purpose is to bring to one association all the Welsh movements in the Metropolis in connection with tennis and other recreative pursuits. To inaugurate the movement a conversazione was held on Wednesday night at the Portman-

rooms, and was attended by a large number of London Welshmen. Addresses were delivered on the desirability of an association on the lines proposed, and it is intended to hold further meetings so as to put the proposal on a practical basis.[8]

On 28th October came an engagement a little out of pattern: opening a new furnishings gallery extension at Brown's, the well-known department store, on the landmark 'Rows' of Chester, albeit in a good cause. The store was founded in 1780 by Susannah Brown – perhaps Mrs Lloyd George was also happy to support a store founded by a woman.

Upwards of 2,000 people were reported to have attended the sale period, including Lady Arthur Grosvenor (widow of the Duke of Westminster), and the Mayor of Chester, who also happened to be the Chairman of the store and great-grandson of the founder.

Mrs Lloyd George's speech survives, in JTR's hand, on six pages of small-sized Downing St embossed notepaper. She said she was not going to talk politics but then immediately defended private enterprise (as did the other speakers). An interesting event for its nuanced addresses, and featuring the biblical Ichabod, as on other occasions, symbolising 'departed glory':

It is a source of great pleasure to me to visit once again your picturesque & famous city. Chester has played a great part in the stirring history of this land. The very Welsh name of the City in English & in Welsh takes us back to very early times. You are citizens of no mean city.

The enterprise which has brought us together today shows you are not content to live in the *past*. It show that you are anxious to keep *abreast*, if not *ahead* of the times. So long as this spirit prevails it is not likely that 'Ichabod' will be written over your ancient walls.

To me this enterprise has more than a merely commercial aspect. In spite of the depression in the worlds of commerce and of industry, this firm carries out a great *extension* scheme. They have not lost faith either in their own future or the future of the country. It is the spirit that made Britain a nation of Shopkeepers that has made Britain second to none among all the nations of the world.

I am not here to talk politics. I am glad to escape from politics if only for a few hours. I cannot however help expressing the hope that whatever changes may take place in our laws we shall never discourage private initiative and private enterprise. Nothing could be more disastrous than that. Scope for initiative and reward for successful enterprises are the conditions of progress.

To celebrate this event Messrs Brown & Co have promised to give one half of the gross proceeds of the day to the Chester Cathedral Restoration Fund, the Chester YMCA & Chester Council of Social Welfare. That is a generous offer. I hope you will all buy everything you want today. I do not think the firm will object if you buy some things you *don't* want. This is an occasion on which we may be excused for being a little extravagant.

I trust the result of the day's proceedings will be of substantial help to the Societies and to the Firm.[9]

During wartime rationing Mrs Lloyd George had campaigned against luxuries and unnecessary consumption. War was now over, but recovery was coming only slowly for most people. We hear a defence of private enterprise (in contrast to nationalisation) and of the 'trade and manufacturers'. The reference (below) by the Mayor to the Gladstone family (former Liberal Prime Minister Gladstone's grand castle/mansion was in Hawarden, Flintshire) was possibly an acknowledgement the presence of the Hon. Mrs H. N. Gladstone, the Grand Old Man's daughter-in-law…

Opening the proceedings, the Mayor said we knew that the late Mrs Gladstone, by her care of her illustrious husband, did much to enable him to sustain the burdens of office, and to carry out his duties to a very advanced period of life. The history of the present day had not been written, but we might safely assume that the Prime Minister, who today directed the destinies of our Empire, could not have sustained the vast burden, and responsibilities which war and peace had laid upon him, had it not been that he had someone near to him prepared to pour out an unstinted stream of care and sympathy and love. [Applause]

Dame Margaret Lloyd George, who had honoured them with her presence that day, besides being a woman of affairs took an active interest in all problems of the day, and she recognised how much depended upon the trade and manufacture of this country. She recognised that it was not by nationalisation or confiscation nor by any other such means that we were to return to our aforetime prosperity, but by the somewhat prosaic method of manufacturing and selling goods. That, he took it, was the reason of her presence that day.

It seemed to him there was far more in our trade and manufacture than profit-making. He believed that the manufacturers and distributors of this country did a public service, as well as create advantage to themselves. That was more, of course, in connection with manufacturing, and as some of them (his hearers) knew, he was connected with the manufacturing interest as well as the retail interest. It was a satisfaction to him to know that year by year they supplied the needs of at least 100,000 of their fellow creatures.

They sometimes were accused of being a luxury trade, but he entirely disagreed with that. Many of the goods they supplied were necessities, and in the present day, in our present era of civilisation, it was not sufficient that our material needs only should be supplied. We had aesthetic sense, and it was quite as necessary we should cultivate that and supply its needs, as to supply the needs of our material bodies. He was prepared to say that a pretty hat was far more inspiring, far more heartening, far more comforting, than an umbrella. [Laughter] That was the reason why he contended that things of beauty were as necessary to us as things of utility.

He concluded by suggesting that having carried on their business near that spot for 124 years, they must have done some public service as well as benefited.[10]

Mrs Lloyd George's reported remarks, very similar to JTR's handwritten version, omitted the reference to 'Britain as a nation of shopkeepers' – probably wise, given that it was first used as a form of derision by Napoleon. Nor does the newspaper refer to Ichabod – perhaps she skipped that too! However, Ichabod, 'departed glory', returned a hundred years later, when the store finally closed.

If Mrs Lloyd George had not committed to being in Chester, she and Lloyd George might have accepted Clementine Churchill's invitation to dinner, sent on 22nd October.[11]

On 3rd November, when opening the St Paul's Presbyterian Church bazaar at Enfield, North London, her hosts were getting to grips with how to address their guest.

In introducing her, the Chairman, Mr A. B. Barrand, MP, said she preferred to be addressed 'Mrs' and not 'Dame.' Officially, of course, she had yet to be formally invested with the title by the King.[12]

That day she also unveiled a three-light stained-glass window at the Epping Congregational Church in the memory of 14 members of the congregation who fell in the war.[13]

On 4th November Mrs Lloyd George celebrated her birthday by being present at the Trade showing of the Butcher's film company version of Allen Raine's well-known story *By Berwen Banks* (a vicar's son marries the daughter of a dissenter), and said she immensely enjoyed seeing such beautiful Welsh scenery on the film.[14]

She confessed to *The Sunday Post* that she couldn't recognise any of the Welsh locations.[15]

Did her birthday presents included Mrs Asquith's new autobiography? The press found another excuse to compare 'Premieresses':

To be as frank as Mrs Asquith herself, she [Mrs Asquith] has never been regarded as the ideal kind of wife for a Premier. She is too clever in her own right, and does not accept the humble domestic role attributed to Mrs Gladstone, Lady Beaconsfield and Mrs Lloyd George. True, Lady Salisbury was clever enough, and ruled with great political power behind the footlights. But exceptions can be made for the wives of aristocratic Prime Ministers. It is only when a Liberal lady Premieress breaks the stupid tradition that all is wrong.[16]

The next day Mrs Lloyd George hosted a Downing Street meeting, planning a Welsh National Exhibition for Cardiff in 1922, a venture supported by the Prime Minister. The project would be shelved as economic conditions worsened. Later that day she appeared on the platform at the YWCA bazaar at the Grand Central Hall, Westminster.[17]

On 8th November Mrs Lloyd George was invested GBE by the King. On the following day, she sported the deep purple ribbon of the Order, when she accompanied the Premier to the Lord Mayor's Guildhall Banquet, along with the Cabinet.[18] (illustration 41)

Two days later, the Dame was auctioning her husband:

An autographed photograph of the Premier will be auctioned at a bazaar to be opened by Mrs Lloyd George at the Baptist Church, Putney, Wednesday afternoon.[19]

On Armistice Day, 11th November, at the Cenotaph, Whitehall, and at the Tomb of the Unknown Warrior, Westminster Abbey, Mrs Lloyd George placed tributes on behalf of the Welsh women of Canning Town.

That day, King George V had laid to rest the remains of the Unknown Warrior.[20]

On the afternoon of the 12th the flower-loving Mrs Lloyd George visited the Abbey with a bunch of vari-coloured chrysanthemums.[21]

JTR retained two tributes to Mrs Lloyd George that marked her Damehood, one by the new feminist paper *Time and Tide*, and one (in Welsh) by the Rev. Thomas Charles Williams, family friend and minister from the Calvinistic Methodist Church, in the pastoral magazine *Drysorfa*. The latter was an updated edition of a very personal tribute that the Rev.

Williams had written in 1914 in *Ymwelydd Misol (The Monthly Visitor).*[22]

*Time and Tide* had been founded in May by Lady Margaret Rhondda, the suffragette and businesswoman daughter of Lady Sybil Rhondda. Margaret Haig Thomas had inherited both her father's title (through a special arrangement he had negotiated) and his south Wales business empire.

The *Time and Tide* tribute was less personal and somewhat more independent, and with a particular focus on her public persona. The tribute (an extract is cited here) was published the day after Armistice Day, in their series 'Personalities and Powers'.[23] (illustration 40)

It has not been the practice in these pages to follow the custom of taking 'wives', as such, seriously; why, then, does the Premier's wife figure as a Personality and Power? Because she is one in her own right. She is a woman who, through the effect of her own character, and quite apart from adventitious aids, counts, and counts for good.

It is probably perfectly true to say that, had she not been the wife of Mr Lloyd George, she would never have been heard of (she is in no sense an ambitious woman), but it is also true to say that as things are she really matters; as the wife of the Premier, she is, in her quiet way, one of the personalities and powers of to-day.

It is not that she is overawed by this wonderful husband of hers; for all her simplicity, one would be just a little sorry for the person who imagined that he could overawe Dame Margaret, or as she prefers to be called, Mrs Lloyd George. It is rumoured that there were people in former days, when partisan feeling ran high, who tried to visit Mr Lloyd George's political sins on his wife's head; people who tried to be rude or impertinent. Possibly they thought it would be an easy task to browbeat such a kindly, unassuming woman – they proved wrong. Mrs Lloyd George emerged the victor from all such encounters, and, moreover, a victor who had never for one moment shed her dignity.

Mrs Lloyd George's position is no sinecure, and she is too conscientious to shrink from the heavy routine it involves. It would be interesting, if depressing, to know how many bazaars she opens in a year. Lately her work has increased. She figures not only at these and other semi-political functions; her sound common sense and practical outlook have been made use of on a certain number of influential Committees, and she attends many political meetings, and on occasion makes political speeches. Like most shy people, she does not find speaking at all easy; it is among the worst of the burdens which her position lays upon her.

It is probable that, although she enunciates sound Coalition Liberal principles, she is really indifferent to politics, as it is certain that though, on occasions, she has expressed adherence to sound – but moderate – feminist principles, she is at heart but little concerned with feminism. The information of her recorded words reveals to the initiated not that she possesses strong views on such matters, but that she is a loyal and hard-working helpmeet.

But in the things which, after all, count for more than just politics, in loyalty, simplicity, dignity, kind-heartedness, Mrs Lloyd George is not the mouthpiece of others, she is her own characteristic self. She is a pattern of a very fine type of woman, and as the wife of the Premier she sets an example which has not always been equalled in the past [and] which it would be difficult to surpass. She is not only a power, she's a power for good.

O.Y.S.

Friendly, polite, complimentary – though O.Y.S. underestimates her political contribution. Whilst she was at first cautious about public speaking, she became confident and effective. However this was written in late 1920, and she was yet to make her most notable impact in 1921. As we shall see, after a week's campaigning in Cardiganshire, *The Times* would reassess her capabilities completely.

Mrs Lloyd George may have eschewed Westminster politics, but was surely not indifferent to the political policies being pursued, yet took care not to oppose her husband's policies and would avoid the tricky questions, as she steered her careful path through life's obligations and choices. Someone with a clear set of priorities and comfortable with her moral compass. Not someone out to rock the boat for change, but someone prepared to compromise in the cause of making progress, viz. her approach to temperance. As to feminism, 'sound but moderate principles' seems to fit all she did, whilst eschewing radicalism and violence. The promotion of opportunities for women was a cause to which she was dedicated.

The Middleton and Prestwich by-election in Lancashire, from which the Labour candidate withdrew in order to avoid door-to-door canvassing during an outbreak of smallpox, was not contested. The newly-appointed Recorder of Birmingham, Coalition Liberal Ryland Adkins, sought, and gained, re-election.

On 16th November Dame Margaret attended a charity dinner in aid of The Queen's Hospital for Children at Bethnal Green, presided over by the Duke of York.[24]

On the 23rd there was the first night of a play to see at the Strand, with Megan.[25] Then there was America's Thanksgiving to celebrate, at the Hotel Cecil, under the presidency of department store owner Gordon Selfridge.[26]

Guests included the economist Lettice Fisher (who would shortly join Mrs Lloyd George on a short tour to the north of England) and Viscountess Margaret Rhondda. Perhaps it was an opportunity to exchange a friendly word with the owner of *Time and Tide* about the tribute to the Dame in the paper?

On 27th November Mrs Lloyd George was a stallholder at the Gilbert and Sullivan fair for the Girls' Realm Guild of Service at the Royal Horticultural Hall.[27]

On 29th November it was announced that Gwilym was engaged to marry Edna G. Jones, the sister of the Mayoress of Caernarfon.[28] Gwilym would soon have a small mission for JTR.

December began on a more sombre note, in the very Victorian Abney Park Cemetery, Stoke Newington. Mrs Lloyd George and Megan attended the interment of Arthur Rhys Roberts, David Lloyd George's former law business partner in London. Herbert Lewis represented the PM.[29]

On 3rd December it was down to Blackheath

Congregational church hall for a fund-raising event; the next day she had a busy time in Cardiff, with a visit to the Prince of Wales Hospital, attending the opening of a number of new departments, followed by a choral prize giving and a concert.[30] She left Cardiff early for royal engagements, before travelling north to rally the Coalition faithful:

> Mrs Lloyd George returns to London early today, being one of the company invited by the Earl and Countess Curzon of Kedleston to meet the King and Queen of Denmark. Tomorrow she will be at the Guildhall for the Prince of Wales' visit, and will afterwards drive direct to the railway station to depart for Leeds, where, with Mrs H. A. L. Fisher, the wife of the Minister for Education, she will carry out a series of political and philanthropic engagements. On Thursday Mrs Lloyd George will be entertained by the Lord Mayor of Newcastle at a luncheon, and will fulfil other engagements in that city.[31]

The economist Lettice Fisher was a leading activist in the suffrage movement and founder of the National Council for the Unmarried Mother and her Child (now known as Gingerbread). She would have been a very good partner for speaking to women's groups.

In Leeds the round of non-political engagements included a visit to the maternity hospital. In Newcastle they both addressed the Northern Council of Coalition Liberals, where Mrs Lloyd George declared, for anyone who might have any doubts, 'I was born a Liberal, and I hope to live and die a Liberal'.[32]

As the tour began she was fending off her customary winter cold. She stayed the course but was abed on her return, her asthma playing her up, though not before joining the men at an after-dinner reception at the (Tory) Constitutional Club:

> Mr Lloyd George was entertained at a complimentary dinner at the Constitutional Club on Friday night. This is the first time that a Liberal Premier has ever been the guest at the great Unionist institution. Mr Bonar Law, President of the Club, was in the

chair, and after dinner a number of ladies were admitted to the banqueting hall. Amongst them were Mrs Lloyd George and Miss Megan Lloyd George.[33]

The JTR Collection includes a short letter from Lettice Fisher, asking after Mrs Lloyd George after their 'northern affair', hoping her cold was better, and saying she almost looked in but she herself was 'wet and loaded up with parcels'.[34]

We may assume Mrs Lloyd George missed the Gala Concert at the Albert Hall on 8th December for the Boy Scouts Association, organised by Dame Nellie Melba and supported by the pianist Arthur Rubinstein; and the YMCA ball in aid of boys' clubs and holiday camps; and the dinner at Buckingham Palace that celebrated the close of the Australasian tour of the Prince of Wales. But she was able to address 'an earnest appeal to women' voting in the upcoming Abertillery by-election – though her message, and one from Lloyd George, could do little to prevent the Coalition Liberal candidate losing 2:1, Labour retaining the safe seat.[35]

Throughout 1920, Mrs Lloyd George had campaigned at all the compass points of the country: in Wales, the north, the east, London and in the south-west. Her next major political engagement would be the Cardiganshire by-election in February 1921.

Plans for Christmas at Chequers were shelved, as she retired to Cricieth for a rest.[36] The PM was not expected to join her, as he concentrated on the unemployment problem.

Shortly before Christmas the reliable JTR was helping ensure Gwilym was duly supplied with a choice of engagement rings for his fiancée:

Dollarog, 16 December 1920

Dear Mr Rhys

I am returning to you tomorrow the rings Carrington's lent me. We have not taken one of them, as my fiancée would like to see one or two more. As we hope to be up in town ere long, it can wait, though you might ask 'Dame Margaret' to bring one or two down at Xmas, like Megan has. That is a ring with no outstanding stone. I have also asked them to send me my Tweed overcoat that I left there. I know you *never* forget.

Lovely weather here. Suits me well.

Kindest regards yrs Gwilym Lloyd George[37]

For Margaret Lloyd George, the busiest year of all lay ahead.

CHAPTER 9

# From Chequers to Cardiganshire

## (January to February 1921)

NINETEEN TWENTY-ONE BEGAN with a clear warning from the Raj:

11 Ulnoor Road, Bangalore, Jan 7th
Dear Mr Rhys
You really are a brick sending your weekly reports as you do – I was ever so sorry to hear of Mamie's illness – I did so warn her against taking on any engagements during the winter months – as she always catches these beastly colds. It is her one weakness. However you must be firm – and not let her have any more – she must 'see off' everything from October until April...

We are all wondering who is to be the new Vice Roy. They do take a time to make up their minds don't they. Makes it look as if no one wanted it.

Well, diolch yn fawr for all your letters – Don't forget I shall expect the whole family to meet me at Tilbury!!! – I hope they'll send a car –

Kindest regards from us both, & from Miss Reis [sic].
Yours sincerely, Olwen Carey Evans[1]

The next viceroy would be Lord Reading, who would appoint Tom Carey Evans as his personal physician, promoting him above higher ranked military men, and whisking Olwen and Tom off to the Viceregal Lodge at Simla in the summer months. Grand as it sounds, Tom did not enjoy the job, in that it did not further his experience as a surgeon – he was much happier when he returned to more regular hospital duties in the UK.[2] (illustration 18)

Olwen's warning went unheeded. Mrs Lloyd George plunged into the busiest of her six years at No. 10; the warning would prove prescient.

The first engagement was comfortable enough as the Lloyd George family formally took residence at Chequers, duly reported in the local Berkshire press:

Mr Lloyd George, with Mrs Lloyd George, have formally received Chequers, the magnificent residence given to the nation as a country seat for British Prime Ministers, by Lord Lee of Fareham. The Premier, with Miss Megan Lloyd George, motored from London, and Mrs Lloyd George, who was on a visit to Wales, arrived at Chequers in the evening. At the formal presentation there were a large number of guests. Lord Lee gave the house to the Premier as head of the Government and amongst those present were Lord and Lady Reading, Sir Robert Horne, Lord Milner, Lord Riddell, Sir Hamar and Lady Greenwood, and the U.S. Ambassador.[3]

In an interview in October 1922, the day after leaving No. 10, Mrs Lloyd George would remark:

I hardly know yet what I shall miss most or the longest. Going to Chequers was very wonderful. It is strange now to think that we may not be there again. No, it didn't feel official, a mere historic background. One could really rest there. It is so beautiful that one felt soothed there.[4]

An early political action was to send a message of support to the women of Dover, where J. J. Astor was the Coalition Unionist candidate in the by-election. The suffrage movement, often Mrs Lloyd George's greatest critic, did not shy from taking her to task over some of her claims. *The Vote*, the newspaper of the Women's Freedom League (first editor Charlotte Despard), wrote:

During the recent by-elections Mrs Lloyd George has been
making a special appeal to the women voters to support the
Coalition candidates, one of the reasons being that the Coalition
Government has brought about increased wages for women!
It is quite true that many women working in the service of the
Government are now receiving more money than in pre-war days.
But men's salaries have increased in a much greater proportion;
and it would be difficult to find any women whose salaries
have increased as much as the cost of living—now 168 per cent
(according to Board of Trade figures) above that of pre-war days.
Mrs Lloyd George omitted to make any reference to the 150,000
unemployed women in this country, for whom the Government, so
far, has not proposed to do anything, and has not even considered
the inclusion of a woman in its proposed Commission of Inquiry
into Unemployment. We do not think that even Mrs Lloyd George
can seriously claim that the economic position of women has
improved under the present Government.[5]

John Jacob Astor, nephew of Nancy's husband, was defeated
by Horatio Bottomley's Independent candidate.

A week later *The Vote* kept up its critique of Mrs Lloyd
George's claims and looked forward to the 'incalculable silent
voters' to save the country.

The Press has become quite excited about the influence of the
women's vote at Dover. *The Times* has devoted a whole column to
this matter, and solemnly assures us that 'the women's vote was
obviously decisive,' and gravely dwells upon 'the new phenomenon
which appeared in politics with the passing of the last Reform
Act – the creation of a large incalculable vote', declaring that 'the
new silent voters are the women; their power is immense; they are
nearly half the total electorate'!

This, of course, is all very gratifying. Just before this particular
election we read in the papers that all the clergymen in Dover,
of varying denominations, had signed a document to the effect
that they would not support the candidate who was ultimately
successful. Then the Prime Minister's wife issued an appeal to
women voters to vote for the Coalition candidate, telling them all
the wonderful (?) things the present Government had done for

women; but neither the local clergymen nor Mrs Lloyd George herself exercised much influence on the women, if they all, as the Press comments appear to imply, voted for the Coalitionist's opponent!

Another paper has just been discussing the party-politics of Welsh women, and relates that one of them said recently: 'At the last election I voted with my heart; at the next election I shall vote with my head.' This evidently means that she does not consider herself hidebound to any party traditions, and she will probably, like most women voters, we imagine, consider each election on its merits, and each candidate on his or her programme. These 'incalculable silent voters' will yet save the country![6]

Women would soon be out in force at the upcoming by-election in Cardiganshire, not least being the first time the women of the county would have had the opportunity to vote, the departing incumbent Liberal, Matthew Vaughan-Davies, having been unopposed since 1910.

On 13th of January, mother and daughter (Megan), attended the first night of a new play, novelist Ian Hay's *A Safety Match*, at Arthur Bourchier's Strand Theatre. The play ran until August.[7] Soon after her night at the theatre, Megan was in bed with flu, missing a bridesmaid engagement at St Margaret's, Westminster.

The next day Mrs Lloyd George was at a matinée at the Alhambra in support of the work of the Ivory Cross, the dental campaign.[8] She also joined an appeal for funds for an endowment for Somerville, the Oxford women's college, which had spent four years of the war as a military hospital.[9]

The rest of the month was spent in a damp Cricieth, from where Mrs Lloyd George was making sure things were in place for the next Court, where she would present some ladies:

Dear Mr Rhys
I am been asked [*sic*] to present Mrs de Worms at the next Court and also Miss Gibbon, daughter of Rev. Morgan Gibbon. Will you put this right, send their names in to the Lord Chamberlain. The

weather is damp here and I have not been able to go out for 3 days now. Cofion M. Lloyd George.[10]

The daughter of Mrs de Worms (herself a daughter of Liberal politician Herbert Samuel) was a great friend of Megan, attending the No. 10 Bastille Day dinner in 1920.

In 1929 JTR would be the election agent in South Hackney for the Liberal candidate and barrister Muriel Morgan Gibbon, daughter of the Congregationalist preacher who had chaired the foundation stone ceremony at JTR's Swansea church in December 1913. Muriel came third to Labour's Herbert Morrison.

Elections were about to become a major activity for Mrs Lloyd George: in February in Cardiganshire, in early March in the Midlands (Dudley) and in Yorkshire (Penistone), and in April in Somerset (Taunton) and then Bedford, to be followed with political rallies around the country.

The two-week Cardiganshire campaign would prove to be Dame Margaret's most notable political achievement, albeit one of the most divisive for the Liberal party, especially in Wales.

On Friday, 4th February, Mrs Lloyd George and Megan took the train from Cricieth to Birmingham, to join the Premier, where he was to address several meetings and receive the Honorary Freedom of the City. He was driven up on Friday from Chequers and he and Mrs Lloyd George drove back to Chequers on the Sunday.[11] From there she returned to Aberystwyth ready for the Cardiganshire campaign. If she had been reading the Midlands' newspapers at the time she may have noted this item in the *Nottingham Journal*:

If being Prime Minister has aged Mr Lloyd George, it has had the
contrary effect on Mrs Lloyd George. Never since her husband
held office has she looked so well. She dresses far better than
she used to do, and her weakness for pretty shoes with gleaming
buckles is quite as pronounced as was Mrs Asquith's for white

silk stockings. It is all very human and adds colour to life; but if there are people who disapprove then the blame must rest with the 'movie' man. Before the advent of the cinematograph, Prime Ministers' wives rarely walked in processions or wore short skirts on public platforms so it mattered not how they were shod. Those were the days when Prime Ministers' wives were expected to live on pedestals loftier and narrower than the pedestals on which the populace set their husbands so, of course, there was a frightful clatter if one toppled over.[12]

Mrs Lloyd George's buckles got a good airing in Birmingham. Her multi-tasked private secretary, a former draper, was entrusted with some wardrobe duties:

Crewe Station
Dear Mr Rhys
There is a small cardboard box on your desk containing 2 shoe buckles. Please send to London Shoe Co. Sloane Square. Yours M. Lloyd George.[13]

Buckles were in fashion, as *The Tatler* commented: 'When this all-important accessory is under discussion our thoughts at once turn to the London Shoe Company, 116 New Bond St. W.'[14] (illustrations 4 & 5)

The 'modest' PM's wife had the best buckles in town.

During the next two weeks Mrs Lloyd George was absorbed in the Cardiganshire by-election. This was triggered when, as expected, Lloyd George elevated Matthew Vaughan-Davies to the House of Lords, as Lord Ystwyth (whose proposal to become Lord Ceredigion was not welcomed). On 26th February the 'tocsin was sounded' in Lampeter, where Mrs Lloyd George had spoken to the Cardiganshire Liberal Association back in 1919. Here the Association met and chose former Carmarthen Boroughs MP Llewelyn Williams as their candidate, rather than Lloyd George's nomination, Ernest 'Ernie' Evans, the private secretary from Downing Street. The Coalition-supporting Tory *Western Mail* reported:

The ill-feeling displayed at the Lampeter meeting was followed
by ugly scenes outside in the streets, the attitude of the 'Wee
Frees' being condemned in unmeasured terms... The rancour
introduced into the Lampeter proceedings has estranged many
family friendships, and the election, therefore, will arouse unusual
bitterness among the electors generally.[15]

As *The Times* correspondent put it, 'In Aberystwyth I was
assured this morning that friends who never quarrelled before
are at daggers drawn'.[16]

The Wee Free Liberals of Spen Valley, scene of the December
1919 Liberal civil war (which let in Labour) were delighted
with the show of strength from their Welsh counterparts:

Numerous congratulatory messages have been received by
Cardiganshire Free Liberals at the result of Tuesday's meeting.
The president and officers of the Spen Valley Liberal Association
wired 'congratulating the association on the stand they had
taken on behalf of true Liberalism', and wishing it success in the
forthcoming contest.[17]

The election would be simple. Lloyd George's Coalition
Liberal versus Asquith's 'Wee Free' Independent Liberal, the
Unionists standing aside and expected to vote for the Coalition
candidate: a contest for the soul of Welsh Liberalism.

The differing loyalties in JTR's family were noticed:

Three brothers – natives of the county are taking prominent
parts in the present contest in Cardiganshire. Mr George Rees
is editor and proprietor of the *Welsh Gazette* at Aberystwyth;
Mr Harry Rees, of Lampeter, is secretary and organiser to the
Cardiganshire Liberal Association; and Mr J. T. Rhys (formerly
pastor of churches at Aberaman, Pontycymmer, and Swansea) is
now private secretary to Mrs Lloyd George at 10 Downing-street.
Mr George Rees is an ardent Asquithian; Mr Harry Rees is believed
to entertain similar views, while it is natural to assume that Mr J.
T. Rhys (who is reported to be in the constituency) is loyal to the
Coalition.[18]

Harry Rees was indeed an Asquithian and was the election agent for Llewelyn Williams.[19]

George Rees's *Welsh Gazette* was for the Wee Frees, whilst *The Cambrian News* backed Lloyd George and thus the Coalition Liberal candidate Evans. As *The Times* would write during the by-election, 'It is said that in the interior of the county, reading is confined to the Bible and the *Welsh Gazette*.'[20]

Of course many families would have been split, as became apparent during the campaign:

> Mrs Lloyd George was addressing a village meeting ... where the chair was occupied by a well-known local lady. A man near the door was a persistent heckler and at the close of her speech Mrs Lloyd George whispered to the chairman, 'Who is that man over there?' Back came the whispered and disturbing reply: 'I am very sorry he worried you, but he is my husband!'[21]

Other notable divisions in the electorate as the campaign developed were within the temperance movement (already not known for much unity) and between the churches.

On Tuesday afternoon, 7th February, Mrs Lloyd George launched her tour of the towns and villages of Cardiganshire, accompanied by the candidate, Ernie Evans, her hosts, the Mathiases of Bronpadarn, JTR, the prominent Methodist the Rev. J. R. Rees of Aberystwyth, and Miss Marian Williams – who, at each meeting, rendered a song in Welsh with eulogistic reference to Evans and to the Prime Minister.[22]

At a crowded meeting at Talybont Council Schools, north of Aberystwyth, presided over by local woman Mrs Evans, The Stores, Mrs Lloyd George made clear the defining challenge of this seminal election: by supporting Capt. Evans they would be supporting Mr Lloyd George.

Later she would ram home her point more powerfully: 'Every vote for Llewelyn Williams is a vote against Lloyd George.'[23]

And if anyone thought that meant Ernie Evans wasn't his

own man, she wasn't having Llewelyn Williams claiming his Wee Free 'independence' was a quality to be admired:

> Mr Llewelyn Williams had said that Capt. Evans was tied to the Prime Minister, and that he (Mr Williams) was an independent Liberal, not responsible, she thought, to any but to himself.
>
> She did not believe the farmers of Cardiganshire would like to have on their farms a servant who was not responsible to anyone but to himself, and she did not think a servant of that kind would be worth much in Parliament either. [Laughter]

Her jibe was later reinforced in a *Western Mail* cartoon. She still had to reassure Liberals that Lloyd George was still a Liberal:

> 'There were people,' she said, 'who said that Mr Lloyd George had turned Tory'. On the other hand, there were extreme Tories who said that Mr Bonar Law had turned Radical. [Laughter] 'That,' she said, 'was all nonsense. They were, both of them, men who had turned everything on one side in order to restore order in Europe and Great Britain.' [Applause]

Later in the campaign Mrs Lloyd George would get personal in other ways:

> Referring to Sir John Simon, who had visited the county in support of Mr Llewelyn Williams, Mrs Lloyd George said it was time for Sir John Simon to do something for Wales. Sir John was a Welshman from Pembrokeshire but she had never heard of him doing anything for the land of his fathers, but as soon as he saw an opportunity to hit another Welshman he came over to Aberystwyth to do so. [Cries of 'Shame']24

Sir John Simon had been the Asquithian loser in the Spen Valley contest.

As both sides sought the vote of the older population, there was a further spat as to who had given them their pension: Lloyd George or Asquith? Mrs Lloyd George would consistently claim credit for her husband, as she would also claim credit on his behalf and for the Coalition for giving women the vote (never fully appreciated by the suffrage movement, who had firebombed his house). The respective merits/demerits of the contestants, Llew Williams and Ernie Evans, was almost a subsidiary issue.

The standard fare of elections, policy issues, also came up, such as Irish Home Rule and Agriculture. Asquith's eloquent daughter, Lady Violet Bonham Carter, even tried to make something of taxpayers' money being spent on Disestablishment (which 'left her audience cold'). But by and large, and without Labour involved, this was a personal contest between the two Liberal factions, with a sizeable Tory electorate offered the choice of either a Coalition Liberal (in coalition with the Tories) or an Independent Liberal.

There was a convention that the Prime Minister and senior ministers did not participate in by-elections, but with Lloyd George's reputation on the line he could not risk a loss. Thus, the PM, in the words of *The Times*, 'strained convention', as the election campaign began, by giving a major speech to the Welsh Liberal Council in London, designed to get wide coverage in Cardiganshire. In support, he sent his wife – 'his deputy', as she would often term herself – into the arena. On 9th February, he wrote:

> They are very bitter outside Wales, and if we lost, all their speakers and newspapers would say, 'Lloyd George spurned and rejected by his own countrymen'. Say that I would like to come down myself to talk to them but that I am overwhelmed with great world affairs: *fy mod yn gweithio yn galed iawn dros y wlad a fod yn rhaid i mi adael i fy nghydwladwyr edrych na chaf fi ddim cam* [I work hard for the country and need my compatriots to see that I am not wronged].[25]

As the *Birmingham Gazette* observed:

Mrs Lloyd George is to be sent into the constituency to work on behalf of Captain Evans, and if disaster does come, the blow will be borne by her just as she has suffered for carrying the Georgian standard in previous by-elections, such as the first of the Wrekin contests.[26]

## The Schedule: Week One

Mrs Lloyd George's published schedule for the first week reflects the planning behind this intense whirlwind campaign:

Tuesday, 8th February: a tour north of Aberystwyth:

Mrs Lloyd George will inaugurate her tour of the constituency today (Tuesday) when she and Capt. Evans will address meetings at Talybont Council Schools at 2.30 p.m; Council Schools, Borth, at 3.5 p.m.; The YMCA Hut, Penygarn, 3.35 p.m. After tea she will go to Penllyn, where she will address a meeting at 4.30 p.m. She will return to Aberystwyth at 5.30 p.m., and at 8 p.m. will address a women's meeting at the Coliseum.

Wednesday, 9th February: down the coast from Aberystwyth to New Quay:

On Wednesday she will address the following meetings: Pentrebont School, Blaen Plwyf, at 2.30 p.m.; National Schools, Llanrhystyd, at 3.20 p.m.; Council Schools, Llanon, at 3.30 p.m.; The Town-hall, Aberayron, at 4.35 p.m. After tea at Aberayron she will resume her journey and speak at the Council School at Llanon at 6.30 p.m., and Tabernacle, New Quay, at 8.30 p.m.

Thursday, 10th February: continuing down the coast to Cardigan:

On Thursday she will leave New Quay at 2.30 by motor, and will address meetings at Llangranog at 3.3 p.m. [sic]; Aberporth at 4.0 p.m.; Blaenanerch at 1.40 p.m.; Llechryd at 5.20 p.m.; and The Pavilion, Cardigan, at 7.30 p.m.

Friday, 11th February: a grand circuit north-east from Cardigan, taking in Lampeter, and back to base in Aberystwyth:

> On Friday Mrs Lloyd George will leave Cardigan at 1.0 p.m, and motor to Newcastle Emlyn, where she will address a meeting at 2.30. She will speak at Henllan at 3.0 p.m.; Penybont Chapel, Llandysul, at 3.25 p.m.; the Town-hall, Lampeter, at 4.20 p.m.; the Jubilee-hall, Llangeitho, at 5.35 p.m.; Cwm Vestry, Tregaron, at 6.0 p.m.; and after the meeting she will return to Aberystwyth.
>
> During the time she will be at Aberystwyth, Mrs Lloyd George will be the guest of Mr and Mrs Mathias, Bron Padarn, Aberystwyth.[27]

The considerable press coverage included the positive spin from the *Western Mail*, a Tory paper backing the Coalition Liberal candidate (Evans), hard critiques from the Asquithian *Welsh Gazette*, and more balanced views from Northcliffe's *The Times* (no friend of Lloyd George but backing the Coalition candidate), and a more independent viewpoint from an Aberdonian living in Aberystwyth. We begin with the upbeat *Western Mail*:

> To-day Mrs Lloyd George commenced very auspiciously her motor tour of the constituency in support of the candidature of Capt. Ernest Evans, and it is no exaggeration to say that her journey through the northern portion of the county was one of triumphant progress. Wherever she spoke she was greeted with unrestrained enthusiasm, and vociferous cheers were repeatedly given for the Premier. The villages visited were gay with flags and bunting and the halls and schoolrooms where the meetings were held were packed to overflowing.
>
> A large number of people had trudged many miles in order to greet the Premier's wife, and at convenient trysting places along the countryside groups of people, young and old, waited in the rain for an hour and more in order to get a glimpse of the distinguished lady as she passed along in her motor-car. Her triumphal progress indicates that the farmers of Cardiganshire are not going to desert the Prime Minister in this grave hour of the country's need of him

and his Government. With her homely and genial disposition, Mrs Lloyd George went right into the hearts of the country people, who clamoured to give her a hearty handshake.

The Premier's wife spoke mostly in Welsh and dealt very effectively with her husband's detractors and the critics of his Government, and the people were not slow to appreciate to the full the cogency of her arguments. There was a touching incident at Penygarn, when an old lady, 83 years of age, hobbled up to the platform and presented Mrs Lloyd George with an exquisite bouquet.[28]

## In Cardigan on Thursday:

The ex-service men met her on the outskirts of the town. She had to leave her motor-car for a carriage, and in this she was drawn in triumph through the streets. A torchlight procession escorted her to the Pavilion, which was packed with 1,400 people, and which was crowded an hour before the proceedings commenced. The Guildhall, requisitioned for an over-flow meeting, was similarly crowded.[29]

*The Times* was slowly taking interest and on the Thursday evening gave one of its considered verdicts, citing the *Welsh Gazette* on behalf of Llewelyn Williams:

In Cardiganshire, perhaps more than in any other county in the Principality, is to be found the quintessence of Welsh qualities. Fervid religious zeal is associated with intense political conviction, the two being so intertwined as to be almost inseparable. The Welsh Nonconformist is by long tradition Liberal, even Radical, in his views. He suddenly finds himself confronted by a bewildering dilemma, being compelled to choose between Mr Lloyd George, the most distinguished representative of 'the land of his fathers', and loyalty to political principle, which is so hard to disentangle from obedience to conscience.

That the electors are proud of Mr Lloyd George, recognize the brilliance of his gifts and the lustre they have shed on Wales, goes without saying. Even he, however, with all his wizardry, cannot conjure them from their attachment to political fidelity. Hence

the concentrated passion with which this election is being fought.
When the vacancy occurred there were many who thought it would
be a walk-over for Captain Evans. Since then Captain Evans's
personality has almost entirely dropped out of consideration.

The fight is between Mr Lloyd George and Welsh Liberalism,
as represented by Mr Llewelyn Williams. Every day brings fresh
evidence of the bitterness with which the struggle is being waged.
Mr Lloyd George's speech last Tuesday is openly described as an
indication of his agitation of mind. Another indication is afforded
by Mrs Lloyd George's tour, by which it was hoped to stay the
defection of voters in the rural districts.[30]

But Mrs Lloyd George's reputation was yet to be made:

Mrs Lloyd George has been courteously received, but she lacks
the personal magnetism of the Prime Minister, and it may well
be doubted whether, as a political missionary, her powers of
conversation are equal to his and to the needs of the occasion.

Mr Llewelyn Williams is also well-served by the Press. It is
said here that in the interior of the county, reading is confined
to the Bible and the *Welsh Gazette*. The latter is a bi-lingual
newspaper, and a redoubtable champion of Mr Llewelyn Williams.
It published to-day a glowing eulogy of him uttered by Mr Lloyd
George at Llanelly in March 1905. It also severely criticized Mr
Lloyd George's speech [his address to the Welsh Liberal Council
in London], pointing out that there was not a single representative
from Cardiganshire present when it was delivered, and urging
the electors to consider, not Mr Lloyd George's personal feelings,
but the good of the country as a whole. Quoting Mr Lloyd
George's assertion that the question at issue is national unity or
the resumption of faction, the *Welsh Gazette* says: 'No! we say,
emphatically no! The question at issue is whether Mr Lloyd George
is to be allowed to rule this country on the same lines as Lenin and
Trotsky govern Russia.'

Both sides admit the contest will be a very hard one and both
think the result will be a near thing.[31]

The *Western Mail* picked up the story as the cavalcade sped
on:

Leaving Cardigan in the zooming car, the Premier's wife addressed a crowded meeting at Newcastle Emlyn, where she was splendidly received. She also addressed rousing meetings at Henllan, Penybont Chapel, Llandyssul, and the Town-hall, Lampeter, and wound up a day of great enthusiasm for the Coalition with another great meeting at Cwm Vestry, Tregaron. Repeated cheers were raised everywhere for Mr Lloyd George.

Mrs Lloyd George has consented to come back to the county on Wednesday of next week, and it is hoped she will be able to visit those places in the division which it has not been possible for her to visit this week.

Friday was market day at Newcastle Emlyn, so the busy little market town was more lively than usual. Farmers hurriedly got their marketing over so as to attend a meeting of the Coalitionists at which Mrs Lloyd George was to speak. The old borough of Adpar was gay with bunting, and the weather was so genial that the meeting was held in the open air. Had it been otherwise there would have been no building in the town large enough to hold the assemblage. She spoke in Welsh and soon captivated the audience, who were particularly pleased she addressed them in the mother tongue.

JTR's hometown tried a little harder than in 1919:

When Mrs Lloyd George arrived at Lampeter in the evening she was met at the entrance to Victoria-hall by a guard of honour formed by the students of St David's Church College. She had a rousing reception from an enthusiastic gathering. D. Evans presided.[32]

In its Saturday edition *The Times* continued with a short geographical lesson, reflecting on this intense, hard-to-predict duel in the fastnesses of rural Wales, noting her good reception and the active participation of women:

The result of the Cardiganshire election continues to be a great note of interrogation, even the most experienced political meteorologists not venturing more than tentative predictions. What makes the problem so baffling is the county's great physical

diversity. From north to south along the coast its extent is over
50 miles, while it runs inland at its widest point for 35. The
constituency is almost wholly agricultural with the exception of
some few towns and urban districts. Every one admits that the
decision rests with the rural voters. Many of them live at long
distances from any town or hamlet; many tend their flocks on the
sides of those Welsh mountains which have so often and so happily
inspired the eloquence of the Prime Minister himself. Will these
dwellers in remote outlying places come to the poll? Numbers of
them live 12 miles from any polling station, far away from rail or
beaten road. I asked the question to-day of one who knows them
well. He answered with surprise, 'Why, they will walk seven or
eight miles to a meeting and think nothing of it, why should they
not walk a dozen to record their vote?'

## But where was Lloyd George?

Mr Lloyd George's speech of Tuesday has not yet penetrated into
these rocky fastnesses, but is being circulated to-day in Welsh
and English by post to every elector. Even so, it is doubtful
whether it will have the effect a personal visit would have had.
People have said in my presence, with evident ill-humour: 'Lloyd
George says he is too busy to come here, but he found time to go
to Birmingham, where he was not always welcome in his Radical
days. What have his own folk done to deserve such neglect?'[33]

The *Welsh Gazette* wasn't letting Lloyd George's absence go
unnoticed either:

He had no scruples in creating the vacancy, and forcing upon the
county an unnecessary contest which involves wasting thousands
of pounds at a time when a quarter of a million servicemen wander
about without a shilling in their pockets... We say it is a scandal
that the Prime Minister of this great kingdom should find time to
meddle and interfere with the poor electors of Cardiganshire in
their free choice of candidate at a by-election which he himself
has created. Even a Tory organ like the *Western Mail* condemns a
sinister proceeding of this kind. Mr Lloyd George says he will be
hurt if the Coalition loses Cardiganshire. But what the electors

of Cardiganshire have to consider in this contest is, not Mr Lloyd George's personal feelings, but the good of the country as a whole.[34]

*The Times* continued:

Women workers are extremely active on both sides. Indeed, one of the greatest of the unknown factors in this election is the women's vote. There are 16,840 men and 14,332 women on the register, and this is the first time the latter have been called on to participate in an election. Mr Lloyd George numbers many adherents among them, and those who admire him are devoted in their work. On the other hand, I hear on good authority that many women are both alarmed and scandalized at the revelations of Government extravagance and waste, and that this issue, which is a live one here, will influence many votes in favour of Mr Williams.[35]

In 1921 the Rothermere-instigated Anti-Waste campaign would start to undermine Lloyd George's drive to build homes fit for heroes, forcing later cutbacks in spending, under the so-called Geddes Axe, a reversal which would also damage the PM's reputation as a reformer.

Should church members abstain or make a choice? Anonymous advice came from a reader:

To the Editor of the *Western Mail*
Sir, I understand there is some hesitation among church electors in Cardiganshire as to whether they ought not to refrain from voting for either of the two Liberal candidates at this by-election. I have come to the conclusion, after careful consideration, that, in my judgment, it is the plain duty of every church elector, as a citizen, not to abstain from voting but to vote as each may think best for the country as a whole, in the present grave position of foreign and home affairs. According to the principles of the church, duty must always come first – before feeling and expediency. – I am, &c., LOVER OF ONE'S COUNTRY.[36]

The temperance movement remained deeply divided over policy: ardent prohibitionists, campaigning for all or nothing, versus the pragmatists, trying to get something on the statute books as a first step. Mrs Lloyd George and JTR were prohibitionists but currently in favour of a compromise (Lloyd George's strategy). It was not an easy choice for the elector. Both candidates were in favour of temperance, and the temperance movement was split as to which candidate to support.

'Do you think seriously,' Mrs Lloyd George asked, 'that Mr Asquith or Mr Llewelyn Williams will do more for temperance than Mr Lloyd George?' 'I do not believe it for a moment.' (Applause) When the temperance party asked Mr Asquith when he was Prime Minister to re-introduce his temperance measure in the House of Commons, he absolutely refused to do so.[37]

Ernie Evans would focus on temperance in his maiden speech in Parliament, assisted by a research paper by JTR. The *Western Mail* reported:

> The position of the Merched y De in this contest has given rise to much speculation. This temperance organisation stands for undiluted prohibition, and the Cardiganshire branch submitted queries to both candidates to ascertain where they stand on the question of temperance reform. The replies of Capt. Ernest Evans and Mr Llewelyn Williams, it is understood, were considered satisfactory, but to-day the following statement, signed by Miss Rosina Davies, the organising secretary, and Mrs M. Lloyd, the county president, was issued.
>
> 'We have unanimously decided by resolution that we pledge ourselves to do our utmost to return Mr Llewelyn Williams, the Free Liberal, to Parliament, because the Coalition Government is practically ruled by Sir George Younger (the brewer) and, therefore, no effective temperance measure is to be expected.'

Not all Rosina Davies' members agreed.

This is very interesting but it does not seem to be in any way conclusive, for today an ardent member of Merched y De informed me that she had definite information that members of that organisation are not acting in accordance with the above decision. I was also informed that a large number of members of Merched y De, which is an organisation claiming to be non-sectarian and non-party, are enthusiastic workers on the side of Capt. Ernest Evans.

Indeed a piquant situation has arisen, for there have arrived in the constituency a large band of temperance workers, including representatives of Merched y Gogledd – an organisation in North Wales similar to that of Merched y De, of which Mrs Lloyd George is vice-president – and they are all out to support the Coalition candidate.[38]

The Cardigan branch announced that they resolved to do all they could to secure the return of Capt. Ernest Evans. Rosina Davies responded forthwith that there was no such branch in the town of Cardigan.

*Merched y Gogledd* translates as 'Women of the North', just as *Merched y De* translates as 'Women of the South'. Cardiganshire straddles both north and south Wales.

Given that in this instance you can't just go and settle your differences over a pint (grandfather, forgive me), in Aberystwyth the local *Merched y De* members had already met in a calm place to decide what to do:

The 'Merched y De', after meeting at Siloh Chapel, Aberystwyth, to consider what attitude they would take at the election and what candidate they would support, found that they were not allowed to discuss politics in the chapel, and the matter has been deferred.[39]

At the women's rally at the Coliseum, Aberystwyth, on the first evening, JTR, in his one published intervention in the by-election (though he spoke on other occasions on the tour), offered his advice:

The Rev. J. T. Rhys, private secretary to Mrs Lloyd George, referring to Merched y De, compared the records of Mr Asquith and Mr Lloyd George in regard to temperance and declared: 'No statesman had done so much to promote sobriety in the country as the Prime Minister.' [Applause] He warned the women of Wales not to follow the example of the women of England, where the temperance cause was being exploited by certain Asquithians, not in the interests of temperance, but in the interests of party.[40]

JTR dedicated his 1912 book *Wales and its Drink Problem* to Lloyd George. He met his future wife Jane Annie Jones when she was an active member of *Merched y De*. (illustration 6)

However, this divisive election was undoubtedly one that JTR would have liked to have avoided altogether. On 10th February his brothers' *Welsh Gazette* had been very clear about where they stood:

Mrs Lloyd George, we understand, is in the constituency. We give her a message to take back to the Premier from Cardiganshire. It is an adaptation of that given by the old Welshman at Pencader to the tyrant who tried to crush Ireland seven centuries ago. 'This county, O premier, may now, as in former times, be harassed, and in great measure weakened and destroyed by your and other powers, but its Liberalism can never be totally subdued through the wrath of men, unless the wrath of God shall concur.'[41]

The Cardiganshire contest was set to move into its final week.

## Chapter 10

# Cardiganshire Decides
## (February 1921)

AFTER A WEEKEND in Cricieth, Mrs Lloyd George returned to the fray on Wednesday, 16th February, Lady Violet Bonham Carter, Asquith's daughter, having arrived in the constituency on the Monday. Over the weekend Lloyd George took the opportunity to give his 'deputy' encouragement, and some further ideas for her speeches:

> Accounts pouring in from every quarter are full of your almost unexampled triumphal tour. It looks as if you have saved Ernie. He & his agents think so. Write me what your impressions are as to the prospects. I enclose a few notes for your further speeches.[1]

Handwritten notes for Mrs Lloyd George's speeches have not survived – as with the 1918 Coupon election whirlwind tour, this was not the occasion for carefully prepared addresses, but the time when Mrs Lloyd George, in Welsh and English, was delivering her well-rehearsed messages to the assembled crowds.

*The Scotsman* reported:

> The final week of the campaign has opened with a rather pronounced feeling that Capt. Evans's prospects are distinctly hotter than they were a week ago. The visit of Mrs Lloyd George last week is now acknowledged, even by the Independent Liberals, to have done much towards consolidating the Coalition vote.
>   Lively scenes marked the arrival of Lady Bonham Carter at

Aberystwyth last night. Enthusiastic students made an escort for her, and attached ropes to a horse brake in which she was seated, pulling it through the town to her hotel. Speaking from the vehicle, she said she was not in the least surprised to find that the forces of youth were on their side. Liberalism had always lived in the hearts and the heads of youth, just as Toryism had lived in the prejudices and the pockets of old men. 'Youth in its great adventure,' she declared, 'is not going to march behind the pied and parti-coloured banner of compromise.'

She described that election as the greatest battle for Liberalism that had ever been fought in Wales. She asked if they were going to send to Parliament a free man, or the puppet and the pawn of a caucus imposed on them from Downing Street, a man who if he was elected, was doomed to run in blinkers with a muzzle on. 'Make it clear that Wales is not a tied house or a pocket borough, but a free democracy,' she urged in a reference to the Prime Minister's speech last week. She said the greatest national danger was the continuance in office of the present Government, and she asked the electors to strike a blow for a free Parliament.[2]

*The Times* was now paying a lot of attention to the contest, its report from the campaign front picking up on the religious dilemmas and on the injection of excitement from the arrival of Lady Bonham Carter:

> There are so many cross-currents in Cardiganshire that no one can estimate with confidence how whole sections of the electorate will vote. Religious bodies formerly unanimous are now divided in their political allegiance. Throughout the county there are hundreds of chapels belonging to the Calvinistic Methodists, Congregationalists, and Baptists. Mr Williams is a Congregationalist [as was JTR], Mr Lloyd George a Baptist, and Captain Evans a Calvinistic Methodist [as was Mrs Lloyd George; it was the largest denomination in the county]. In some cases the pastor and deacons favour Mr Lloyd George, while other leading members of the Congregation will support Mr Williams. There is not an inconsiderable body of Unitarians, whose votes will go to Mr Williams. Since the vote of the sects is obviously of the first importance, the candidates have left nothing undone to win it to their side.

The clergy of the Episcopal Church are believed to be
lukewarm in their Coalition sympathies. Reports that they are
disposed to abstain from voting are producing exhortations
from Captain Evans's supporters to them to go to the poll. One
of the most remarkable features of this election, however, is the
complete indifference of the electorate to the Church question,
which for more than a generation was the chief if not the only
one in Wales. 'He (Mr Lloyd George) re-endowed the Church with
taxpayers' money,' exclaimed Lady Bonham Carter in her speech
at Aberystwyth last night, but it left her audience cold. The issue
seems a dead one. Nevertheless, Lady Bonham Carter's visit has
done much to heighten interest in an election in which feeling ran
already very high. Her presence has infused a new element into the
contest, her arguments are received with attention, and her shrewd
thrusts at the Prime Minister and his policy are much relished by
his opponents.[3]

After the election Llewelyn Williams would claim that the
Free Church congregations largely voted for him, including
Mrs Lloyd George's Calvinistic Methodists, the only exception
being strong Baptist loyalty for Lloyd George.[4]

Mrs Lloyd George, a week earlier dubbed by *The Times* a
'political missionary lacking the personal magnetism and
powers of conversation of the PM', was now regarded as a
force in her own right.

All testimony agrees that in Mrs Lloyd George, the Prime Minister
has found a surprisingly effective substitute. It is not too much to
say that Mrs Lloyd George, who has not hitherto been regarded
as an expert in electioneering, has exercised a far more potent
influence upon the contest than any other individual on either
side. She has been indefatigable in her perambulations of the
constituency, has addressed more meetings than most men would
care to face, and is now returning again to Cardiganshire with
the object of counteracting the effort of Lady Bonham Carter.
Mrs Lloyd George has a great advantage in her knowledge of the
vernacular [Welsh], and she has had much success in the villages.
In all future elections, feminine influence and appeals are bound

to become more prominent, but this is probably the first election in which women on both sides have played a more important part than the men, both on the platform and in the work of organization.[5]

The *Manchester Guardian* was also dubious as to whether rural Tory voters would vote:

A tramp of four to six miles from a hill farm to a polling booth is going to be a pretty severe test of Tory enthusiasm for the Coalition, and incidentally for a candidate pledged to temperance and Welsh Home rule.[6]

Mrs Lloyd George did, however, have a comfortable car: Winifred Coombe Tennant made two diary entries: on the 14th, she remarked after touring from 3.30 pm till midnight: 'all of this in an open car – awful!'; followed by an entry for the 15th: 'Mrs Lloyd George is to lend me her car for the present, and it is on its way from Criccieth... a very comfortable street car.' Mrs Lloyd George was of course still in Criccieth on the 15th.[7]

The *Western Mail* detailed the day's tour:

Mrs Lloyd George left Criccieth shortly after eight a.m., and on her arrival at Machynlleth was met by Sir Richard Mathias, Major Lewis Mathias, Mrs Dr Ellis (the Coalition Liberal candidate's sister), and Mr Dan Thomas, who has the tour of Mrs Lloyd George under his direction. Mrs Lloyd George's first act was to call to see Mr Pugh, the stationmaster, who had been knocked down by an engine at the railway station last week and badly injured. A large crowd had assembled near the town clock with flags, and cheered the party as they proceeded on their way to address meetings at Glandyfi and other villages between Machynlleth and Aberystwyth.

And then a series of local meetings, all hosted by women:

No time was lost in motoring to Eglwysfach, where an excellent meeting, presided over by Mrs Pugh, was held. At Taliesin the

Rev. Rees Jones took the chair, and, after a good reception in the important village of Talybont, which had been visited by Mrs Lloyd George during her previous tour, a move was made to Elerch, where Mrs Simmett Jones presided. At Penrhyncoch the chair was taken by Mrs James.

The next move was to a ploughing match at Gogerddan, the seat of Sir Lewes Loveden Pryse. The ploughmen left their furrows and crowded around when she entered the field to speak to them.

Mrs Lloyd George told them that another match was going on – a sort of ploughing match. 'I dare say,' she added, 'you are judging who is going to win here, just as we are judging who is going to win the election. From what I can see, even from the opponents' newspapers, they are now prepared for a defeat, and that, after all, Cardiganshire is going to stick to Lloyd George.'

Speaking in Welsh, she drew a homely analogy from farm life in Cardiganshire. The chief servant on the farm, she said, was called the *hwsmon*, and the opponents in that contest were trying to turn away the *hwsmon* (or chief officer of the State). Not only had he proved an excellent servant but he had been working hard and long days. Eight hours had not satisfied him – more often than not they had been twelve hours. 'You all know what he has done,' concluded Mrs Lloyd George, 'and I feel sure Cardiganshire people will make certain that he is supported in his present work and enabled to carry out his task to the end of the furrow.'[8]

And as *The Times* concluded their account: 'Then, with a friendly smile and a nod, she entered her car and drove away amid cheers'.[9]

The *Hwsmon* story was echoed the next day by Lloyd George in a telegram to Margaret:

Wish I could be with you in your tour through that beautiful country, but must stick to the plough. DAFYDD YR HWSMON.[10]

The *Manchester Guardian*, with rather less coverage of the whole affair, saw the telegram as 'a stroke of the master electioneerer'. (This paper, in a city with a large Welsh population, shouldn't have slipped up with the spelling, of

*Hwsmon* as 'Twsmon'; but then, the 'Grauniad' still has a bit of a reputation with its typos.)[11]

The *Western Mail* continued:

At 1.40 lunch was partaken of at Bronpadarn, Aberystwyth, the residence of Major Mathias. It is almost impossible to convey an idea of the inaccessibility of some of the districts visited. Up in the hills the party were enveloped in mist, and it was almost a miracle that the cars stood the strain of the inclines and declivities. Some of the outlying villages were known to be regarded by the Wee Frees as their strongholds, but it requires a vivid imagination to believe that Mr Llewelyn Williams will poll more than half the votes to be recorded in any of them.

There was a very encouraging meeting at Devil's Bridge, and still further up in the mountains at Cwmystwyth. There was a remarkably cordial reception accorded to her at Pontrhydygroes.

After tea another large gathering had assembled at Ysbyty Ystwyth. At Pontrhydfendigaid she said she would like to ask how many of Mr Llewelyn Williams's supporters and speakers were conscientious objectors during the war and placed every obstruction instead of encouragement in the way of the Government.

No punches being pulled there.

After roadside chats at Ystradmeurig, the party proceeded to Swyddffynon... one of the best meetings of the day.

At Llanafan there was some opposition, but the chairman (Mr Percy Wilkinson) had it well in hand.

The last two meetings were at Llanfihangel y Creuddyn and Llangwyryfon, and they were the best of all. The schoolrooms were packed.

Aberystwyth was reached shortly before ten o'clock, after a tour of some of the most difficult country that motor-cars ever traversed, some of the people had walked many miles over mountain tracks to greet Mrs Lloyd George, and on all hands it was evident that the effort she was making was deeply appreciated.[12]

On that final day of touring, by her tally Mrs Lloyd George addressed another 23 meetings to the south of Aberystwyth. After the final rally at Aberystwyth on Thursday night, the ex-service men of the town escorted Mrs Lloyd George in torchlight procession from the Coliseum to Bronpadarn.[13]

*The Times* reviewed the 'battle of the Amazons':

What may, perhaps, without discourtesy, be described as a battle of the Amazons is proceeding during these last few days of the Cardiganshire contest. Eloquent, enthusiastic women, representing the Coalition and the 'Wee Frees' respectively, are touring the county, delivering roadside speeches, canvassing electors in hillside villages, and addressing meetings in local schoolrooms.

Lady Bonham Carter made 12 speeches yesterday and Lady Simon has spoken at 15 meetings in the last two days, mainly in remote mountainous districts.

Captain Evans, on the other hand, is equally well served by his lady supporters. Chief among these is Mrs Lloyd George, who visited many villages to-day. Nothing could have been at once more homely, simple, and effective than her little address to those attending the Gogerddan ploughing match this afternoon.[14]

Touring continued on polling day:

Polling in the Cardigan election opened in sunshine. A heavy poll is expected. Ten per cent of the electors had voted in Aberystwyth by 10 o'clock. The candidates were out and Mrs Lloyd George made a tour of the polling stations before leaving Aberystwyth for London. About 200 motor cars are in service. Women were the first to vote in many cases.[15]

Winifred Coombe Tennant noted in her diary for 18th February: 'Went down to the Committee room at 9.30 am... then Mrs Lloyd George came in, buxom, grey haired, with a slight squint, very pleasant. She greeted me warmly and we had a few minutes' talk. Then Ernie came and thanked me and I was photographed with him!'[16]

The *Manchester Evening News* had its finger on the Amazon pulse:

Mobilized Political Amazons: For the work of the election the Coalition mobilised their women agents from all parts of the country. Captain Guest has far more women attached to his staff than any other political chief, and the hotels of Aberystwyth have been full of them for a fortnight. All these nice ladies are having a holiday (election law does not permit paid canvassers), and no busman ever threw himself into holiday ecstasies with more zest than these pioneers of a new profession for women have thrown themselves at the door knockers of Cardigan. Their work, it is believed, has turned the scale in the favour, not of the Coalition especially, but of its chief figure, for they have made no appeal except the personal one.[17]

With an unexpectedly high 77 per cent turnout, Evans took 57 per cent of the vote, winning a 3,590 majority, 14,111 to 10,521. With the Liberal voters fairly evenly divided, and Ernest Evans capturing the majority of the estimated 6,000 Coalition partner Unionist votes on offer, Llewelyn Williams could justifiably claim it was the Unionists who decided the outcome and elected his opponent.

The Cardiganshire by-election was not only seminal for Welsh Liberalism, but also gripped the country. At stake was Lloyd George's Coalition, for a loss in his home country would have been very damaging. It was also a marker in terms of the role of women in elections.

JTR's brother Harry Rees had recognised the importance of women's contribution back in April 1919 when trying to rally the Liberal women of Aberystwyth into action. But Harry was up against his brother JTR's trump card, Welsh-speaker Margaret Lloyd George. Violet Bonham Carter, the Wee Frees' Amazon, was undoubtedly an eloquent speaker, and made an impact in the urban areas, but was no match for Mrs Lloyd George's friendly approach in Welsh, in a county where, in the 1921 Census, 83 per cent of people had reported their first language as Welsh. Harry's equivalent 'weapon' was perhaps the Rees family newspaper, the bilingual *Welsh Gazette*, which, as noted earlier, was the main form of reading in rural homes, alongside the Bible. But then, Mrs Lloyd George could undoubtedly deliver the Bible in Welsh, too.

This view from the *Aberdeen Press and Journal* offers a good perspective to an outside audience:

Cardiganshire, where one of the liveliest by-elections in recent years has now entered its final week, has one curious link with Aberdeen. The dwellers north of the Tweed have been facetiously divided into 'Scots, damned Scots, and Aberdonians,' the unspeakableness of the last being due, I believe, to their alleged grippiness. Tradition classifies the Welsh in corresponding categories, with 'Cardis' in the third place, and for the same reason. The proverb has it that your Cardigan host serves the pudding first, that the guest may not be too hard on the succeeding beef. Living in Wales and writing to Aberdeen, I had rather not give an opinion to whether the gibe is any better deserved the one case than the other.

The political point in this is that the good folk of Cardiganshire are in many respects peculiar people. They are, so to speak, more Welsh than the Welsh. There is a 'civilised' fringe along the Cardigan Bay coast, where, in this town of just under 10,000 inhabitants, the English visitor is taken in and done for. But inland the county is one of the wildest in the Principality, with mountain scenery that called forth some of Borrow's most rapturous descriptions. There are wide moorland wastes without a single human inhabitant, interspersed with lonely valleys tenanted often by a solitary shepherd and his dogs. Over all in this countryside Welsh is the tongue of daily discourse, often the only language spoken or understood. That fact gives point to the report (and I have seen nothing make me doubt its truth) that the Independent Liberals are sending down an army of fifty speakers, not one whom can speak Welsh!

The county, like almost the whole of rural Wales, is nearly to a man Liberal and Nonconformist, and both with a fervour that amazes the Sassenach. Every hamlet is hopelessly divided into the various sects of Calvinists, Baptists, Methodists,

Congregationalists, and the rest, and, therefore, has almost as many chapels as dwelling-houses. Little barn-like Bethels are scattered over the countryside as if shaken out of a supernatural pepperpot. And the point to be kept in mind by the outsider is this – that these meeting-places are centres of political activity even more than religious. These folk are as keen on political polemics as the Scots of an elder generation were on theology, and their rapacity in the matter of meetings and speeches amazes even the hardiest electioneerer.

One of the strongest forces in the election, as might be inferred, is the influence of the ministers of religion. Time was when the occupant of a Nonconformist pulpit did not hesitate, 'in holy rapture', to give his flock plain and vigorous guidance to their choice of political representative, and enforce the advice with all the weight of religious sanction. Those days have gone; but the minister still sees no bar in his high calling to a vigorous week-day canvass among his flock.

So far, although both sides are going dingdong at the campaign, there has been little of the roughness which used to mark electioneering in the Welsh backhills. Not so very long ago – within this century at any rate – a party of the 'free and independent' electors in the neighbouring county of Montgomeryshire gave vent to their political enthusiasm by placing a heavy tree-trunk across the road along which one of the candidates was due to drive on a pitch-dark night. That sort of thing has happily joined other observances of the 'good old days'. This time the only untoward incidents have been rowdy demonstrations by students at the Aberystwyth meetings of both candidates. Aberystwyth, I may mention, has one of the colleges which constitute the University of Wales and it also houses the National Library of Wales, so that the county capital, at least, has some pretensions to learning and enlightenment.

Personality, not political principle, will be the deciding factor on Friday. Mrs Lloyd George has toured the constituency for Captain Evans, and Lady Bonham Carter doing so for Mr Llewelyn Williams. Other notable visitors, past, present, and prospective, are Ian Macpherson, Mr Wedgwood Benn, Sir John Simon, and Sir A. Griffith-Boscawen. The last-named has made a considerable mark, for the farmers of Cardiganshire, though a good few of them cannot sign their names, are a shrewd race, and they appreciate the blunt honesty of the new Minister of Agriculture.

It may be an omen or it may not, but a good many people here are noting that it is just a year, almost a day, since the Paisley fight.[18]

Sir Arthur Griffith-Boscawen, the new Minister of Agriculture, would soon be off to seek re-election in his own seat, Dudley, with the help of Mrs Lloyd George.

The 'Paisley fight' was in 1920 when Asquith regained a seat in the House having ignominiously lost in the 'Coupon' election.

The correspondent for the *Dundee Evening Telegraph* recalled his own challenge when reporting the countryside tour:

> Amongst the villages visited by Mrs Lloyd George during the Cardigan campaign were – Egwysfach [*sic*], Cwmystwyth, Ysbtythyystwyth [*sic*], Pontrhydfendigaid, and Llanfigelycrnddyn [*sic*], and she actually talked to the inhabitants of these villages in the language which has given rise to such place-names. For myself, I'd rather do a sum than try to pronounce one of these names – but other people, other tastes.[19]

*The Times* had not only discovered that Mrs Lloyd George was a formidable campaigner, but also, with hindsight, revealed that the result had been wholly predictable. There was probably little disagreement on all sides as to the messages that could be drawn: that Lloyd George and his Coalition was losing much support in Liberal Wales, that his victory was gained thanks to still strong personal support for him, that the Tory votes cast in Capt. Evans' favour were probably more than the final majority (or as the Wee Frees consoled themselves, it was the Tories that won it), and that victory was achieved by 'the indefatigable efforts of Mrs Lloyd George than to any other factor', who 'won a great many votes from wavering women not attached to any other party'.

And of course, the victory was also helped by the organisational support from the Tory Party, including its fleets of cars – a reminder that Lloyd George had yet to develop his own campaign chest and organisation.

As to the dispute, 'Who gave the pensioners their pensions?', the 'truth' is that the pensions were introduced with Lloyd George as Chancellor, under Asquith as PM. Mrs Lloyd George would say her husband gave them their pensions (though he is recorded as having once given the credit to Asquith). Both were involved. Today, of course, Lloyd George can perhaps rest easier in that he is generally regarded as the real 'founder' of the welfare state, and fought hardest for it. His daughter Olwen quipped that every time she went to the Post Office for her pension she would say, 'Thank you, Father'.

At the election, therefore, it was a pretty petty squabble that neither side could win or lose...

For divided Liberal families, such as the Rees/Rhys family, the whole experience was stressful. In the 1860s newly-enfranchised Welsh Liberal tenants had defied their Tory landlords and won. In 1921, when they had seen finally the departure of the unpopular Liberal incumbent (himself, once a Tory), the seat was won by the Tories for Lloyd George's man.

The experience also underlined that Lloyd George needed to retain and regain Free Church support, a task which JTR would take on for the party in 1922.

For our comfortably motorised Amazon, it could have ended in tragedy shortly afterwards when Mrs Lloyd George reportedly encountered one farmer too many:

Mrs Lloyd George had a remarkable escape in a motor car accident in Cardiganshire on Friday afternoon. Her car was being driven along a quiet country road near Bronwydd when a farmer's cart, drawn by two horses, emerged suddenly from a by-road. The car ran into the horses, knocking both off their feet and overturning the cart. The car was not overturned, and neither Mrs Lloyd George, nor her chauffeur was hurt. The driver of the cart also escaped, but both horses were badly injured.[20]

We may leave the final word to Mrs Lloyd George herself, from her interview with the Press Association, published by the *Western Mail* and others. She also had better news on the horses:

Mrs Lloyd George, who looked wonderfully well after her strenuous electioneering work in Cardiganshire, when seen by a representative of the Press Association at 10 Downing-street, on Tuesday evening, declared that she had thoroughly enjoyed the contest, and was not fatigued as the result of her long journeys and many meetings.

'How many meetings did you address in all?' she was asked. 'About sixty-five, I think. During the first four days I spoke at seven meetings, each day, making twenty-eight in all during that week. After a short rest at home [Cricieth] I returned to the fray, and on the Wednesday before the election I addressed fourteen gatherings. On the final day of the campaign I spoke at twenty-three meetings, making sixty-five in the six days.'

Asked about the physical strain of so much speech-making, Mrs Lloyd George said, 'the fourteen tired me more than the twenty-three, but the conditions, rather than the actual talking, are the chief consideration. The weather was good, the prospects were good, and the winning cause was a potent tonic. The strain is not as great as you imagine when the meetings are comparatively small, but the effort to make the voice carry to all parts of a very large room or to the limits of a crowd in the open is more tiring.'

'I noticed a statement that your tears won the election.'

'Yes,' said the Premier's wife, with a merry laugh, 'it is stated that tears were streaming down my face at Aberayron. That is simply untrue. I did not shed a tear during the campaign, and why should I. We were winning all along the line.'

'You appear to have experienced a bad accident while electioneering, Mrs Lloyd George, and to have knocked over and seriously injured a pair of horses.'

'The fact is we never touched them, and I cannot understand the version of the affair that got into the newspapers. We were motoring along a narrow road, bounded by high hedges, and a carter drove his team out through a gap in a hedge onto the roadway. Two cars had passed and he apparently thought that there were no others. Ours was the third car, and our chauffeur pulled up very smartly within a few feet of the team. The carter saw his danger when clear of the high hedge, and pulled his horses sharply round, with the result that the cart was drawn up on to a bank and overturned. The shaft horse pulled over with it, but the leader did not come down, and as to serious injuries, we saw the horse walk away from the scene. Apparently none the worse for its fall.'

In conclusion, Mrs Lloyd George said: 'I neither wept nor ran down a team of horses. But what we did do, and it was most satisfactory, was to win, and to win handsomely.'[21]

And in a reminder that she was not actually the one getting elected, Mrs Lloyd George told the *Western Gazette*:

I am delighted with the result. I felt sure that Cardigan was going to be true to the Prime Minister. Captain Evans has just the qualities needed in the House of Commons, and will be a most useful member. I am sure he will shine there.[22]

On 24th February the North Wales Methodist preacher of Tremadog and then Bangor, the Rev. Edward Lloyd, bardic name Tegfelyn, composed a poem based on the famous *Hwsmon* exchange, which was published in the Welsh papers. A handwritten version, 'Gwraig yr Hwsmon' (or, 'The Husbandman/Steward's Wife') is in the JTR archive. (illustration 7)

Pencilled in the top corner are the words, probably in JTR's hand, 'Based on an incident in the Cardiganshire election.'

The first verse refers to Violet Bonham Carter: that she came seeking to overthrow those supporting Lloyd George's man, but the Welsh were not so stupid as to be fooled by her posh Paisley shawl. (Violet had campaigned in the Paisley by-election, which returned her father to Parliament.)

In the second verse, Mrs Lloyd George came without any false pretences – as cheerful as the flowering heather, her language like sweet wine, and the language of her forefathers on her lips. Even so, if needs be, she could without oppression win over the English.

The third verse refers to the jealous opposition / Asquith supporters who would like to be rid of Lloyd George – but a strong one came from Mynydd Ednyfed (Mrs Lloyd George's birthplace) to show them who was boss.

The final verse continues with the praises of Mrs Lloyd George, and hopes that the 'Steward' remains in. charge, bringing happiness and peace back to the country.[23]

The *Sunday Post* gossiped that even if Mrs Lloyd George can't be expected to be permanently on the hustings, that doesn't end family ambitions in that regard:

> Mrs Lloyd George is, I hear, taking a well-earned rest after her activities in Cardigan. To those who know how deeply she follows her husband's fortunes, her whirlwind campaign in her native Wales came as no surprise. But she confided to friends when it was over that she wouldn't like to fight an election every day.
>
> Miss Megan Lloyd George is evidently desirous of emulating Lady Bonham Carter's platform triumphs. The Premier's youthful daughter, who was with her mother at Cardigan in the Evans-Williams fight, made a tiny speech backing up Captain Evans. The little she said was cleverly spoken, and Miss Megan does not appear to be troubled with nervousness.[24]

Lloyd George wrote to Olwen:

> As you may have perceived from the papers your mother has completely eclipsed me as a public performer. I am already a back number & a drudge. Dame Margaret is the star. She is having a remarkable success. England has never seen before a swell quite of her sort – simple, unostentatious – talking plain… Common sense without frills – & Englishmen like it. The contrast to her predecessor helps![25]

So perhaps it was just as well JTR hadn't stopped Mrs Lloyd George from engaging in anything between October to April, as Olwen had advised, though she would feel the effect later in the year.

For all that, it was something of a Pyrrhic victory, intensifying the Liberal divisions.

In her future electioneering Mrs Lloyd George would concentrate on keeping the electorate's confidence in Lloyd George and in the Coalition, and in 1922 JTR would focus on getting the wavering Nonconformist vote back onside.

On 22nd February Ernie Evans took his seat in the House and a celebratory dinner was planned for March:

> Captain Evans, the victor of Cardigan, will take his seat in the
> House to-day, and Mr Lloyd George intends to escort him to the
> table. By right of course, Mrs Lloyd George should carry him there
> in her arms. From all accounts it was she who carried him through
> his election.[26]

It was perhaps at this dinner that Mrs Lloyd George reflected on the opposition with the quip (as Ernie Evans recalled in 1922):

> The Wee Frees are prepared to bury everything, except the
> hatchet![27]

On 25th February there was another Welsh wedding to attend at St Margaret's, Westminster, that of Sir Rhys Williams, MP for Banbury; it was so dark coming up the covered walk to the church door that Mrs Lloyd George was challenged as to her right of entry. She was too taken aback to explain, but Miss Megan (very smart in flame and mole velvet), put the matter right with a word and a laugh.[28]

In June of that year Mrs Lloyd George would stay with the groom and his new bride, Juliet Glyn, at their home, Miskin Manor, near Cardiff.

CHAPTER 11

# The By-elections Continue
## (March and April 1921)

THE 1921 ST David's Day celebrations had a Breton twist, being attended by the French PM Briand and by Marshal Foch.[1] In the morning the PM, Mrs Lloyd George, and Megan, had welcomed, in a tradition that had started in wartime, the children of the Heritage Craft Schools, Chailey, Sussex, who brought their gifts.[2] Ten days later, on 11th March, Mrs Lloyd George and Megan visited Chailey, the institute for crippled children, a cause that Megan would now champion, being steadily introduced into the public role she would pursue for the rest of her life: as she once said, from the very youngest age it was politics around the meal table.

From 2nd March, St David's Day celebrations over, Mrs Lloyd George was back on the by-election trail. But the next three seats were three straight wins by Labour, in the Midlands seat of Dudley, in Kirkcaldy in Scotland and in Penistone in Yorkshire. Whilst Mrs Lloyd George did not campaign in by-elections in Scotland, she was back on the hustings in Dudley on 2nd March, and a day later, in Penistone, for another 'flying tour'.[3]

In Dudley, Worcestershire, the Coalition Unionist but Lloyd George-friendly Welshman, Sir Arthur Griffith-Boscawen, sought re-election after being appointed Minister of Agriculture. He had also campaigned in Cardiganshire for Ernie Evans. Coalition spirits were up, having just won the Woolwich by-election, vacant after the retirement of the ailing

Labour MP Will Crooks. There the pacifist Labour candidate (and future Prime Minister) Ramsay MacDonald had, contrary to expectations, lost to an ex-soldier, a Coalition Unionist first-time candidate.

But the voters of Dudley narrowly rejected their newly promoted MP, and Sir Arthur had to look for another way back into Parliament if he was to rescue his career. The loss was in part ascribed to Beaverbrook's Canadian Cattle Campaign – or, as Sir Arthur jokingly referred to it, the 'dear meat stunt'.[4]

Megan's friend Thelma Cazalet would recall the event with clarity: 'A nice old Tory type, Sir Arthur Griffith-Boscawen, on appointment as Minister of Agriculture, had to seek re-election. He refused to allow the importation of Canadian store cattle, and Lord Beaverbrook [Canadian] entered the fray against him with a vast coruscation of posters. "Boscawen favours dear meat." Poor Sir Arthur lost his election.'[5]

Mrs Lloyd George then drove up to the West Riding of Yorkshire, where she was joined by Ernie Evans, to campaign for Coalition Liberal Sir James Hinchliffe, in Penistone, near Barnsley, against an Asquithian Liberal and a Labour candidate. As in Cardiganshire, the local Liberal Association had picked their own candidate and Lloyd George put up his own man, backed by the Unionist Party (which did not contest the seat).

Mrs Lloyd George's well-organised tour, variously hyped as a 'record hustle' and 'an unprecedented hurricane trip', packed in 24 meetings during one day:

Shepley, 10.07; Kirk Burton, 10.22; Shelley, 10.32; Skelmanthorpe, 10.42; Scissett, 10.52; Clayton West, 11; Cawthorne, 11.25; Silkstone, 11.35; Thurgoland, 11.55; Wortley, 12; Tankersley, 12.20; High Green, 12.35; Chapeltown, 12.45; Ecclesfield, 1.15; Grenoside, 1.30; luncheon interval; Wadesley Bridge, 3.15; Oughtibridge, 3.40; Deepcar, 3.50; Stocksbridge, 4.10; Langsett, 4.25; Millhouse, 4.40; Thurlstone, 5.05; Penistone, 5.20; Denby, 5.45.[6]

At Chapeltown, Lady Mabel Smith, surrounded by working men, women, and children, gave a hearty greeting to Mrs Lloyd George, in spite of the fact that her ladyship is a strong supporter of Labour.

Grenoside mothers proudly displayed their babies to the admiring, motherly gaze of Mrs Lloyd George, and all were eager to shake her by the hand. Many, however, were slightly embarrassed and tongue-tied when they found their ambition so easily realised.

'Now, she's a lady, she is,' said one delighted woman to her neighbour after her presentation. 'No airs or hoity-toity about her. She might be one of us. Reckon we could do worse than vote as she tell us.' And her neighbour cordially agreed.

Outside a house at Wadsley Bridge, old Mrs Smith, eighty-three last birthday, was brought to the notice of Mrs Lloyd George, who congratulated her on her splendid appearance at so great an age. Another lady had come prepared with her autograph album, and went proudly away with the desired signature inscribed in the book.

There can be no doubt that the visit of Mrs Lloyd George to Penistone will have gained the good will and support of hundreds of Yorkshire women for Sir James.[7]

The public interest wouldn't necessarily translate into votes, and the people weren't always welcoming:

The spice of variety was furnished by Skelmanthorpe, a notoriously strong centre of Socialism. Here the crowd was distinctly hostile, and the visitors were received with cries of 'Get out of here'. As a carefully prepared time-table had to be rigidly adhered to if the day's programme was to be carried out, the uselessness of wasting precious time here was at once realised, and no stop was made.[8]

The Penistone Coalitionists played their highest card yesterday, when Mrs Lloyd George made a tour of the division to try to revive some interest in the cause. They had reposed great hopes in her intervention, and Captain Evans had been commissioned to remind the electors of her success at Cardigan. But Penistone is not Cardigan. Mrs Lloyd George has little in common with

Yorkshire men and women, and those who did turn out yesterday were actuated mainly by curiosity. 'We don't see a Premier's wife every day', aptly remarked one hardy roadman. They are scarcely likely to see her again this year – or next year for that matter, even if they vote for Sir James Hinchliffe.[9]

As in Yorkshire's Spen Valley, the division in the Liberal camp allowed in Labour, Hinchliffe coming third, the votes distributed roughly equally, three ways. Penistone indeed was not Cardigan.

Back in London, on Monday 7th March the Prime Minister's wife attended a 'glittering' reception hosted by the Foreign Secretary, Lord Curzon, with the Duke of York and visiting foreign dignitaries. 'I am told that Mrs Lloyd George looked the calmest and most placid of them all', wrote 'Evelyn' of *The Tatler*, in a long gossip column.[10]

At a dinner celebrating the Cardiganshire victory at London's Hotel Victoria, on Northumberland Avenue, Lloyd George acknowledged his wife's importance:

When the toast of Our Guest was reached, Mrs Lloyd George said laughingly: 'You will see my name is down to propose the next toast, but I have a deputy here, and, as President of this dinner, I am going to allow him have a "look in". "Mrs Chairman," the Prime Minister continued, "It shows what a change has come over the world when a man is ordered about in public by his own wife. Still," he added, "the best thing I can for the sake of peace is obey, make no fuss about it".'[11]

The anecdote sounds suspiciously like that recounted by Thelma Cazalet: 'I happen to have been at a lunch in Downing street when a German delegation, headed by Siemens and Hugo Stinnes, came over to make one of their numerous overtures early in March 1921. Lloyd George told the luncheon party that the German proposals had been simply preposterous, that he would tell them so and send them home the next day. Philip Kerr interrupted to say their plan was politically unsound but probably quite sound economically. Lloyd George rounded on him and said that the plan was impossible in both senses, and that he had 'not felt in such a rage for a long time'. This so enraptured Dame Margaret that she rose from her place and circled the table to kiss her husband. The act moved him to one of his whimsical turns. He said that he had once been quite a great man, but now it was his wife who was the great one, and he was only a second fiddle, existing to arrange her political meetings and cut press notices out of the papers.'[12]

Mrs Lloyd George and her daughters did indeed cut press notices out of the papers. Though Lloyd George was quite resilient – as JTR later put it, having a great ability to bounce back from failure – his family did censor some of the worst criticism from his gaze.

Meanwhile a cable from Bangalore announced the arrival of Mrs Lloyd George's third granddaughter, Eluned Jane Carey Evans. Doubtless she would have received congratulations at the Cardiganshire celebratory dinner. JTR was among the many guests, including Megan, Sir John Lynn-Thomas, Winfred Coombe Tennant, Tom Macnamara and Sir Alfred Mond. Winifred Coombe Tennant, pleased to be seated next-but-one to the PM, with Vincent Evans between them, later recorded 'Talk with Evan R. Davies and Rees [sic] the Private Secretary of Mrs Lloyd George, who wants to see me about going in to Parliament!'[13]

On 12th March Mrs Lloyd George visited the Chailey Heritage Craft School with Lady Riddell.[14] (illustration 30)

On 16th March it was another wedding at St Margaret's, Westminster, of Miss Florence Anaise Le Gallais, from St Helier, Jersey, to Capt. Stanley Sykes, son of Charles Sykes, the MP for Huddersfield, for whom Mrs Lloyd George had campaigned in 1918.[15]

That evening Mrs Lloyd George and Megan were at the Wigmore Hall supporting the public London debut concert of Welsh harpist Miss Nancy Morgan, from Telynfa, Aberdare.

Miss Morgan had on several occasions played at Downing Street on the invitation of Mrs Lloyd George.[16] JTR may have attended her No. 10 performances, his second parish having been in Aberdare.

The following day, 17th March, there was another move towards Liberal disunity when Lloyd George hosted the inaugural dinner for his 1920 Club, for Coalition Liberals, edging towards a new party. Mrs Lloyd George and a number of ladies attended.[17]

On 18th March she distributed the prizes at the London Musical Festival. The month ended with a visit to the ailing former Labour MP Will Crooks, in Woolwich. Though a member of the Labour Party – indeed, the fourth Labour member of the House of Commons – he had long been an ally of Liberal government policies, and of David Lloyd George.

April 1921 began with the Coal Strike, which continued until July. Since the war the former private coal mine owners had been pushing for the return to them of the mines that had been nationalised (temporarily) during wartime. In 1919 Lloyd George set up the Sankey Commission; their report surprised many, the main recommendation being continued state ownership. The Coalition government didn't take up the recommendation, apart from introducing a shorter (7-hour) working day.

By 1921 there was a slump in demand for coal exports. On 31st March 1921 the mines moved back to private ownership, wages were cut, and miners who refused to accept the cuts were locked out. It was expected that the railway and the transport workers would also strike in support of the miners – all together being the three partners of the Triple Alliance of union solidarity forged in 1919.

In this tense time, Mrs Lloyd George campaigned in two by-elections, albeit in the more rural market town constituencies of Taunton and Bedford. She warmed up with a speech to the Llandudno Women's Liberal Association on 1st April.

The handwritten version of Mrs Lloyd George's Llandudno speech shows it to be an early run of her stump speech for the imminent Taunton by-election.[18] (illustration 26) After congratulating her audience for building their association, and spelling out clearly the intended role of these associations, she reassured her audience that 'supporting the Coalition does not mean selling our principles but pooling our resources':

One of the most satisfactory features of our political life today is the fact that Liberal Women are forming assoc all over the country to further the Lib cause & to promote Lib principles. Some people I know say that because we support the Coalition Government we have no right to call ourselves Liberal. The answer to that is a very simple one. We are justified in supporting the Coalition Gt because of the crisis through which the nation is passing. We are not false to our Liberalism simply because we subordinate the interests of the party to the interests of the country. Supporting the Coal does not mean selling our principles but pooling our resources; it means that for a time the political parties agree not to fight each other but to fight together the enemies of our beloved land. If doing that is a sin against Liberalism then so much the worse for Liberalism. What I want especially to say is this. Associations such as this can only live & thrive by steady and solid work.

What can women do to keep this association alive & to help the Gt in the great work it is doing? One useful & essential part of its work ought to be to educate the electors of this country, so that when they vote they vote wisely. Thanks to this much abused Gt there are about 13 millions more voters than there were a few years ago. Of this number about 6 millions are women. That measure was the most Radical Reform Act ever passed in this country. It has made Britain the most democratic country in Europe. But nothing is more dangerous to a people than political power not accompanied by political knowledge. Political wisdom makes for progress. Political ignorance makes for disaster.

To avert the disaster & to secure progress the electors must be educated. I think there are two great subjects on which we ought to be educating the people diligently just now.

We ought to be telling the people the wonderful record of the present Gt. As I have been going up & down the country I have been amazed to find how few people know what the Gt has actually achieved. Our enemies are never tired of pointing out the failures real & imaginary of the Gt. We must never tire of telling the people of the reforms passed by the Gt. When that is done it will do a great deal to inspire confidence in the Gt & allay a good deal of the unrest in the country. We might also tell the people of the perils of an alternate Gt. Most people now agree that a Labour Gt is a not unlikely successor to the present Gt. Well in my opinion that is a very grave prospect for the country. With the aspirations of democracies I have always had the deepest sympathy. I am a democrat. But democracy is one thing. Socialism & communism are very different things.

I know that the ILP [Independent Labour Party] has refused to identify itself with the Russian Revolutionaries. There was a large majority against. But do not forget this. There was a large minority in favour & if people want a revolution they do not wait until they can get a majority, a minority can do that. They have done it in Russia & they are doing it much nearer home. Let us therefore use all the means in our power & adopt all the methods we can to educate the voters so that they will vote intelligently not blindly, wisely not recklessly. To educate people alone is not enough. We must organise them so that they will be able to meet their opponents when the elections take place. The Labour party is scoring heavily largely because they are well organised. Let us follow their example & we will do well.

There is one other thing we must attend to. We must agree among ourselves what measures we want the Gt to pass & bring pressure on the Gt of the day to pass those measures. Let me explain what I mean.

We in Wales agree that we ought to get a Temperance Measure. There is no doubt we need it badly. We simply cannot afford to spend as much money on drink. Nor can we hope to compete successfully with sober nations unless we ourselves drink less than we do now. But Wales is not united as to what form the Temperance measure shall take. Some want P[rohibition], others state control. Others want minor reforms such as Sunday closing for Monmouth. We may be sure that if the Temperance people are not agreed the Gt will not act. I think if we could unite the sections on Local option it would be a real service to Temp. Then after you unite the nation, bring all the pressure you can to get the Gt to adopt the measure as the matter will come up in Parliament again in May. I hope you will take the hint. Now is the time to act not when it is too late.

(P refers to Prohibition. Until 1915 Monmouthshire had been exempt from the 1881 Sunday Closing Act for Wales, but adhered to it during the war, and reaffirmed in 1921 that it would continue to stay closed.)

There is another Reform to which I would like to refer before I sit down.

The handwritten speech ends here, but a press report reveals the other reform to which she referred:

In Llandudno they had been agitating recently against the leasehold system, rightly, too – applauded – and the Government had recently passed a Bill for the Enfranchisement of Chapel Sites built on lease, and now they had realised the principle that the people of Llandudno should keep pegging away until the Government introduced a Bill dealing generally with this important question. Women could do a lot by making use of their newly granted rights. The vote carried great responsibilities. They should make good use of their votes, and things would be well.[19]

With rail transport possibly subject to industrial action, Mrs Lloyd George set off by car for Somerset, to help the Coalition Unionist Sir Arthur Griffith-Boscawen, defeated at Dudley, to regain a seat in Parliament and thereby rescue his career. An audience of 2,000 awaited her in Taunton on the first evening of the campaign.[20] What neither Mrs Lloyd George nor the Welsh agricultural minister foresaw, nor could control, was the large numbers of sheep being driven to pasture in the hills of Wales. As a result, she arrived far too late for the evening event.

Taunton had always been a Unionist–Conservative seat, and elections had always been a straight contest with the Liberals (except for the 1909 by-election, Labour versus Unionist). In the 1918 Coupon election a Coalition Unionist faced Labour, with no Liberal candidate standing.

In this 1921 by-election, Coalition Unionist Sir Arthur was opposed by Labour: in effect a rerun of 1910 and 1918 with different candidates. It was presumed to be a safe seat, and the incumbent Col. Boles stepped aside to offer Sir Arthur a route back to Westminster.

Over the next two days Mrs Lloyd George – billed by the *Daily Herald* as the Coalition's 'star turn' of the week[21] – toured the villages of Somerset to the west of Taunton, with an accompanying party, concluding with a large meeting in Taunton on the eve of the poll.

Mrs Lloyd George, echoing some of her Llandudno speech, carefully indicated what she thought of the opposing party in this election, and of strikes – raising the bogey of Communism, whilst not being against the labouring classes. Though she was supporting a Unionist, this approach was one of the ways in which Liberals of all hues were seeking to hold back the threat of Labour.

The meetings could be lively:

In Wellington, where a great crowd had gathered… it was clear that a large part of the opposition were going do their utmost to prevent any speeches being heard. The opening stages saw a shouting match between the Colonel [Boles] introducing Mrs Lloyd George, and some shrill-voiced women in the crowd. The Colonel wore down the opposition, and said that he would forgive them for not listening to him, but he hoped that they would listen to Mrs Lloyd George.

Mrs Lloyd George addressed the crowd, the cheers of the Coalition supporters drowning the cries of their opponents. An interrupter asked her why Mr Lloyd George did not go to South Wales, and insinuated that he was afraid. 'He is not afraid,' retorted Mrs Lloyd George. 'He has been to South Wales before to-day and had had a tremendous reception. Perhaps it would be a good thing if he did go. It might bring some people to reason.'[22]

In Taunton there was some heckling from Labour members of the audience. The hecklers were removed, but abuse of the hecklers was also deplored. Mrs Lloyd George said:

'Mr Lloyd George and myself have always been democrats, and have stood for the people, and will do so again… The only alternative to the Government is a Labour Government, which I think at the present time would be a serious calamity.'

She thought that most of those present knew that Mr Lloyd George had always been a Liberal and had always been in favour of democracy, but democracy was one thing, and Socialism another. [Applause] She knew that a short time ago the ILP had decided to have nothing to do with the Russian revolutionaries, but there was a large number in the minority, and minorities could do what had been done in Russia.

She wanted to make it perfectly clear that she was against the Labour Party and not the labouring class, for they were two distinct parties. [Cheers] There were many, many working men against the policy of the Labour Party. She was anxious that they should do things constitutionally, as they had been used to doing in this country, but there were some people who wished them done unconstitutionally. The present strike was an unconstitutional way of going about things.

Mrs Lloyd George, continuing, said she was perfectly sure that there was no woman in Taunton in favour of such a strike, for it affected the women and children and the home more than anything and therefore she appealed to the women of Taunton to vote seriously on the morrow and not vote recklessly. [Applause] They must remember that the vote had been purchased at great price, and that it was a weapon of reform.

In conclusion Mrs Lloyd George appealed to her hearers to send a message of confidence to Mr Lloyd George and the Government, remarking that they had a lot of work in front of them. They had still to settle with Germany, and if they did not make the Germans pay they would be encouraging other people to enter into war, and she was sure they did not want that. The present was no time for social experiments, for common sense told them they ought to confine their energies to clearing the ravages of war, and that was what the Government wanted to do, and she hoped that they would send Sir Arthur back to help them with that work. [Cheers]

At this juncture a few Labourites, who had been interrupting the meeting, left the hall, their departure being signalised by boos and hissing and whereupon Dr Macdonald [the Conservative chairman] observed: 'Taunton! Taunton! Don't do that; let them alone. You will never imitate their methods.' The people immediately resumed their seats, and Mrs Lloyd George rose to return thanks, observing that she could not have had a greater reception in Wales than she had received in the Taunton Division that day. The best thanks they could give her would be to send Sir Arthur back to cheer the Prime Minister. [Applause][23]

The country's Agriculture Minister won his seat quite comfortably, albeit on a reduced majority: Griffith-Boscawen 12,994, James Lunnon 8,290.

Two days after the Taunton result, on 15th April – dubbed 'Black Friday' in the annals of the union movement – the rail and transport unions surprisingly voted against a supportive strike. However, the miners continued their action, holding out until July, when the squeeze on their own incomes would force them back, having won nothing.

Industrial tensions, however, were still current. Mrs Lloyd George moved on to Bedford, another largely rural/market town constituency – this time supporting a Coalition Liberal, not Unionist, against a Labour candidate, Frederick Fox Riley. The incumbent, Frederick 'F.G.' Kellaway, MP since 1910, was seeking re-election after promotion to Postmaster General. Conscious of Mrs Lloyd George's potential power to attract the women's vote, Labour brought in Dr Marion Phillips (an Australian-born LSE-educated, prominent suffragette and women's campaigner, and later MP) to speak for Riley, who followed Mrs Lloyd George's progress in four cars. At times, both entourages good-naturedly arrived together at the village greens.[24] (illustration 15)

In her opening remarks on 19th April, Mrs Lloyd George went onto the attack:

Mrs Lloyd George arrived in Bedford yesterday, and to-day
will tour the whole constituency in support of Mr Kellaway's
candidature. Speaking to a mass meeting in the County Theatre
yesterday, she said we had beaten Prussianism, and the next thing
to be defeated was Russianism. Disciples of Lenin and Trotsky
were in our midst, doing infinite harm to the country. We were at
the present moment in the middle of a great struggle with them,
and if they succeeded we might as well write 'Ichabod' – against
the nation.[25]

Bedford delivered victory for the new minister, the Coalition
Liberal. But Labour put in a protest:

At the meeting of the Bedfordshire Education Committee Friday
week Mr G. Dixon, member, who is Chairman of the Bedford
Divisional Labour Party, said he understood that the school-
children were paraded at Cople, Cardington, Willington, and
Dean, to sing and make presentations to Mrs Lloyd George. So
long as party politics contributed to the making and unmaking of
Governments he thought the least they could do as an Education
Authority was to see that the children did not enter into the
question. He desired to know whether permission was sought that
children might be so paraded, whether permission was given by
the Director of Education, or the School Managers, or whether the
head teachers did it themselves.[26]

The Committee agreed to make enquiries.

In between by-elections, in London Mrs Lloyd George and
Megan received the guests at a festival dinner for more than
200 at the Savoy Hotel, in aid of the Chailey Heritage Craft
School.[27]

On 21st April, back in London after the Bedford tour, Mrs
Lloyd George had to defend her husband's record in another
way:

Mrs Lloyd George was one of the speakers at the annual meeting
of the Early Closing Association at the Grocers' Hall, London.
Mrs Lloyd George said, 'The improvement in the hours of shop

assistants is largely due to the work of this Association. I will tell you a little story about this. It not "official". It is true. [Laughter] One day, very soon after the Early Closing Bill was in operation, I was in the shop Peter Robinson, and two very smart ladies came in. As they passed me I heard them say, "Yes, they close the shop at one o'clock on Saturday. Lloyd George has made them close at one o'clock." [Laughter] Poor Mr Lloyd George gets blamed for everything, but Mr Winston Churchill happens to have been the culprit.' [Laughter and applause][28]

Perhaps, fresh in mind, was the debate in Cardiganshire as to who should get the credit for the provision of old age pensions, Asquith, the PM at the time, or Lloyd George, the Chancellor, and this was one where she wanted to set the record straight. Debit where debit is due, one might say.

She also noted that they were under an obligation to the shop assistants, 'who sell us things we want, often things we don't want, and sometimes sell their customers.' She added that London recruited its shop assistants to a considerable extent from Wales, and many of them had risen to the highest positions in the distributive trades of London.[29] Welsh leadership in the drapery business was indeed impressive, e.g. Dickens and Jones, John Lewis, D. H. Evans.

On 27th April the Calvinistic Methodist Mrs Lloyd George made 'peace with her adversaries', at the Baptist Women's League meeting at Bloomsbury Central Church, London. She had spoken there in February 1918, when accepting the Presidency of the Women's Free Church Council; in 1920 she had had to pull out of attending the Baptist Union Annual Assembly in Birmingham, when she had overdone it and had had to take almost a couple of months off.

We are advised on High Authority to make peace with our adversaries quickly. My first duty this afternoon is to make peace with my friends of the Baptist Union. I made a promise to attend your meetings last year at Birmingham. It was an engagement sandwiched in among a number of others. I failed to keep my engagement. The failure was not due to want of will but want of time & of strength. I now apologise for any inconvenience I may have caused you.[30]

Mrs Lloyd George reminded her audience of the progress being made by women under her husband's government:

Well, I want to congratulate the Baptist Union on having a Women's League. That shows that you are abreast of the times. It proves your chivalry and your wisdom. This Government as you know has revolutionised the place of women in the land. It has given millions of them political power for the first time. It has opened to them doors which were closed to them throughout the centuries. Practically every profession is now open to women. Women now sit on the Benches as Magistrates & one has even entered the House of Commons. Lady Astor is now like a pelican in the wilderness. I hope that there may be a flock of them!

Well, if women can render service to the *State* they cannot be ignored by the Church.

She concluded by urging her audience to be ambitious:

If I may offer a word of advice to you – it would be this. Don't be afraid of new enterprises, & big enterprises. An appeal to the heroic received a wonderful response during the war. I have all kinds of letters from all sorts of people every day of the week. I am amazed and pained at the number from people who are friendless in the world. The help they need very often is not any Government can give. They need the help which the Church can give. Seek them out. Help them & you may win them.

I venture to appeal to all women in the Baptist Churches to join this League and so all they you can to make it a real power for good.

This speech was reported widely in the press at the time, particularly picking up the epithet for Lady Astor as a 'pelican in the wilderness'.

On the evening of 27th April, Mrs Lloyd George was at the

Coliseum supporting more Welsh artistes: 'a performance of Mr J. O. Francis's play, *The Poacher* by a company compiled of the well-known Hopkins family, of Cardiff'.[31]

The next day, 28th April, her secretary will have had to make peace on her behalf again, as she had to miss a planned engagement at East Finchley, visiting the Manor Farm and Dairy. A promise was made to visit at a later date, which she duly honoured.[32]

April closed with her attendance, with many other notables, at the private view of the Royal Academy's 1921 Exhibition.[33] Works by a number of Welsh artists were on display, including the portraitist Christopher Williams' study, from life, of the PM, to be unveiled later in Caernarfon, and Sir William Goscombe John's memorial figure of a lady, and a war memorial for Lampeter. The planned RA dinner was cancelled 'in consequence of the present coal strike and the distress caused thereby'.[34]

The coal strike continued into May. The *Montrose Standard* speculated as to whether the women, including Mrs Lloyd George, could succeed where efforts to solve the long coal strike had so far failed:

Conferences between coal-owners and miners are plentiful just now, and both parties have frequent interviews with the Prime Minister. How would it be if there were a Conference between coal-owners' wives and miners' wives, and if they took their mutual troubles to Mrs Lloyd George? 'Impossible!' you say. Well, I suppose so. But is it so impossible that each should try to put herself into the other's shoes, and see where the shoe pinches? Above all, is it impossible that both alike should remember that there are other wives and children who are suffering because the miners are standing out for a principle that the owners said that they would never grant. I don't attempt to decide who is right or who is wrong. Tragedy, a great philosopher has said, does not consist in the conflict of right with wrong, but of right with right. And here we are, face to face with a tragedy which the men who argle-bargle across the conference table hardly see. But we women can see it, and we know that it is going to affect not only this generation throughout its life, but the next as well.[35]

On another front, Mrs Lloyd George's wartime experience was called upon, when she was appointed to an Emergency Kitchens Committee set up by the Board of Trade 'to encourage the provision of cheap cooked foods in districts when the need is apparent'.[36]

May's engagements began on the 4th at the Brompton Oratory, at the society wedding of Violette, the second daughter of Gordon Selfridge, to the Comte de Sibour. The bride's satin dress was trimmed with lace that had belonged to Marie Antoinette. The flowers 'came by aeroplane' from the South of France.[37]

After that little bit of extravagance, there was a little sobriety. On 5th May Mrs Lloyd George addressed the Women's Total Abstinence Union at Central Hall, offering encouragement to a cause that continued to struggle to make its full impact, and offered her suggestions as to how they might 'get the laws we need'. The two versions in the JTR Collection, one in MLG's hand and one in JTR's hand, are virtually identical texts apart from a little tidying up and with minor additions in the version reproduced here.[38] The subject was important both to the speaker and to her secretary and is a good example of a thorough speech offering encouragement to campaigners fighting an uphill battle:

I accepted Lady Clwyd's very kind invitation to attend this conference with great pleasure. I have come, however, not to make a long speech but rather to show my sympathy with the movement, and to offer my congratulations to the Women's Total Abstinence Union on the success which is following their efforts.

As I go about Temperance workers I meet with many who are greatly discouraged for one reason or another. Now nothing paralyses effort like loss of faith & courage in the work. Temperance people are very liable to catch this complaint. Yet no people have less reason to be discouraged that those who are promoting sobriety in the land.

What is there to encourage us? The great progress made in the opinions & the habits of the people since this cause was started.

For one thing the teaching of the Churches has altered completely during the last 50 years. It is not so very long since drinking amongst Church people was quite the ordinary thing. Even drunkenness was tolerated among all denominations not so very long ago. Even Ministers thought at one time that total abstinence was a fad *if not a sin*. Today, the vast majority of Ministers & students are total abstainers. Drunkenness is not tolerated in any Church. Even people who drink do not enjoy the respect they once did. People engaged in the business are not allowed to be Church members in all denominations.

That *I think* is very encouraging.

Then Science has come over completely to our side. As you know scientific men have been busy making researches into the effect of alcohol on the human body. Experiments have been made in a hundred directions. The results have been such as to astonish and to convince the most sceptical. Science today declares emphatically & explicitly that alcohol has little use as a medicine, none as a food, & less as a beverage.

That surely *is* very encouraging.

Again, social experiments of great value have been made in this and other lands to find out the effect of alcohol on work, & on how to effect sobriety. The experiments made in this country during the war, these experiments are without exception in our favour. They show that sober people are more efficient than drinking people. The less men drink the better they work. They also show that restrictions of facilities to obtain drink make for sobriety. We now know that people can be made sober by Act of Parliament, or an order of the Control Board.

That again is very encouraging

As a result of all these things, there is a marked improvement in the habits of the people. There is of course far too much drinking going on now. We wish it were less. But let us not forget that we are at least moving in the right direction.

If you feel discouraged let me advise you to read the history of the last 100 years & especially the history of the Temperance Movement. If you read the biographies of men like Sir Wilfred

Lawson or Mr W. S. Caine [the father of Lady Clwyd] you will realise that we are making progress. It may be slow but it is sure.

*What we need now is legislation that will embody our experience.* If people can be made sober by Act of Parliament, we must get an Act of Parliament to make them sober. We have every reason to be *encouraged*, but none to be *satisfied*. We cannot be satisfied until our laws are satisfactory.

*How can we get these laws we need?*

Of one thing we may be certain. We cannot get a Temperance Bill without strenuous & well directed effort. We know from experience the power of the enemy. We must adapt our methods to the needs of the hour.

I suggested in this building a few nights ago the directions in which we ought to work. I repeat the suggestions to you.

1. We must *educate* public opinion. The people as a whole still believe in the merits of alcohol. Heresies die very hard. We must convert a majority of the electors to our views. Denunciation of the Government is no substitute for the education of the people. We must make every citizen familiar with the established facts of science & our experience. I have great faith in education.

2. We must *organise* our forces. At present we are not united nor organised. I am inclined to suggest Unity of Command as a help to victory.

3. We must *stir up* the public to demand reform. Ask, seek, knock, especially *knock*.

In this work none can render more effective help than women. I hope the Women's Total Abstention Union will take a lead in this Crusade & lead us to Victory.

The similar talk 'in this building a few nights ago' referred to an evening meeting at Central Hall on 22nd April, where Lady Astor spoke, under the chairmanship of Cardinal Bourne.

On the political front, Lloyd George's Liberals were preparing for a tougher fight.

1. With Megan and Lloyd George.
*The Sphere* 4.1.1919.

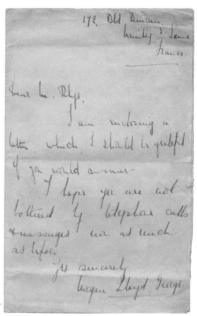

2. A missive from Megan to JTR, Neuilly-sur-Seine, France.

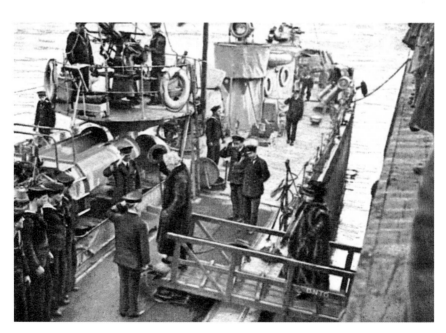

3. Homebound from Paris on the destroyer, 8th February 1919. *The Sketch*, 19.2.1919.

Crewe Station.

Dear Mr Rhys
    There is a small cardboard box on yur desk containing 2 shoe buckles. Please send to London Shoe Co. Sloane Square. Yrs
    M. Lloyd Geo

4. Mrs Lloyd George note to JTR.
JTR Private Collection

5. The well-shod campaigner. Buckled in Birmingham with the Lord Mayor of the city, 5th February 1921. *Illustrated London News*, 12.2.1921.
© *Illustrated London News Ltd/Mary Evans*

6. Jane Annie Rhys' South Wales Women's Temperance Union / Merched y De medallion, inscribed: 'A good name is better than precious ointment.'
JTR Private Collection

GWRAIG YR HWSMON.

GWRAIG YR HWSMON HONNO AETH A HI,
UCHEL IAWN YN NGHYMRU YW EI BRI;
ABERTEIFI SWYNWYD GAN EI DAWN
I GYFLAWNI YR HYN OEDD IAWN;
GWRAIG BONHAM CARTER DDAETH MEDDE NHW,
ER EI DISODLI, OND PW, PW, PW.
TYBIAI HON FOD CYMRY YN DDIGON FFOL
IW HUD-DDENU GAN RYW BAISLEY SHAWL.

7. Verse 1 of 'Gwraig yr Hwsmon', by Tegfeln, celebrating the 1921 Cardiganshire victory.
JTR Private Collection

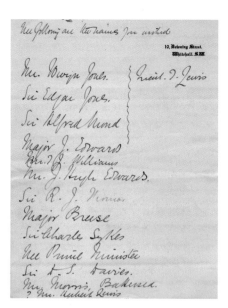

8. JTR's list of the invitees to the House of Commons dinner, 26th February 1919, for Mrs Lloyd George and her winning 1918 'Coupon Election' candidates.

JTR Private Collection

## TO THE ELECTORS OF THE
### Criccieth Urban District Council.

BRYNAWELON,
CRICCIETH,
March 27th, 1919.

LADIES AND GENTLEMEN,

In deference to the wishes of a large number of electors, so many of whom are old and valued friends, I have consented to become a candidate for a seat on the Criccieth Urban District Council.

The powers of these Councils, already very considerable, are continually being increased by new Legislation. The Councils already possess, or soon will possess, large powers for dealing with such reforms as Housing, Lighting, Health, Infant Welfare, and Cottage Allotments.

Though Parliament has conferred these powers on Local Bodies, it rests with the latter to adopt and enforce the Laws.

The possibilities of Criccieth as a Health Resort make it very important that the maximum benefit should be derived from these and similar Laws.

My association with Criccieth has been long, close, and happy, and if I am honoured by a seat on the Council of my native town, it will be my pleasure as well as my duty and interest, to do all in my power to further the prosperity of the town and the well-being of its inhabitants.

Yours faithfully,
**Margaret Lloyd George.**

Printed & Published by Matthew Roberts, Criccieth.

9. Mrs Lloyd George's message to the Criccieth electors, 27th March 1919.

JTR Private Collection

10. Speaking at an Exeter garden party, 11th July 1922.

*My South Western Tour*, NLW Album 1291 C

11. On the beach in Normandy, August 1919. *The Bystander*, 3.9.1919.

© *Illustrated London News Ltd/Mary Evans*

12. Picnic by Loch Maree, Scotland, September 1921. Seated in the car, Mrs Lloyd George and the PM. On the running board, LlG's private secretaries Sir Edward Grigg and Frances Stevenson. *Illustrated London News*, 17.9.1921.

© *Illustrated London News Ltd/ Mary Evans*

13. Targeting coconuts at St Dunstan's fair, 8th July 1922. "CAN WOMEN AIM STRAIGHT? Mrs Lloyd George can; she knocked a coconut down with her second shot at St Dunstan's yesterday – but the little boy ate it." *Sunday Illustrated*, 9.7.1922.

14. The wireless tent at Clifton Zoo, Bristol.

*My South Western Tour*, NLW Album 1291 C

15. The Bedford by-election, April 1921: Campaigning at Cardington Aerodrome. *Daily Mirror,* 21.4.1921.

© *Mirrorpix*

16. Arriving at Tiverton, Devon, 11th July 1922.

*My South Western Tour*, NLW Album 1291 C

17. The reception given in Aberaeron to Mrs Lloyd George, 17th June 1919.

Archifdy Ceredigion Archives, Ref ADX/66

18. Simla: Olwen Carey Evans seated right; Tom Carey Evans, standing, far left; Miss Mary Mond, daughter of Lady Mond, who later married the son of the Viceroy, standing left, back row. Seated centre, the Viceroy and Countess Reading. *The Tatler*, 12.10.1921.

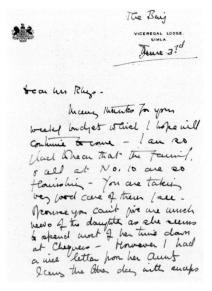

19. Letter from India: Olwen Carey Evans to JTR, 3rd June 1921.

20. The audience, and press, at Falmouth, Cornwall, 13th July 1922.

*My South Western Tour*, NLW Album 1291 C

21. With Megan at the Harlech Pageant, August 1922. *The Illustrated London News*, 26.8.1922.

22. Patients exercising at the Prince of Wales Hospital for the Limbless and Disabled, Cardiff, 1918.

Screen and Sound Archive, National Library of Wales

SIR WILLIAM TRELOAR and MRS. LLOYD GEORGE

Copies of this picture, showing Mrs. Lloyd George carrying one of the patients of Sir William's Cripples' Home, were autographed, and are being sold at 10s. at 61 Moorgate Street on behalf of the Home. One of the photographs was given to the child's mother by the "Daily Graphic."

23. The photograph at the Treloar School was sold to raise funds. *The Graphic*, 30.7.1921.

© Illustrated London News Ltd/Mary Evans

24. Witham Nurses' Bungalow opened by Mrs Lloyd George, July 1919.

Image 1932–1934, with the kind permission of Roy Gage and sourced from *The History of Witham, Essex*, by Janet Gyford.

25. Garlanded with roses by Mrs Lall at the YWCA fair, Lansdowne House, 28th June 1922.

TopFoto

26. From Mrs Lloyd George's draft speech for the Llandudno Women's Association, 1st April 1921.

JTR Private Collection, with copies in NLW

27. From JTR's draft for the 'speech that never was', to the Derby Free Churches, February 1919.

JTR Private Collection, with copies in NLW

28. Weekend at Chequers: the grandchildren meet Crown Prince Hirohito, May 1921.

© British Pathé Ltd

29. The Welsh dragon at No. 10: St David's Day 1922. The Chailey Guild of Play children present the Premier with an armchair, with Megan and Dame Margaret, 2nd March 1922. Also presented was a miniature set of stoolball, commemorating Dame Margaret's participation in the game in 1921.
TopFoto

**PREMIER'S WIFE ON STRIKE FOR WALES**

Mrs. Lloyd George opening the stoolball match for a women's team representing Wales against a men's team dressed as Sussex farmers during a visit to the Heritage Craft Schools, Chailey. The Welsh national costume was worn.

30. Stoolball at Chailey's. *Sunday Mirror*, 13.3.1921.
© *Mirrorpix*

31. Dr Williams' School at No. 10, 24th June 1921.

*Gwynedd Archives Service*

32. The cheering girls of Cullompton School, Devon, July 1922.

*My South Western Tour*, NLW Album 1291 C

33. Cheering students at Milton Mount College, Worth Park, Crawley, Sussex, 23rd June 1921. *The Sphere*, 2.7.1921.

© *Illustrated London News Ltd/Mary Evans*

34. Unveiling the Roll of Honour at the Royal Dental Hospital, 5th November 1919.

Photograph by British Illustrations Ltd from the London Metropolitan Archives, with the kind permission of the St George's Hospitals NHS Foundation Trust.

WHILE YOU WAIT.—Dame Margaret Lloyd George standing patiently while an artist draws her portrait at the garden fête held at St. Dunstan's.

35. A rapid portrait at the St Dunstan's fair, 8th July 1922. *Sunday Mirror*, 9.7.1922.

Sophie Ries succeeded JTR as private secretary to Mrs Lloyd George in mid 1922. Known to the Lloyd George grandchildren as "Toffs", in 1920 she had accompanied Olwen Carey Evans to India.

36. No.10 children's Christmas party, 1921, Sophie Ries in dark hat. *Sunday Pictorial*, 25.12.1921.

© Mirrorpix

37. Truro, July 1922, Sophie Ries (in chequered coat) standing behind Dame Margaret.

My South Western Tour, NLW Album 1291 C

38. Mrs Lloyd George with grandchildren and Sophie Ries at Brynawelon.

JTR Private Collection

39. Passing the time in Genoa, one of the rare trips abroad when LlG was working, May 1922. *The Sketch*, 22.4.1922.
© Illustrated London News Ltd/Mary Evans

MRS. LLOYD GEORGE, G.B.E.

40. Drawing from *Time & Tide* 12.11.1920, by J.W. Ginsbury.
JTR Collection

41. Dame Margaret, Dame Grand Cross of the British Empire, by Bassano Ltd., National Portrait Gallery, 1924, No. 84282.
© National Portrait Gallery

42. Leaving No. 10 for the last time, October 1922. *The Sphere*, 4.11.1922.

© *Illustrated London News Ltd/Mary Evans*

43. 'My dear Mrs Weinidog'. Isabel Law to Mrs Lloyd George, May 1920.

JTR Private Collection

44. Redruth, and the Camborne Commitment to the mining community, 12th July 1922.

*My South Western Tour*, NLW Album 1291 C

45. Mixing religion and politics: The Rev. J.T. Rhys (standing, right) with MPs and Free Churchmen at the National Free Church Council annual assembly, Llandrindod Wells, March 1926. The Rev. Elvet Lewis seated, centre. Rhys Hopkin Morris (bow tie, back row, left), an Independent Liberal opposed to Lloyd George, contested the Cardiganshire seat in 1922, losing narrowly, but in 1923 he unseated Ernest Evans.

Photo by P.B. Abery, Builth Wells. JTR Private Collection

46. The introduction to JTR's 1922 report for the Chief Whip Charles McCurdy, on his countrywide meetings with Nonconformist ministers.

JTR Private Collection

47. JTR, in a photograph also included in the album of 189 photographs of his fellow Free Churchmen, and MPs, presented to Lloyd George on 28th July 1922.

JTR Private Collection

48. A signed menu from the 14th July 1920, Bastille Day dinner and dance for Megan at No. 10.

JTR Private Collection

49. The silk programme for the No. 10 concert in aid of the Middlesex Hospital, 18th December 1919.

JTR Private Collection

50. Presentation gift to JTR by the concert committee of the Welsh Industries Association, June 25th 1919. The first concert at No. 10 to be open to the paying public.

JTR Private Collection

CHAPTER 12

# The Gloves Come Off
## (May 1921)

ON 6TH MAY Mrs Lloyd George was the hostess at the
Connaught Rooms, London, for the launch of the new London
Council of Coalition Liberals, the reception and dinner
attended by 500 guests, as the Lloyd George Liberals began to
build their organisation around the country. Chaired by the
Liberal politician Lord Rathcreedan, the meeting welcomed
Charles McCurdy to what was his first major event since taking
over from Freddie Guest as the Coalition Liberal Chief Whip.
JTR left behind an undated speech, in his hand, on the Prime
Minister's paper, which has all the hallmarks of this occasion,
and which may have been given by Mrs Lloyd George, but
it is unattributed and a bit of a mystery. Perhaps the speech
was prepared for delivery by Mrs Lloyd George, but then not
delivered, hence unreported.

The *Pall Mall Gazette* merely reported her quoting a short
couplet:

> After a series of resolutions setting up the council and various
> committees had been passed, Mrs Lloyd George was induced to say
> a few words. Very happily she borrowed an old couplet to describe
> the feelings of the meeting:
>> We hold not with statesmen whose infatuation
>> To party give what was meant for the nation.[1]

The unpublished, unattributed speech reads:

My Lords, Ladies and Gentlemen

I think this is almost the first gathering at which Mr McCurdy has appeared since his promotion to the office he now occupies. While we shall all miss Capt. Guest we shall watch Mr McCurdy's career with interest. He has already proved himself a thorough Liberal & a statesman of no mean order. We trust that the success which has already marked his political career will continue & increase.

Tonight's gathering is no ordinary political gathering. I believe it is going to have a far-reaching influence on British Politics. Since the unfortunate cleavage in the Liberal Party Coalition, Liberals have studiously refrained from doing or saying anything that might tend to widen the breach. They did that in the hope that with the passing of time, the breach might be healed. That was our wish & that was our hope.

But while we have been passive, the so-called Independent Liberals have been active. Their activity has been marked by an amount of intolerance and arrogance which are in striking contrast to the ideal & the spirit of Liberalism. I do not want to be unjust. I do not want to be harsh. But when I recall Leamington, the name of T. J. Evans, and the Christopher Williams painting of the Prime Minister, you will admit that I have not exaggerated.

There is a limit to human forbearance. Our self-respect, not to say our self-preservation, demands that we should defend ourselves. This meeting is an acceptance of the challenges thrown out by our foes, and a call to our friends to rally to the defence of their principles.

While I deeply regret the need to defend ourselves I have no misgivings as to the issue of the conflict. I will tell you why I say that. As some of you may know, I have almost unique opportunities of meeting the Liberals. My experience convinces me that the majority of Liberals are with us. The Independents are labouring under a delusion. They think that Abingdon St is the United Kingdom, that the National Liberal Club is synonymous with National Liberals; that to capture the machine is to convert capture the electors. Well, there is a great disillusionment in store for them.

The Germans made an initial & fatal mistake before the war. They failed to under [*sic*] British Psychology. The Independent Liberals are committing the same blunder. They have overestimated the political effectiveness of bluff, intrigue, & rancour.

Because the British people love above all things fair play I am confident we shall win.[2]

It is a good synthesis of the 'gloves off' approach now being taken. Reference to actions taken against two Welshmen perhaps suggests it was for Mrs Lloyd George to deliver.

T. J. Evans, a journalist from Cellan, Cardiganshire (his wife was from JTR's hometown of Lampeter), was the secretary of the Coalition Liberals. The Asquithian-minded National Liberal Club had, in September 1920, suspended him for three months from the Club. The dispute went on into the courts.[3]

During the refurbishment of the National Liberal Headquarters, the 1913 Christopher Williams painting of the Prime Minister had been taken down. Now the National Liberal Club was refusing to rehang the painting, and that of Winston Churchill. The decision would have been taken before the Cardiganshire election got into full swing.[4] In a slightly different telling of the story, in a tribute to JTR after his death in 1938, the author of one newspaper's 'London Letter' wrote:

> It will be remembered that during the Great War the authorities of the day, who controlled the National Liberal Club, removed the oil painting of Mr Lloyd George from the smokeroom to the cellar. JT was on his hind legs at once and made, in various ways, things very uncomfortable all round. He was the most uncompromising man I ever knew, and somehow, now, I think that that attribute of his make-up stands out more than any other.[5]

The painting today hangs prominently again at the Club.

A short message from the absent PM was also read out at the meeting. Lucy Lady Markham, Vice-Chairwoman of the new Council, received the guests with Mrs Lloyd George.[6] Perhaps Lady Markham, wife of Sir Arthur Markham, the former MP and Nottinghamshire coal industrialist, delivered the speech. Lady Markham was active in promoting events for the Coalition Liberals at her Portland Place home, and had recently begun hosting a series of lectures on economic issues for women, in conjunction with the Economic Study Club.[7]

On 9th May Mrs Lloyd George left for north Wales for a series of Coalition meetings, accompanied by MPs Ernest Evans and J. W. Pratt, and by No. 10 staff member E. R. Davies. Before then she and Megan accompanied the PM to Maidstone for another political meeting, staying the weekend at the Tonbridge home of the parents of Thelma Cazalet.

Also on 9th May the *Western Mail* gave an update on the 'who's who' in the secretarial staff at No. 10, now that Captain Evans had moved on (the new MP would also return to the Bar):

> Mr Lloyd George hopes to be able in the future to get his secretarial work done by four secretaries, namely, Mr J. T. Davies, CB, Capt. Shakespeare, Mr Silvester [*sic*], and Miss Stevenson. Mr Evan R. Davies remains on the Downing-street staff, but his duties are more concerned with the preparation of Cabinet work than in personal service to the Prime Minister. There is also still at No. 10 Mr J. T. Rhys, who is private secretary to Mrs Lloyd George, and assists a good deal in her charity work. Col. Sir Edward Grigg, CMG, DSO, having been pressed by the Roads Trust to continue his services for them, is unable to accept an appointment in succession to Mr Philip Kerr as the private secretary to the Prime Minister on the foreign affairs side.[8]

In 1973 John Grigg, the son of Sir Edward Grigg, published the first book of his four-volume biography of Lloyd George.

On 10th May the campaign in Wales got under way, rallying support rather than with any specific election in mind. Mrs Lloyd George made a 'spirited defence of the Premier and the Coalition'. She shored up support in Lloyd George's urban constituency, the Carnarvon Boroughs (the Municipal Boroughs of Bangor, Caernarfon, Conway, and Pwllheli; the Urban Districts of Cricieth, Llandudno, Llanfairfechan and Penmaenmawr; and the Lleyn Rural District), as well as in the neighbouring more rural ones, at a time of industrial strife, and increasing division in Liberal ranks.

Her speech represents an issue that was important to Mrs Lloyd George – unfair criticism. Not because she had a thin skin, but because of the dishonesty it represented. A passage in JTR's Notes for her putative autobiography sets out her thinking under the heading of 'Misrepresentation Calumnies etc':

> As I look back & try to review dispassionate events of 40 years few things amaze me more that the large part played by misrepresentation in discussion of private and public affairs. Due to many causes:
> 1. Sheer mental incapacity to grasp what was said or read;
> 2. Love of going one better, of improving on what was read or heard, love of exaggeration;
> 3. If some w/out thought or malice, deliberate i.e. w. malice aforethought for sake of personal or party ends. 'My country right or wrong', an old Norfolk farmer. So many think if party ends are served, the end justifies the means, however mean they may be. ['Carelessness' written in the margin]
> Once started lies grow bigger – breed others & can't be arrested. Often feel that if public discussion could be restricted to truth, whole truth & nothing but the truth it would be most beneficial revolution world has ever known.[9]

This was perhaps one reason for steering clear of front-line politics.

JTR's handwritten version of her remarks in the Carnarvon Boroughs,[10] as well as a copy of her further speech at Llanfairfechan on this trip, in her handwriting and in Welsh,[11] are in the JTR Collection. Her own speaking notes are also in the NLW Collection, offering some indications as to how she prepared her own speeches, and JTR preparing more final versions, most likely for future use and reference.

In an article in 1927 Mrs Lloyd George wrote that she generally spoke extempore, and when she did make some

preparatory notes she invariably lost them by the time she was
ready to speak.

### Tragedy of Lost Notes!

Among the questions often put to me is one as to what method I
adopt when preparing my speeches before any public function or
meeting.

To tell the truth I seldom, if ever, prepare a speech beforehand.
I simply say what I have to say, extempore. My husband works
quite differently to this as he generally prepares his speeches
carefully beforehand.

I remember one occasion when I attempted to prepare a
speech. I sat down and carefully thought out headings for various
subjects, and then jotted down my notes concerning them on a
scrap of paper to take with me to the meeting.

But when I arrived there and got on the platform that scrap of
paper had completely vanished! So I had to extemporise as usual.

And it was always like that whenever I tried to arrange my
speech. No matter what care I took of my notes, they would
perversely disappear just as the moment arrived to make use of
them.[12]

For many of her engagements, especially opening bazaars
and where her speeches were short, this may be true – but it
is hard to believe for much of her political speaking, except
perhaps in the frenetic whistle-stop campaigns of December
1918 and Cardiganshire 1921. However, as long as she had her
notes, then the style suggests she did not need to speak from a
full text. Formal speechmaking was not her style – instead she
spoke directly to her audience. In 1922, Ernie Evans recalled:

She married the young Welsh lawyer at an early age, and for
34 years has shared his life during the romantic episodes of his
remarkable career. It was not long before she was called upon
to take her part in public life. The time came when she had to
make her first public speech. Reminding her husband of the
engagement, she asked him to prepare a speech for her. This task
he promptly and wisely declined, pointing out that in the course of

time many similar calls would be made upon her, and that, if he made the first of her speeches, would probably have to make all of them, and it would be wiser for her to rely on her own gifts from the commencement.

Subsequent history has confirmed the wisdom of this advice. Few women have made so many speeches in recent years, and few women's speeches, or men's, for that matter, have exercised so much influence.

Their influence springs from her attractive and sincere personality. All her speeches are couched in simple language, delivered in homely fashion, characterised by great common sense, and reveal an intimate knowledge of domestic affairs and home life.[13]

Her Llanfairfechan speech is a classic example of her speaking style, spiced with biblical history and Greek mythology, attacking criticism of the Government before spelling out its achievements, and ending with her favourite Walpole analogy:

I am very glad to be down once again in my husband's constituency and to discuss with his constituents some of the great and grave problems with which he is wrestling.

The Prime Minister would have been glad if it had been possible for him to come down himself. That is not possible.

As you know the Prime Minister is a very busy man. Few people I think realise how very busy and how very burdened he is. No Prime Minister in the history of our country has had such heavy & such exacting responsibilities. The affairs of the State, indeed the affairs of this world, absorb all his energies, all his time & all his thoughts.

Mrs Lloyd George then carefully defends her husband and his Government's record by forensically addressing the criticism, as opposed to the critics, warming up with a biblical reference:

You remember that when Nehemiah was rebuilding the Walls of

Jerusalem certain men devoted their energies to thwarting his efforts: by criticism, by misrepresentation, & by ridicule. Their names were Sanballat, Tobiah and Geshem.

History is always repeating itself. While your member is devoting himself unreservedly to the task of reconstruction, his enemies are doing their utmost to harass and to hinder him. Instead of patriotically lending a hand they are doing their best (& their worst) to annoy the builder & to delay the building & so prolong the agony of the people.

I do not propose to say much about the critics of the Government but I do want you to hear what I have to say about the criticism.

Some criticism of the Government is *inevitable*. The Government of this Empire touches very closely the lives of tens of millions of people. It is impossible to frame & to administer laws affecting so many millions in such a way as to please everybody. Besides, human nature is so constituted that men can't help grumbling. Some people grumble at some things; some people grumble at everything. Fault-finding is a privilege we value. It is almost the only thing we can indulge in without paying a tax upon it! There never has been a Government, there never will be a Government free from criticism.

I have said some criticism of the Government is inevitable. Let me now add quite frankly that some criticism of the Government is *reasonable*.

All legislation is an experiment, an adventure, a leap in the dark. It is like getting married. You can foretell how a problem will work out in Mathematics or in Chemistry. Given certain factors there can only be one result. It is very different in politics. You pass a law and you can never foretell exactly how it will operate. No law has ever worked out precisely as people expected. Some laws disappoint even those who advocated them. They produce the very evil that are intended to prevent. That was the case e.g. with Gladstone's Grocers' Licences [the first off-licenses, established in 1860]. EPD is a more recent example. To object to such a law is *reasonable*. To have allowed such a law to remain would have been futile & foolish. The Government did the only thing a sane & fair Government could do. It repealed the EPD law. [EPD was Excess Profit Duty, introduced in wartime and repealed in the 1921 Finance Act.]

Now the criticism of that law was reasonable. But the conduct of so many of the critics was not so reasonable. They pointed to the repeal of that law as a proof that the government had blundered. If it was a blunder it was the blunder not of the Government but of Parliament as a whole. If the Government had not tried it would have failed in its duty. If it retained it after it had proved its failure it would have failed in its duty.

After admitting some criticism that is inevitable, and some that is reasonable, she warms up her adjectives:

… let me now say that there is a good deal of criticism that is *contemptible*.

There are some people who are not only critical but *hypercritical* – and *hypocritical*. They find fault not with some things but with all things done by the Government. Well, even this Government must some times do some wise & good things. Even if it tried it could not always succeed in doing wrong things.

Here she refers in particular to the Peace Settlement with Germany, including:

They are hypocritical because if they had the power they would not do otherwise than the Government is doing in regard to the key things they criticise. Those who were *Pro*-Germans and then *Pan*-Germans during the war are now protesting against making Germany pay. Do you think if they were in power they would let Germany off without paying?

They are blaming the Government because peace has not been made with Germany. Would they make peace with Germany on terms made in Germany? No they would not if they could. If you think our terms harsh will you remember that the crime was a great one; what would Germany have imposed on us if our positions had been reversed? Germany is not asked to pay a fine, only the cost & given time to do that. As politicians they denounce profiteering, as Directors they make all the profits they can.

When I read what these critics are saying I remember one of the fables of Aesop I read as a child. I will recall it to you because it has a moral.

Jupiter, Neptune & Minerva, so the story goes, once contended which of them should make the most perfect thing.

Jupiter made a man; Minerva made a house; and Neptune made a bull.

Momus was chosen judge to decide which production had the greatest merit.

He began by finding fault with the bull; because his horns were not below his eyes so that he might see when he butted with them. Next he found fault with the man, because there was no window in his breast that all might see his inward thoughts. And lastly he found fault with the house, because it had no wheels to enable its inhabitants to remove from bad neighbours.

But Jupiter drove the critic out of heaven telling him that a fault finder could never be pleased, & that it was *time to criticise the works of others when he had done some good thing himself.*

Having invoked the Greek gods with the help of Aesop, Mrs Lloyd George leaves a final question for critics, targeting the Independent Liberals:

I want to ask one question before I leave the critics. Supposing Mr Asquith were at the head of this Government, & the Government had pursued exactly the same policy, would the critics still criticise?

The critics dealt with, it was now time to focus on the Government's achievements and to rally the faithful:

*So much for the critics.* Let me now turn from the critics of the Government to the Government itself.

Most of you helped to return the Government to power 2½ years ago. I am here to ask you to continue to support it. I do so on two grounds.

*In the first place, because it has justified the confidence you placed in it by the volume & the character of the legislation it has passed.*

Other speakers will enter into details of the Government record: housing, education, franchise, taxation, insurance &c. I will content myself with making three claims for the Government record. The first claim is this. No Government in this or any other country or any other age has passed such a volume of legislation in the same time as this Government has passed.

The second claim is this. Every Bill passed into Law by the Government has been a *democratic* Bill. There has not been a single Bill passed in the interests of the rich: every bill has been framed in the interest of the common people. That is a significant fact, it is a satisfactory fact. I will not dwell on it. You think about it.

I am told by students of world politics that the legislation of the past three years has made Britain politically the most advanced nation in the world.

There is a third claim I make. It is this – that the effect of all the legislation has been to make the after-War Conditions better in this than in any other country. We are all burdened by the cost of living. *But food is cheaper & more abundant in this than in any country in the world.* Let me give you a few very recent figures. In Britain the cost of living is 133 per cent above pre-war prices. But in Naples it is 481 per cent, in Greece from 400 to 500 per cent; in Constantinople about 1000 per cent above pre-war prices.

I ask you to continue your support of this Government because *the problems still confronting us can be dealt with more successfully by a Coalition than by a Party Govt.*

It is said that 'no assertion was too wild, no insinuation too incredible, no lie too glaring' for his enemies to use against Walpole. I think the same can be said of your member. But for 30 years you have stood by him. I think I can say he has brought no discredit either to the Constituency or to his Country. He has done all in his power to justify your confidence. You have given it generously. He values your confidence more than anything else in the whole world. I am here tonight to ask you to continue to trust Mr Lloyd George.

On the back of the final page are pencilled notes, cut possibly from another occasion:

Few people realise the volume and extent of legislation passed. 3 reasons
House overshadowed by foreign politics – Peace

Legislation passed more quietly than before: Education – Reform...
Have not seen harvest – education

Her son Richard recounted her attitude to the Northcliffe press attacks on the PM: 'I don't believe in taking attacks and abuse in a resigned, humble way.'[14]

In London, on 12th May, it was back to the Baptist Church in Bloomsbury, central London, for the annual meeting of the National Sunday School Union.[15] Her speech is preserved on six sheets of Downing Street embossed notepaper, handwritten by JTR.[16] The Sunday school was highly regarded by Mrs Lloyd George, as it was by many of her compatriots:

> As you know I come from a country where the Sunday school is held in higher regard than any other Society, in higher regard than it is held in any other country in the world. In other lands the Sunday school is mainly for the younger generation. In my Country few are too old to go to a Sunday school. I know of many people in Sunday school where many of the scholars – so far as age in concerned – have qualified for the Old Age Pension.
>
> They are serious students too. They study the Scripture and Theology. They do not indulge in the easy method of the day. Crams-books make no appeal to them. They will wrestle with a verse for weeks.
>
> My own house was no exception to the rule. My father was a Sunday school teacher throughout his life. He had a class of men and preparation for the class was not the least important part of the week's work. Nothing was allowed to interfere with that. I was teaching myself, until I married.

After some customary words of encouragement, and noting that she would have declined the invitation except that 'when Sir George Croydon Marks calls in 10 Downing Street surrender is inevitable', Mrs Lloyd George offered 'one or two words to the Teachers & Officers of Sunday school':

> There are hundreds of organisations & thousands of people in this land today doing other valuable work for humanity. Some

are engaged in political work. Some in social reform. Some in philanthropic enterprises. Some are working in public places & their names are household words in the land. Others are toiling bravely in obscure places & their names are not known outside their own parishes. Both the well known & the unknown are doing good work. But I know of no institution & no people are doing better work that those doing the work of the Sunday school.

Why do I say that? I say that because you are engaged in moulding character after the Highest Model known in the world. A nation morally poor is a decaying nation. The strength & glory of a nation is the moral character of her people. Military power, material wealth and mere intellectual culture are tawdry & trivial compared with character. It is righteousness that exalteth a nation. Seek first.

You are *forming* not *re*forming character. You have heard it said that a fence at the top of a precipice is better than an ambulance at the bottom. So to keep children from falling into vice is better than to rescue them from the pit.

Your work is not only *valuable* but *vital* to individual and to nation.

You meet with many disappointments which tend to discourage you. Nothing more discouraging than this – seeing failure – toiling & caught nothing. So you go through life. None of us can know whether we fail or succeed.

Is there a place for the SS in modern life? My answer is in affirmative. Not fewer but better: not fewer but more teachers. I trust your help this year will result in an increase of Scholars & be an inspiration to teachers.

Again, rallying the troops, encouraging them to keep up the good work, in the knowledge that 'a fence at the top of a precipice is better than an ambulance at the bottom. So keep children from falling into vice is better than to rescue them from the pit.' A phrase she would use on other occasions.

Sir George Croydon Marks was Liberal MP for North Cornwall, an engineer who had served in the Ministry of Munitions during the war. He was a lifelong Congregationalist and Chairman of the Sunday School Union.

The next day and over the weekend there were foreign guests again to be entertained, this time it was Crown Prince Hirohito of Japan. After a dinner at the Japanese Embassy (with the Prince of Wales) on Friday, 13th May, the Japanese party was invited to Chequers for the weekend. A short *Pathé* film of the visit to Chequers shows the grandchildren, Margaret and Valerie, being introduced to the future Emperor, and Lloyd George ensuring Mrs Lloyd George is in the front row. The front row is perhaps the right place for someone of whom it was said at the time: 'It is only history that will reveal the fact that Mrs Lloyd George was one of the greatest assets of her husband's successful career.'[17] (illustration 28)

On Thursday 26th there was another gathering of the Coalition, an 'At Home' at the Langham Hotel, hosted by Lady (John) Henry, and attended by Mrs Lloyd George and by Megan. The next day, Friday 27th May, she attended an evening of theatre at the opening by the Prince of Wales of the Royal Academy of Dramatic Art (RADA) theatre in Gower Street, London.[18]

To round off May, she opened a bazaar for the Clive Vale Congregational Church, at the Albany Hotel in Hastings. Her late arrival meant she missed much of the morning, resulting in many leaving early for lunch, reducing hoped for sales at the bazaar. In her apology she sought to lighten the mood, with a quip that might easily have backfired: that it was good to come down from smoky old London, except that it wasn't so smoky now as they didn't have any coal. [Laughter etc][19]

CHAPTER 13

# Pure Milk, Pure Minds
## (June 1921)

ON 1ST JUNE, back in the less smoky London, Mrs Lloyd George fulfilled her promise to visit the new 'Grade A Certified Milk Dairy' at Manor Farm, Finchley, postponed from April:

> [She] had the opportunity of seeing the precautions that were taken to safeguard the public, and to ensure that the public had milk of the finest quality, absolutely clean, free from harmful bacteria, and bottled by machinery, to enable the milk to be delivered to customers in a hygienic state.
>
> She gave her endorsement in the Company's visitors' book: 'June 1st, 1921. Margaret Lloyd George 10, Downing-street. Delighted with the way things are done here.'[1]

It was still unclear how the 'Dame Grand Cross of the British Empire' might best be addressed, if, indeed, the title would be used at all. The press advertisements for her forthcoming visit to Hull played safe: 'Visit of Mrs Lloyd George, to meet Dame Margaret Lloyd George'.[2]

On 3rd June Olwen Carey Evans wrote another missive to JTR, thanking him for his weekly input, giving news on the new baby Eluned Jane, and mentioning that her friend 'Miss Ries is very fit'. And there was the oft-proffered instruction: 'Keep a strict eye on the Dame – & don't let her do too much.' The letter also suggests that JTR was probably seeing less of Olwen's daughter Margaret, the latter spending more time at Chequers.[3]

That day, the new lady of the manor went to the county town to pay her respects, when Mrs Lloyd George, of Chequers, visited Aylesbury to speak to some 500 women of the newly formed local Women's Association. She encouraged women to do their bit, now that the vote was won, and more professions were opening up. She recalled her pleasure in presenting the top prize to the dental student Miss Grose back in November 1919 at the School at the Royal Dental Hospital.[4] Mrs Durand of the National Council of Women followed with a similar talk, expressing faith that women when voting would see sense and 'not listen to the claptrap of extremists'.[5]

At the meeting Dame Margaret was referred to as Dame Lloyd George, another variation on a theme.

On Saturday, 4th June, it was the Trooping of the Colour for the King's official birthday. The Lloyd George family watched the ceremonies taking place in Horse Guards Parade from the wall of Downing Street.

The King's birthday meant new titles for some. That weekend the *Sunday Post* enquired: where were the missing new Dames, and why so reluctant to use the title?

In glancing through the long list of new knights to-day, a woman who holds a number of important public positions remarked to me that there were no new dames.

A man who joined our little party hazarded the explanation that perhaps for some reason this title could not figure in the birthday honours list, but it was generally agreed that it might rather be due to the fact that this distinctive title for women is not too popular with members of the sex who might be considered eligible for it.

Every one of the fifty-four new Knights will immediately drop his 'Mr' and take up his new dignity, but it is a curious circumstance that hardly any women who have been promoted to the Knighthood of their sex use their title Dame.

Dame Nellie Melba provides a notable exception which proves the rule. The Premier's wife is one of the most prominent women in public life, but she is never referred otherwise than as Mrs Lloyd

George. To speak of her as 'Dame Margaret', as one would say 'Sir Henry' would sound odd, though strictly correct.

What is wanted is a new title for women which shall not give the lugubrious suggestion of frumpy old lady to the smart, capable woman of modern times.[6]

It was now her husband's turn to have a chill. Mrs Lloyd George sent a note to JTR to put off her engagements for Monday and Tuesday, but saying she 'would come up for Eastbourne Wednesday... Please tell Davies to apologise for my absence at the Palace [presumably an event relating to the King's birthday]... Sawyer would like you to dine with him tonight at the Piccadilly Hotel and take anyone you like with you.' G. A. Sawyer, silversmith, was a fund-raiser and organiser who took on projects for the Lloyd Georges – and was coordinating with JTR in assisting Richard Lloyd George in making some purchases at a house sale near Richard's house in Springfield, Essex.[7]

On Wednesday, 8th June, it was down to Eastbourne to open a bazaar for the Upperton Congregational Church, accompanied by Mr and Mrs Sawyer.[8]

At the weekend the Lloyd Georges were back in Wales, listening to the Criccieth Choral Union rehearse for the Harlech Castle festival. Lloyd George remarked that it was his custom to sing Welsh tunes on the hearth at Downing-street with Mrs Lloyd George, accompanied by Miss Megan. There were no hymns in the world, he said, which could be compared with those of Wales. During the troublesome times of the war, the Premier concluded, those unsurpassable Welsh hymns were balm to his wounded soul, and there was no better means to secure peace and goodwill on earth than by singing them.[9]

From Criccieth Mrs Lloyd George sent a message of support to the Coalition Unionist Sir Hildred Carlile, defending the Hertford seat against the Anti-Waste candidate Rear-Admiral Murray Sueter (another candidate supported by the right-wing

Horatio Bottomley, a thorn in the side of the Coalition). Her support, and messages from Lloyd George, from Tory leader Austen Chamberlain, and from Coalition Liberal Chief Whip Charles McCurdy, were not enough to stop a 2:1 rout by the Anti-Waste candidate, campaigning against increasing state spending.

On home soil, Mrs Lloyd George sought to right the world's wrongs, delivering a strong speech in Pwllheli and in Porthmadog, addressing the drink problem, immoral attitudes, and the need for the churches to combat their decline in membership and role in education. We have the handwritten text, in JTR's hand. The first part was in Welsh:[10]

> The name of this meeting is Temperance. But we are here considering three matters, being 'Temperance', 'Purity', and the 'Religious Situation'. These topics are timely and important, and hold a close relationship with one another.
>
> They are timely as drunkenness, untruthfulness and religious apathy are very prevalent these days. They are living enemies in our land, and are causing much harm. They are important as they are the enemies of the best in man and nation.
>
> They hold a close relationship with one another. Where we find one, we are almost certain to find the others. The three belong to the same family. They are all children of the same father.
>
> The Committee has invited three brothers to talk to us tonight. The three are specialists in their fields. They have kept their promise, and are ready to start. It is not appropriate for me therefore to stand between you and these three gentlemen.
>
> However, I should like to make one short point.
>
> If we look at the state of the country today from the viewpoint of Temperance, Purity and Religion, things are not satisfactory.
>
> Think about Temperance. The [brewing] business is about as prosperous as ever. When every other business is wilting, this one blooms. Other countries are shaking free of the business; people in our country seek to give more freedom for drinking. It is almost impossible to awaken the country to fight this enemy. The Temperance leaders complain that even the Church is being indifferent.

Think about Purity. The points made by Lord Birkenhead the other day are enough proof in themselves to prove that things are far from what we would wish them to be.

The Lord Chancellor had been speaking about the rapid increase in divorce petitions and the burden this was placing on the courts. *The Times* reported him as saying that 19 of the 20 cases were the result of the war, that the backlog had been dealt with, but that while there was hope for the moment that the domestic relationship may be affected 'perhaps for an indefinite period'.[11]

Think of Religion. We have more Churches than ever. The denominations have more wealth than ever. Our preachers are more enlightened and hard-working than ever. Despite all this, neither the Church or Sunday schools are holding their own in our land.

Everyone acknowledges that the War is mainly responsible for the state of our country today.

The second point I should like to make is this. Despite everything looking so unfavourable today, it has been worse in Wales.

It is said that John Elias always appealed to visitors to the Quarterly meetings of Welsh Presbyterians not to get intoxicated. This shows that many who attended these meetings in their days were drinking to excess.

There is no need for such advice today at Pwllheli / Porthmadog.

A hundred years ago there weren't many abstainers even amongst the clergymen. Today preachers who are not total abstainers are the exception in our midst. If the world has not dried them, the Church is almost dry.

Things have improved regarding Purity too. If we read Literature from the beginning of the last century, we see that things are much better today in this respect.

The text continues in English:

History is always a good remedy for Pessimism.

If Religion is not prospering today as we would wish, even so there is more real religion in the land than there was in the days of Rowland, Llangeitho [one of the foremost leaders of the eighteenth-century Welsh Calvinistic Methodist revival]. When we are depressed by the state of religion in the land, it is well for us to remember that Christianity has always seemed to its contemporaries to be in a state of decay.

The next pages are not numbered but probably follow:

My last remark is this. Though things are *bad*, and if they have been *worse*, it is our duty to make them *better*. The Church is in the world to better the world. When it ceases to do that it forfeits its right to exist (?). The fact that we are here tonight facing these problems is proof that our Church is alive to its duty.

I trust that when we leave here tonight, and return to our homes, and to our different spheres of activity, we shall go back determined to do what lies in our power to promote Temperance, Purity, and Religion in our land.

And from a further page, in Welsh:

The drink traffic must be controlled. The nation cannot afford to have so much money spent on drink. The interest of the nation depends that the people should be made sober.

The Vicar Prichard of Llandovery said: 'Drunkenness is the surest and the most certain of traps [or nets] from which all faults sprout.'

Mrs Lloyd George would reference the Porthmadog event later in the month when opening Milton Mount College in Sussex on 23rd June, though not delivering this particular message to the schoolgirls that day.

On Tuesday evening, 14th June, during the General Assembly of Mrs Lloyd George's Calvinistic Methodists, she also unveiled the portrait of the assembly's retiring moderator, Dr John Morgan Jones, who had died at the age of 72, shortly before the tribute could be made. The portrait, by Christopher Williams, is today in the National Library of Wales. Mrs Lloyd George's remarks, in Welsh, upon presentation of the portrait, are in the JTR Collection at the NLW.[12]

The important personal occasion that month was the wedding of the Lloyd Georges' son Gwilym and Edna Gwenfron Jones, of Denbigh (sister of the Mayoress of Caernarfon) at the Welsh Wesleyan Chapel, Caernarfon, on Tuesday 14th June. His friend Captain Ernest Evans was best man; Megan was one of the bridesmaids.[13]

That evening Mrs Lloyd George unveiled a war memorial shrine at Beddgelert, in the heart of Snowdonia.[14]

The next day, 15th June, in Porthmadog, Lloyd George also addressed the Welsh Calvinistic Methodist General Assembly on the divide in religion over politics:

> Politically Nonconformity had never been divided as today. He had made some inquiries about recent by-elections, and he had found in many of them most hopeless division in the churches. Much of this might have been avoided, but most of it was inevitable, and it was no use blaming anyone.[15]

Mrs Lloyd George then travelled to Yorkshire, on another short political mission, from Monday to Wednesday (20th to 22nd June). She began in the West Riding, meeting Liberals in Wakefield, Brighouse (a garden party) and Bradford (an evening reception with a short speech). The latter was attended by MPs from the district, as well as Col. Scovell, the General Secretary of the Liberal Federation, with whom JTR would have dealings in 1922 when undertaking his own campaigning on behalf of the party.

On Tuesday the Leeds schedule included meeting Coalitionists at lunch, followed by a garden party. The seats of Leeds North, Central and West were held by Coalition Liberals, the Leeds North East seat by a Coalition Unionist.

That evening Mrs Lloyd George travelled east to Hull, where

at a 'monster' At Home she laid a coping stone at the City Hall. She stayed at Hunmanby Hall overnight, where she planted a tree before returning home on 22nd June.

The next day Mrs Lloyd George and Megan travelled down from London to Sussex to open the new premises of Milton Mount College, a boarding school for the daughters of Congregationalist Ministers, then attended by JTR's eldest daughter Margaret.

JTR's letter to his daughter on No. 10 notepaper, two days earlier, noted:

> your letter, which in the classic phraseology of MMC was positively 'ripping'... Well, the great 23rd is drawing near. Dame Margaret & Miss Lloyd George & Dr J. D. Jones will be leaving here in one car at 10/30, then your humble and his pride proud [sic], Mr and Mrs Tudor Jones in another at the same time. I hope you will be there to meet and greet and do the honours. Let's hope the weather will be fine.[16]

Mrs Lloyd George had invited Margaret Whitley, the Congregationalist wife of the House of Commons Speaker, to join her, but she was unable to attend, having to meet delegates from Virginia.[17] She would speak at the school speech day in 1923.[18]

Politics is not the first choice of topic you might expect at a speech for the daughters of the Manse, but Mrs Lloyd George took the opportunity to introduce a little politics, in relation to religion. Though referencing her recent Porthmadog meetings, she spared them any moralising on the three evils: drunkenness, impurity and lack of religious zeal. JTR, his own interests straddling politics and the pulpit, may well have had a hand in this speech – and perhaps was asked to draft something he thought appropriate.[19]

The school's original premises in Gravesend, Kent, had been commandeered by the Admiralty during the war. After exile at Cirencester's Agricultural College, the pupils were now in the splendid house and gardens of Worth Park, near Crawley, Sussex.

> I am delighted to be down here on this historic and auspicious occasion in the life of Milton Mount College.
>
> As you know there is a lively discussion now proceeding in the press as to whether Churches should take part in politics. Well I, for one, am very glad to escape for one day from the strain, & stress & strife of politics to the quieter atmosphere of this educational establishment retreat.
>
> When I was a child, my parents often entertained over the weekend the preachers who came to officiate at our church. I continue that good custom in my own home. Last week Mr Lloyd George and I had the pleasure of entertaining some of the delegates of the Annual Meetings of the Welsh Calvinistic Methodists. From my conversations with many of those ministers I understand that one of the chronic troubles of a preacher is first to find a text & then to divide it to find proper divisions.
>
> I am glad I am spared that difficulty today. My text and my divisions are at hand. The text is Milton Mount College & and the divisions are – *its past record, its future prospects & its present needs*.

She then spelt out the excellent record of the school, its voluntary board, its staff and pupils, noting that:

> many have done brilliantly at College, & have risen to positions of such usefulness & importance in the world. Of those trained here not a few have become foreign missionaries – a magnificent proof of the religious influence exercised by the school.

The Prime Minister's wife introduced a little politics:

> I have been down in Yorkshire this week addressing a number of political gatherings. I have been telling the people there that I do not feel called upon to *apologise* for the Coalition Government, that it is justified by its works. Well, you may not all agree as to that I know; however, you will all agree that in view of its past

record there is no need to *apologise* for the work of Milton Mount College.

Well now, I come to my second point – the future prospects of the school.

Like the Israelites of old you have often changed your place of abode. This is your third place *since* the War began & *because* the War began. It is a magnificent building & and you have magnificent grounds. I doubt whether there are many schools in the country so pleasantly & so favourably situated as you are.

I find that the object of the College was not simply to educate the mind but the heart & the will. It exists not simply to turn out scholars but to fashion character. I hope that policy will never be changed.

She then made a pitch to the audience to contribute to a new fund to support the school, being launched by the Rev. J. D. Jones, a leading Congregationalist minister from Bournemouth:

Lastly: 'Now concerning the collection.' That is my final point.

Well, there is to be no Collection! Dr J. D. Jones must be feeling very strange here. I think this must be the first gathering he has ever attended at which he has not taken the hat round!

I am given to understand that two unofficial requests/hopes have been sent from here. One was that I would bring my daughter down here with me & secondly that none of the speeches would be long!

Well now that must be my excuse for concluding my remarks.

I will now declare the College open & pray that it may long remain & that the richest blessing of Almighty God may rest upon the efforts of the College.

In early July *The Sphere* gave the school generous coverage. Hopefully, the adults in the audience responded to the collection of the Rev. J. D. Jones. A favourite quip of the Rev. J. T. Rhys, fund-raiser, was, 'When I look at my congregation I ask, where are the poor? When I look at this collection I ask, where are the rich?' (illustration 33)

In December, JTR would help to set up a meeting between Dr Jones and Lloyd George, in Bournemouth (Dr Jones' parish) when the PM was there resting and trying to avoid all visitors.

On the final day of this busy week, Friday 24th June, Mrs Lloyd George welcomed to Downing Street alumni of her old school, Dr Williams' School: the girls' boarding school at Dolgellau, Wales. Olwen also attended the school for a short while (as would others in the Rhys/Rees family). (illustration 31)

The JTR Collection includes a nine-page typed briefing note for Mrs Lloyd George on the national education system, dated June 1921: perhaps a briefing paper in preparation for meeting the schools.[20] Mrs Lloyd George prepared well for her engagements.

It is quite possible that it was whilst entertaining her school alumni that the pacifist George Maitland Lloyd Davies called at No. 10 hoping to meet with her and the PM. George Davies was seeking to help negotiate peace with the Irish and also engaged in a correspondence with fellow Welshman Thomas Jones, Deputy Secretary to the Cabinet, who had the ear of Lloyd George. Davies followed up with a two-page letter in Welsh for Mrs Lloyd George, He wrote from Gregynog, near Newtown, in Wales, the home of the philanthropists, music promoters and art collectors, Gwendolen and Margaret Davies, his cousins, where he was then working:

Gregynog, nr Newtown, 28th June 1921

Dear Mrs Lloyd George

... I tried to get to see Mr Lloyd George and yourself last Friday morning at Downing St., in the utmost hope of appealing to him to do what he did that day – i.e. invite Mr de Valera to a place of reconciliation in the spirit of conciliation. I thanked God from the bottom of my heart on seeing Christ's way being proclaimed...

Yours sincerely, George M. L. Davies[21]

On Monday 27th June Mrs Lloyd George was down in

Hampshire, for the Founder's Day at Lord Mayor Treloar Cripples Hospital and College, Alton, planting a tree and giving out prizes and bonuses to long-serving domestic servants. Treloar had been Lord Mayor of London, and his school and hospital continue today.[22] (illustration 23)

That evening, she and the Premier dined at the Churchills' Sussex Square house, with other guests, entertaining the PM of Canada and his wife.[23]

There was now one more great city to visit, one more favourite cause to support, before a break in Cricieth.

On 29th June Mrs Lloyd George made a splash in Liverpool. After being met at Lime Street Station by the Lord Mayor, she attended the June fair at the Philharmonic Hall, in aid of St Monica's Refuge, Prince's Road, and St Hilda's Maternity Home and Crèche, Penny Lane, Wavertree, and later spoke at a meeting of the British & Foreign Bible Society. Opening the Fair, she acknowledged the great support Liverpool had given to her wartime Troops Fund.

The Lord Mayor, in introducing the Prime Minister's wife, said that by coming to Liverpool she had shown, as the wife of the leading man in the land today, that her sympathies were not wholly with the south. She had come to the Welsh metropolis [hear, hear] to assist in a great work. Mr Lloyd George himself was greatly respected in Liverpool. His lordship doubted whether, as a Conservative, he could have said that a few years ago. [Laughter] But whatever had happened in the past, and whatever might happen in the future, he ventured to say that all classes and creeds would remember Mr Lloyd George for the great work he did during the war. [Applause] Liverpool contained a large population, and by her presence on that occasion Dame Lloyd George had not only given encouragement to the work of the charity, but had conferred upon her fellow countrymen and country women a very great compliment. [Applause]

'It is a great pleasure, I can assure you, to come to the Welsh metropolis once more,' said Mrs Lloyd George, amid applause. She went on to recall that she was in Liverpool many years ago opening a big bazaar at St George's Hall, and later on during the war, she came to visit her Welsh friends in Liverpool. 'They were very good to me during the war. I had a comforts fund for the Welsh soldiers, and I got more support from Liverpool than from any other English town, excepting London. So I have every reason to be thankful to my friends in Liverpool, and the least I could do was to come here today and do a very small service in return for their kindness to me. My family are always telling me I am very anxious to come somewhere near north Wales! [Laughter] Well I'm not ashamed to say that after a very hard two weeks' work I am looking forward with great pleasure to spending a quiet week-end at my Welsh home in Criccieth.'

Mrs Lloyd George proceeded to commend the objects of the June fair, and said she hoped the four days' market would prove a great success. It was difficult to get money for anything almost in these days. During the war time they got money very easily for things concerning the war, but nowadays it was much more difficult to get funds, even for a good cause like that which her hearers were supporting. However, she felt sure that now, after the settling of a strike which had lasted three months [Hear, hear], they would all look forward with more hope for the future. This more hopeful outlook would, she trusted, make for generosity on the part of the public towards the June fair. Although in functions of that kind the gentlemen helped in a small way [Laughter], the burden of the work fell upon the ladies, and she was sure from what she had already seen that the efforts of the ladies would be crowned with the very greatest [*sic*]. [Applause][24]

In the afternoon, the Welsh of Liverpool held a reception in Mrs Lloyd George's honour, at the Exchange Station Hotel, presenting her with a piece of silver inscribed:

Presented to Dame Margaret Lloyd George by the Welsh National Society in Liverpool, on her visit to the city as a token admiration and respect of the Welsh people, June 29th, 1921.

Ever the fund-raiser, and speaking in Welsh, she made an appeal on behalf of a fund to benefit the widows and orphans of Welsh soldiers which was being organised by Mr Thomas

Edwards. There followed 'a vocal and instrumental recital of Welsh national airs and afterwards some interesting Welsh elocution'.

In the evening the wife of the Prime Minister visited the Sun Hall, to address the British and Foreign Bible Society.[25] In JTR's Notes, the Bible Society is one of the seven movements listed in which she was particularly interested, noting it as: 'Largest meeting I have addressed.' The Society was originally inspired by the actions of Mary Jones, who in 1800, aged 15, had walked to Dolgellau, 26 miles across mountains, to obtain a Bible in her first language, Welsh.

The Sun Hall, built in 1904 as a gospel hall, used for concerts and later becoming a cinema, could have been the venue for a large crowd. It had also witnessed notable suffragette disturbances in 1909. JTR kept the newspaper clippings from her Liverpool trip.

It is a great pleasure to me to find myself in Liverpool once again. It is now many years since I paid my first visit to the City, & since then I have been a fairly frequent visitor. I almost feel I am one of yourselves.

During the last 30 years I have come to Liverpool on various missions. All of them I hope have had good objects. I feel tonight that I have never come on a more congenial mission nor for a better object than the one that has brought us together this evening in the Sun Hall.

We are here under the auspices & in the interest of the British and Foreign Bible Society. It is a Society with which I have been connected for many years. I used to collect as a child for the Society; & all my children have also been collectors at one time or another.

I think I shall not be exaggerating when I say that the history of this Society is one of the romances of Christianity. At any rate, I do not know of any Society with such an interesting, thrilling and inspiring record.

I think it may be worthwhile reminding ourselves at this great meeting of some of the facts.

The Society was founded over a century ago. It is now in its

118th year. It was born at a time of great religious awakening in this country. (In passing, will you let me say how glad I am to read in the papers that there are signs of another awakening in Britain. We need nothing more urgently. Nothing else I know of can do us so much good. From my heart I say with the Welsh poet *'Cerdded ymlaen, Nefol dân'* ['Walk on, Heavenly fire'].) Since the Society was founded vast changes have taken place in the life & thought of the world. But in spite of all changes this Society persists. Other Societies have come and gone, but this goes on, & I hope will go on for *so long* as it is needed.

From the day of its birth it has never gone back. During the 118 years of its activity it has a record of slow, silent yet steady progress. It now prints the Bible wholly or in part in 538 languages. It has issued over 300 million copies of Scripture. Its expenditure falls not far short of half a million pounds a year.

It is a truly wonderful record. We used to be taught that the Bible was a miracle. It is certainly true to say that the Bible Society is little short of a miracle.

It is possible for the Society's officials to give us statistics dealing with the translation, publication or circulation of the Bible. But it is not possible for a society to tell how much good has been accomplished. To tabulate the effects of reading the Word is beyond the power of man. Today some of the most harassed men I know find comfort & inspiration in this that they cannot find anywhere else.

The Society has a wonderful record. None of us need apologise for helping on this work.

But the work of the Society is not yet finished. Nor will it be finished so long as men and women need guidance, comfort & inspiration in life.

The Bible is still required by the individual, by the Nation & by the race. *'Pa fodd y glanha y llanc ei ffordd?'* [roughly translated as 'How can the young man cleanse/change his path?']

Man needs the Book.

The Nation is confronted by grave & difficult problems today. There are tens of thousands of men who have fought for the Country until they are unable to fight for themselves. There is a great deal of bitterness & hatred in the land. The acceptance of the ideas, principles & spirit of the Bible will help us to solve our national problems more than anything else I know of. We want peace on earth & goodwill among men. Then again the Bible can help us as nothing else can. The Society has done splendid service in promoting unity among the sects. The Bible can in the same way promote the unity of the race & make wars to cease throughout the world.

I am sorry but not surprised to learn that there is a heavy deficit in the accounts of the Society this year. I am not surprised because all enterprises have deficits these days. I am however sorry because it may mean curtailing the work. I venture therefore to appeal to you all to help in the work of making the income balance the expenditure.

May I venture to make a special appeal to my compatriots to help. Wales owes more to the Bible than to any other single factor for the position it is in today. As a Nation we are all debtors to the Bible. Then the Bible Society is a child of Wales. Do not let it die. Help it to thrive. Then, we have great traditions to maintain. Think of how John Elias & others worked for this cause & let their example be an inspiration to us.

Do your best, remembering that the Bible is indispensable to the race & the Society is indispensable to the *Bible*.

It is a good example of a strong speech in aid of a cause dear to Dame Margaret, underlying the importance of the Society (and the Bible) in difficult times and including a bid for more funds – in particular asking her Welsh compatriots to help in the name of John Elias, the early 19th-century High-Calvinist Methodist preacher, literal believer in the Bible and strong champion of the Bible Society.[26]

After a busy month, it was off to Cricieth for the weekend.

# CHAPTER 14

# The Summer Round

## (July 1921)

ON 6TH JULY Mrs Lloyd George attended a quite unique function at the Langham Hotel.[1] it was a sell-out, and at first reading you might have thought Nancy Astor was after Mrs Lloyd George's job:

> Leading women from all over the Empire met yesterday at a luncheon given in London by the British Women's Patriotic League to Mrs Lloyd George and the wives of the Dominion Prime Ministers. Hundreds of society women who applied for tickets had to be refused owing to the lack of accommodation.
>
> Princess Louise presided, and the guests were received by Mrs Lloyd George.
>
> Lady Cowan, in welcoming the Colonial guests, said that while English women wished to honour them, they also desired to learn from them – to know how they were facing problems confronting women all over the world.
>
> Lady Astor, in reply to the toast of 'The Guests', said that she had a profound admiration for the wives of the Imperial Prime Ministers. 'I admire them for what they have made of their husbands' she said, 'and I commiserate with them for what they had to do. I would like to be a Prime Minister's wife because it would be a glorious chance of getting things done, but it is one of the most difficult jobs in the world. Prime Ministers rise to such dizzy heights that their wives are the only persons who can speak out flat to them. [Laughter] I am sure Mrs Lloyd George would agree with me.' [Laughter][2]

The wives, with their husbands, would be entertained at Chequers by the Premier and Mrs Lloyd George on the coming Saturday, 9th July – where presumably they could 'speak out flat' to their husbands, in Nancy Astor's words.[3]

In his Notes JTR reported Mrs Lloyd George's reflections on this aspect of her role:

> Public men sometimes have a task of such a confidential nature that they entrust them only to a wife. Neither colleagues, not even secretaries can be entrusted to discharge them with strict fidelity. To me were several connected with the Temp. Cause. He knew of my lifelong interest in this & he knew too few can be trusted to report faithfully.[4]

The same day, Wednesday, 6th July, Mrs Lloyd George was also due in Harpenden, Herts, to open a garden fête in the grounds of the National Children's Home and Orphanage in aid of the extension fund of the Wesleyan Methodist Church. A *Pathé News* film – planned to be shown in local cinemas – survives,[5] but her tight schedule delayed her arrival:

> Harpenden was on Wednesday afternoon afforded its first opportunity of giving a public welcome to the wife of a British Prime Minister, and the pleasure and excitement naturally created in the town and its environments by such an eventful experience will probably live all the longer and more vividly in the memories of all associated with the enterprise because of the keen anxiety it must have entailed...
>
> Many more than a thousand must have gathered from Harpenden, Luton, and all parts of the surrounding district to do honour to Dame Margaret, and right up to the last even the most faithful believers could have been excused fears of a disappointment. It was known to the inner circle that Mrs Lloyd George, after a long over-night journey, had an important engagement in London at a luncheon to the wives of the Prime Ministers and other notabilities who are visiting this city from the Dominions, and would probably be a little late, and by the advertised time for the opening ceremony such an immense crowd

was gathered round the improvised platform built up in front of the Principal's house that it was considered advisable to give them a gentle hint of the delay they might expect.

No greater compliment could be paid the wife of any British Prime Minister than the stoic patience with which folks kept their places in a broiling sun, but when half an hour had passed, even the optimists began to borrow the cloaks of doubting Thomases, and the services of the boys' brass band from the Farnborough branch of the National Children's Home and Orphanage were enlisted to distract if not to dispel the fears that lay uppermost.

To a waiting crowd wiles are but a temporary antidote, and as the minutes passed and still no signs of Dame Margaret, it was decided to risk all on the chance of a grand finale turning up. It proved the idea of a genius. There was a hymn, and a prayer. Mr J. C. C. Davidson, CB, MP, had not got much further beyond his introductory remarks than an explanatory statement of the position and an expression of hope that Mrs Lloyd George would yet arrive in time to perform her promised duties, when he found all eyes and ears attracted to an approaching car, and as Mrs Lloyd George stepped out, fifty minutes late, a pent-up sigh of relief was given expression to in cheers of mingled gratitude and welcome and the boys' band struck up with 'Land of Our Fathers'.

Dame Margaret was jointly presented by little Misses Margaret Raban and Rita Nott with a beautiful basket of roses, and Margaret supplemented this with a gift of a bunch of carnations to the organising secretary, Mrs Edwin Nott, and then all went swimmingly.

In appropriate words of welcome to Mrs Lloyd George, the Member for the Division said he did not think the people of the country understood the strain which was put upon the wife of the first citizen of the British Empire. But as he had lived next door to 10 Downing Street [as Parliamentary Private Secretary to Bonar Law], he knew the Prime Minister owed a very great debt to Mrs Lloyd George for carrying him through the most terrible times this country had ever been through. [Applause]

Remarking upon the fact that the object of the fête was to help the spread of Christian knowledge in the schools, Mr Davidson said he was told just after the last great stoppage was settled that all the really red Socialists in South Wales forgot all about their Socialism and worked very hard directly they got busy feeding the children. That was really the essence of the thing, Christian knowledge and the work of the Christian church was the only thing which was going to stand between this city, in fact, the world, and 'Red' doctrines.

Apologising for being so very late, Mrs Lloyd George said they worked her rather hard. She had had to attend a public luncheon given to the ladies who were over here from our Dominions and she could not come away before the Royal toast had been proposed and she found Harpenden was a longer journey than she thought. She was very delighted to help in a small way the good cause of the Wesleyan Methodist Church because she was, too, a Methodist, although not a Wesleyan Methodist. She happened to be a Calvinistic Methodist, who she believed were only to be found in Wales, but she believed they were cousins – they were followers of John Wesley and she was a follower of John Calvin – and the very least they could do was to help each other. The churches had suffered very much during the years of the war. In those days they had to put their hands in their pockets for all sorts of things concerned with the war and leave the work of the churches alone. Now they had peace once more in this country they could turn their hands to the work of their own different churches, and they were very much needed because they were the force that was going to help to keep England a free, happy and prosperous country, the foremost country in the world and stand between us and revolution and the Red Flag. Talking of their Welsh singing, she was saying only the previous day that she thought it would keep Wales free from Bolshevism. If they could sing their Welsh, their national songs and hymns, she thought they would be fairly safe in Wales, and she was quite sure the same thing applied in England.

Mrs Lloyd George's arrangements would not permit of her spending more than half an hour at the fête... She was especially interested in the Luton hat stall and carried off a beautiful lace Panama...[6]

The pressing engagement that evening was at 6 Carlton House Terrace at a party with her compatriots of the Cymmrodorion Society, the Welsh cultural group. It had been a busy Wednesday.[7]

After perhaps a day off, catching up with the postbag, on

Friday 8th July Mrs Lloyd George continued to support the cause of education and children, attending the speech day of the Furzedown Training College for Teachers at Mitcham in South London, and was impressed with the singing:

During the last fortnight, she said, she had spent most of her time among girl students, which had brought back recollections of the day when she attended a high school in north Wales. On the last day she was at school the headmistress had made a speech about her, and then the girls called upon me for a speech. 'How terrified I was, and that gives me all the more appreciation of the speeches made by the students here this afternoon.'

Mrs Lloyd George thought that a great change had taken place in the education for girls during the past forty years. At one time there was no profession but teaching open to women, but to-day women could enter the professions of medicine, dentistry, art, literature, and law.

'A few days ago,' Mrs Lloyd George went on, 'I was present at a school in a rural district of north Wales, where the scholars sang very well indeed, but the singing here to-day is as good, if not better. There is an idea in this country that the Welsh nation can sing better than any other country in the world. I'm not so sure of that after my experience here to-day.'

Before leaving in company with Miss Megan Lloyd George, who arrived in a motor car from Downing Street to meet her mother, Mrs Lloyd George witnessed the display of dancing in the grounds of the College, evincing particular interest in the performance of the Welsh national dance.[8]

Mrs Lloyd George's working weeks were almost seven-day affairs. On Saturday afternoon, 9th July, she was back in Tom Macnamara's south London Camberwell constituency, where she had campaigned in March 1920. At this garden party, held for Coalition Liberals, Macnamara did the talking, saying a few words about the on-going Irish situation, leaving Mrs Lloyd George to collect the floral tributes.[9]

Then it was back to Chequers, where the Dominion Premiers were the first, it seems, to be entertained with films at the house (a premiere for the Premiers, perhaps?). Films shown included *Across India With the Duke of Connaught,* and *The Topical Budget.*[10]

Lloyd George was a fan of movies at home.

No rest for the wicked, nor for the wife of the Prime Minister, it seemed. On 12th July the *Western Mail* announced Mrs Lloyd George's busy schedule for the rest of the month as the summer season got going:

> Mrs Lloyd George has a number of important engagements in the next fortnight. On Wednesday she is giving an 'At Home' at Downing-street for the ministry of the Welsh Churches in London and Welshmen who are ministers of English Churches. Miss Megan Foster will sing.[11]

Attendees included the Rev. Morgan Gibbon, and his daughter Muriel (for whom JTR would be election agent in 1929); the leading Congregationalist the Rev. Enyon and Mrs Davies, and the Rev. John and Mrs Thickens, Calvinistic Methodists, of William Lewis' church in Willesden, North London.[12]

> Mrs Lloyd George addresses a big meeting at Edmonton Town-hall to-day, and is due to address a large gathering at Northampton for Mr McCurdy, as well as meetings at Witham, in Essex, and a luncheon at Prince's Restaurant given by Mrs Herbert Lewis.[13]

A garden party at No. 10 was also in the offing, as well as a Palace garden party where Mrs Lloyd George would present some of her compatriots at Court:

> I hear that invitations are being sent out by Mrs Lloyd George for a garden party at No. 10 Downing-street. All the supporters of the Government and their wives are being invited, and the affair promises to be most brilliant. This is the preliminary to a series of interesting functions in connection with the Coalition.

Parliament is also represented strongly in the invitations for the garden parties at Buckingham Palace which are to take the place of the Courts [where the presentations would now be made]. At the first, on July 21, Mrs Lloyd George will present a number of well-known South Wales people, including Lady Roper Wright, Lady Witham, of Newport, the Hon. Mrs Cooper-Smith (the late Lord Glantawe's daughter) and Mrs A. T. Davies, the wife of the member for Lincoln.[14]

A. T. (Alfred Thomas) Davies, the Coalition Unionist member for Lincoln (not to be confused with Alfred Thomas Davies, Permanent Secretary to the Welsh Department, Board of Education, and a great friend of the Lloyd Georges) was an active supporter in arranging Mrs Lloyd George's events. We may assume he had been understanding when she had pulled out of her visit to Lincoln in October 1920. Now his wife would be presented at Court.

On 12th July, after the scheduled speech in Edmonton Town Hall, Mrs Lloyd George may have had lunch with Marie Willingdon (the wife of the Governor of Madras) and her son Inigo.[15] Marie Willingdon's husband would impose martial law in Madras later that summer after riots.

In the afternoon Mrs Lloyd George and Megan joined the Dominion Prime Ministers and their wives at an afternoon reception at the Speaker's House, hosted by Margaret Whitley.[16]

India at this time was not a Dominion of the British Empire, but there were representatives from India at the conference, the Maharao of Cutch, Mr S. Shastri, and Edwin Montagu, the Secretary for India.[17]

That evening, 12th July, Mrs Lloyd George attended the after-dinner reception at Lady Astor's London house, in the corner of St James's Square, for American professors of history.[18]

On Thursday 14th July the Coalition Liberals met at the Hotel Cecil, on the Strand, to hear the Prime Minister. The dinner was in honour of Charles McCurdy, the Coalition

Liberal Chief Whip, for whom JTR would work in 1922. There was a big Welsh turnout, including JTR, and accompanying Welsh musicians.[19]

On the 16th Mrs Lloyd George was at the Guildhall to witness the Freedom of the City of London being conferred on the Prime Minister of Canada.[20]

On 19th July she and the PM, with Megan, welcomed friends and some MPs and their wives to an 'At Home' at No. 10. Guests included future Tory Prime Minister Stanley Baldwin and his wife, and JTR's future potential election opponent, Joynson-Hicks – in all, 1,000 invitations were issued.[21]

The next day, it was off for a maiden (official) visit to Essex to open a Nurses' Bungalow as a war memorial in Witham (at the invitation of the colourfully-named Unionist MP Sir Fortescue Flannery, who had attended the No. 10 'At Home' the day before), and to lay a wreath at a more traditional war memorial in Maldon. (illustration 24) As always, Mrs Lloyd George expressed her approval at the provision of a war memorial in the form of a useful facility:

> Mrs Lloyd George said they had been told that she was being worked very hard, yet when Sir Fortescue Flannery asked her to come to Witham she could not refuse such an old friend of the Prime Minister. They owed a great deal to the nurses for all they did during the war, and what they would do without them she did not know. Everyone should sacrifice something to make the nurses more comfortable and their surroundings brighter and better. She was glad to know that they were now united in Witham and that they had got such a nice and useful memorial. [Applause] No place ought to be without a memorial, something that the future generations should look up to, something to commemorate the great sacrifices that had been made.
>
> Referring to the fact that many professions were now open to women, Mrs Lloyd George thought that the future for women was very bright. With regard to the difficulty of keeping hospitals open she thought it was a deplorable matter. She hoped that in the future they would be more generous to their hospitals. [Applause]

Concluding, Mrs Lloyd George said this was her first visit to Essex, and hoped to see more of it in the future, her son Major Lloyd George and his wife having come to reside at Springfield, near Chelmsford. [Applause][22]

Mrs Lloyd George's party then went on to Maldon, near the Blackwater estuary, where, accompanied by Sir Fortescue, she spoke alongside a fellow woman JP, Mrs Hudson Lyall, a Conservative politician elected to the London County Council in 1919, a Life President of the Mothers' Union and Vice President of the Primrose League. After the unveiling of a more traditional war memorial, Mrs Lloyd George, speaking at the local village hall, used her time to defend her husband's Coalition government – the attending party included the local Liberals. She warned that 'some objected to the Coalition, but they must put up with it, for if they did away with this they would have another Coalition', and urged the women to use their votes, especially for the sake of their children. The future of the country was in the hands of the women.[23]

Mrs Lloyd George's postbag showed that, on that evening of 21st July, Ivy and Austen Chamberlain, the residents of No. 11, were celebrating their wedding anniversary, and perhaps the Lloyd Georges were free?[24] A week earlier Ivy had also written in the hope that Mrs Lloyd George could come and help entertain the Grand Duchess George of Russia, who 'has invited herself to lunch'. Mrs Lloyd George would have been unable to assist entertaining the Duchess (Greek by birth, but then exiled royalty), as she was planting a tree in Hull at the time.[25] But perhaps the Lloyd Georges were able to join the Chamberlains later for their celebration.

On that day Éamon de Valera had arrived in London, with Irish negotiator Mr Barton, and that afternoon they met with Lloyd George from 4.30 to 7 pm. With more meetings to come that week, and people singing Irish songs and praying in the streets of Whitehall, it was a tense time.

Also on 21st July there was an invitation to join a party for

a visiting Egyptian delegation at the house of Lord and Lady
Carnarvon, who a year later would celebrate his successful
discovery of the tomb of Tutankhamun. If they could not
attend, Lady Carnarvon hoped that 'Miss Lloyd George could
come and dance'.[26]

Whatever nocturnal entertainment she may have enjoyed
that night, the next day, Friday 22nd July, Mrs Lloyd George
travelled to the Exchange Cinema, Northampton, the first
venue for a somewhat controversial visit – meeting the divided
Liberals. After the usual opening niceties Mrs Lloyd George
defended their MP, Charles McCurdy, strongly criticised
the Liberal Women's Association (though not by name) and
defended the Coalition. Though she was amongst Coalition
allies, at this stage in the all-out Liberal civil war, the times
were gone when the Coalition Liberals were going to be polite.
They had taken off the gloves and her message to her Coalition
audience was that this was now the way forward.

The women of Northampton had, in the run-up to her visit,
been disputing who spoke for them, as demonstrated in this
contribution to the *Northampton Echo*:

> They take strong exception to the form of the invitation to the
> Reception at the end of this month in honour of Mrs Lloyd
> George. This is, of course, a Coalition Liberal function. Invitations
> are sent out as from Mrs McCurdy and 'the Liberal women of
> Northampton'. Liberal women in this town have for many years
> been represented by the Women's Liberal Association, of which
> Mrs George Swan is the president and Miss Amy Hewitt is the
> Hon. Sec. As this is the only known organisation of women
> Liberals in the town, its officers and members think they should
> have been consulted before anybody issued invitations in the name
> of 'the Liberal women'.[27]

The same paper reported further on this ping-pong spat:
McCurdy saying he had been refused the opportunity to speak
to the Women's Liberal Association, the Liberal Women
responding that he had never asked, and then the Liberal

Women reported as saying that they were not coming – not out of disrespect for Mrs Lloyd George, who was wonderful etc, but because she was being exploited to support the Coalition, and supporting the function would mean showing support for the Coalition, which they were against.

Also speaking in Northampton was Winifred Coombe Tennant, boosting her credentials for a seat to contest for Lloyd George's Liberals. Her diary for 22nd July read:

> Left Euston at 9.20 for Northampton. Lunched to meet Mrs Lloyd George with people called Marlow at Preston Deanery Hall. Mr and Mrs McCurdy there. Thence to cinema, holding over 2,000 people. Made my speech and McCurdy absolutely satisfied... Mrs Lloyd George told me PM wants to see me and invited me to Chequers for weekend – joy![28]

At the weekend, before going to Chequers, Mrs Lloyd George found the time to open a tennis club at St George's, Weybridge, hitting the first ball over the net.[29] The *Western Mail* later reported a comment perhaps made at this opening: 'Tennis is a fine game, but in my younger days there was not much tennis, and girls had to join boys in cricket.'[30] Lloyd George was playing golf here since moving from Walton Heath to Cobham. She may have recalled watching Britain defeat France in the first post-war Davis Cup, in Deauville in 1919.

The rest of the weekend of 23rd/24th July was spent at Chequers, with Winifred Coombe Tennant as a house guest. Winifred would accompany Mrs Lloyd George on the political West Country tour in 1922. On Monday 25th July Winifred 'motored up [to London] with Mrs Lloyd George'.[31] This was probably the weekend when Winifred wrote liberally to many people using the Chequers notepaper, which, to her discomfort, was lampooned in the so-called 'Junior Member from Treorky' satirical column in the Tory *Western Mail*.

On the eve of Mrs Lloyd George's departure for Wales, the

Herbert Lewises (with the help of JTR) hosted lunch for many Welsh friends at the popular Prince's Restaurant, Piccadilly. This is one of the few occasions when my grandmother, Jane Rhys, is mentioned during these years. JTR had been making the arrangements.[32]

> On the eve of her departure from London for a tour in South Wales, and the summer holiday which will follow it, Dame Margaret Lloyd George was entertained to a complimentary lunch at Prince's Restaurant, Piccadilly, today by Mr and Mrs Herbert Lewis. A large company attended, including Lord and Lady Davenport, Mr and Mrs Towyn Jones, Mr and Mrs John Hinds, Lord and Lady Clwyd, Mr and Mrs T. A. Lewis, Mr and Mrs J. T. Rhys, and Mr and Mrs Cooper-Smith.[33]

The final few days of the month would be spent in western Wales:

> Dame Margaret will leave London tomorrow morning for Bristol, where she will unveil the memorial stone of an institute in connection with the Horfield Baptist Church.
> On Tuesday evening she will stay with Sybil Viscountess Rhondda at Llanwern.
> On Wednesday evening she will be at Pembroke Dock, opening a YWCA bazaar. She will stay on Wednesday night with Sir Ivor and Lady Philipps at Cosheston Hall, Pembroke.
> On Thursday Dame Margaret will open a county hospital bazaar at Haverfordwest, and on Friday will preside over an eisteddfod at Fishguard.
> On Thursday and Friday nights Dame Margaret will be the guest of Mr and Mrs Walter Williams at Fishguard [the family of Anita Williams, wife of Lloyd George's brother William George].
> It is not unlikely that Mrs Lloyd George will also spend the week-end in West Wales.[34]

In Bristol, at the memorial stone ceremony for the Horfield Baptist Church Memorial Institute, attended by the Rev. Dr Carlile, President of the Baptist Union,[35] she encouraged her listeners to continue their efforts to promote social well-being, as the state cannot do it all:

> These are days when we are all talking, planning, & then dreaming of Social Reform. We need reforms in many directions very urgently. We are urging the State to do a thousand and one things for the people.
>
> Well I am not here to belittle the work of the Statesman. Parliament can do a very great deal to improve the conditions under which we live. Politicians have done a very great deal for us. I am not sure they always get the credit, & the sympathy, & the support they deserve & need. From the days of Burke, Bristol has done well in this regard. May I say you have never been more wisely, jealously, & courageously represented than today.
>
> Still I would urge you to remember that the best things of life are beyond the reach of parliament. But they are things in the reach of every single individual.
>
> I pray that this Institute will be the means under the blessing of God in enabling thousands to find the things that make life worth living & death worth dying.

The full western Wales tour continued as planned. Mrs Lloyd George then returned to London.

# CHAPTER 15

# Time for a Break
## (August to December 1921)

ON 2ND AUGUST, Mrs Lloyd George travelled to Cricieth from London with Lloyd George in a party of seven, on the overnight train from Euston, arriving at six in the morning.

On Thursday, 4th August, they attended the Eisteddfod in Caernarfon. The PM did the talking, whilst Mrs Lloyd George held the ceremonial Corn Hirlas, or Horn of Plenty – presenting it to the Archdruid during the ceremony of the crowning of the Bard.

The next day, Friday 5th, she joined 'Billy' Hughes, the 'other Welsh Premier', the Welsh-born Prime Minister of Australia, at his boyhood home in Llansantffraid, and unveiled a stained glass window in memory of his mother. He in turn unveiled the church war memorial window.[1] The following day Welsh PM Hughes unveiled a bronze statue of Welsh PM Lloyd George in Caernarfon.[2]

Mrs Lloyd George and Megan also attended a local fund-raising concert in Pwllheli.

JTR continued to keep things running smoothly from Downing Street, but at times encountering problems, as this letter of 18th August shows:[3]

Dear Mr Rhys
I am sending you a few things to reply to. I think it was a mistake to send my letters to you first as I got a letter today from Sir A.
J. Boscawen wanting me to attend his wedding. I could not have

done that but I could have written to say so and wish him luck but I got his letter today only, 18th, and he was getting married today. Now you had better still carry on. I am going away next week for a time to Yorkshire & Scotland.

Yours sincerely, M. Lloyd George

After their three weeks in Cricieth, Mrs Lloyd George and the PM set off on 27th August for Scotland, via Barnsley in Yorkshire, for a holiday supposedly well away from it all, prescribed for Lloyd George by his doctor.

It was no picnic. The press described the glorious Scottish Highlands through which they drove to get there, picking up the Freedom of Barnsley on the way, and attending the wedding of William Sutherland (one of the PM's secretaries). Eventually the party was ensconced in the remote Flowerdale House, Gairloch. En route, the Rolls Royce had to halt while the men in the party filled a hole in the road. The party on the holiday included ministers, Lloyd George's secretaries (including Frances Stevenson), and Gwilym and his wife.

A Cabinet meeting had to be held in Inverness (the first held outside London). Due to tense negotiations with de Valera, an Irish delegation was met. A delegation of London mayors came to seek action on unemployment. Lloyd George suffered a serious tooth abscess, requiring surgery. It rained most of the time. Mrs Lloyd George broke her glasses (though borrowed her husband's), and was concerned over the imminent arrival of Olwen from India – not least trying to track down a parcel sent to India that had arrived but with the packaging opened, missing the dress and diamond brooch – which Olwen hoped was insured.[4]

The Irish negotiations were at a difficult point, and as messages were relayed back and forth to de Valera (in Dublin) via his emissaries, 'a telegraphic controversy nearly wrecked the small Gairloch post office. But the local postmistress rose to the occasion and did the work extremely well.'[5]

JTR meanwhile handled the daily postbag from London,

including cancelling engagements in Tonypandy and Birmingham that could no longer be fulfilled. The Prime Minister did some fishing and had films flown in, accompanied by a skilled team with four sets of apparatus to rig up an indoor cinema. A warship was moored in Gairloch Bay, having brought General Nevil Macready (the Commander in Chief, Ireland) from Ireland.

*The Yorkshire Post*, describing the scene as the Cabinet members left the Inverness meeting, added a personal touch:

> Presently another motor car drove up, and in it was Mrs Lloyd George, waiting, it seemed to me, like any ordinary wife, for her husband after office hours were done.[6]

However successful the work, the attempt to get 'away from it all for a good rest' was clearly a total failure. The nearest thing to a picnic (according to a photograph) involved Mrs Lloyd George and her husband sitting in the back of car, parked on the roadside by Loch Maree, with the Downing Street secretaries Sir Edward Grigg and Frances Stevenson perching on the running board with their lunch. (illustration 12)

Mrs Lloyd George returned to London on Wednesday 28th September and left the next day for ten days in Cricieth. Megan, meanwhile, had spent the summer in north Wales, and was preparing JTR (who had fitted in some holiday) ahead of her own return to London:

> Plas-y-Lyn, Carnarvon, Monday
> Dear Mr Rhys
> Many thanks for your letter. I should be so pleased if you could send my two letters on here. I shall be here a few days more. I am so glad you enjoyed your holiday & I hope the children did so also. I suppose they will be going back to school shortly. The weather here has been perfect, and I have spent most of my time bathing, playing tennis, motoring, with a very little dancing now and again – still there is nothing to beat Wales in the summer months. I shall

be back in town the first week of Oct I expect – not sooner. I hope you are enjoying 'peace' in Downing Street now. It will not last long I'm afraid.

Yours sincerely

Megan Lloyd George[7]


Plas-y-Lyn, Carnarvon, Weds

Dear Mr Rhys

It seems to me that you are the only reliable being from whom an answer to any question may be received at Downing Street. It was such a relief to know that you had taken the matter in hand; I felt sure Weller would be found & sent on to Criccieth. I am going on to Torquay tomorrow, starting off six o'clock in the morning. I mean to do it in a day. You were asking me about my small car. I have driven it all over N. Wales and have derived a great deal of pleasure out of it. By reason of the make (Rover) the car has been christened Don Juan – which is now its official name.

Yrs sincerely, Megan Lloyd George[8]


Weller was the family driver.


Grand Hotel Torquay, Friday, postmark 30th September 1921

Dear Mr Rhys

I wonder if you be a brick for me! I'm sure you will. I am motoring my small car to London on Sun. & Mr Brownhill is very kindly lending me his chauffeur to accompany me & I want to have a room for him. Could you please arrange either to have a room ready at Downing Street or the garage. Don't tell *anyone* I'm coming up except of course Sarah. I shall be there sometime late Sun evening. Could you also please send me some money. My Swansea journey exhausted my stock. I shall be in town next week & bother the life out of you.

Yours very sincerely Megan Lloyd George[9]


Finally Lloyd George dropped a note to Megan, with instructions for JTR:

Friday, Brynawelon, Criccieth, N. Wales
Dearest Megan
I forgot the most important thing I wanted to tell you. Please do
not let your Mami speak in public just yet, and tell Mr Rhys that
he is not to ask her to speak much less make any engagements for
her, she has still the tired feeling, but you will see her on Tuesday.
Love to you both, Your loving Shian.[10]

The letter is undated, but could well be on this occasion.
JTR recalls that when he met with the PM on his appointment
as Secretary to Mrs Lloyd George, he was told in no uncertain
terms that he should not let her overdo it.[11]

The respite at home didn't last very long for Mrs Lloyd
George.

Mrs Lloyd George is returning from Criccieth within the next few
days, and expects to spend the winter months between Downing
Street and Chequers. Unfortunately Mrs Lloyd George has not
derived much benefit from her holiday, and is cancelling all but
her most important public engagements. Both the Prime Minister
and his wife are looking forward to the arrival from India of their
daughter, Mrs Carey Evans, and their granddaughter, whom they
have not yet seen.[12]

Mrs Lloyd George has been suffering rather badly from
asthma, and it is rather doubtful whether she will be able to do
as much public speaking as the Coalition hoped. Being a quiet,
domesticated woman, she knows how to appeal to the average
woman voter.[13]

The announcement that Mrs Lloyd George could not undertake
public engagements at present does not mean that she is seriously
indisposed. She is fairly well now, but not sufficiently rested to
resume her normal activities.[14]

Mrs Lloyd George has promised to open a Saxon fair
and pageant at Leicester on October 25. The pageant will
commemorate the defeat of the Danes at Leicester in 920AD.[15]

On 8th October the PM, or failing that, Mrs Lloyd George,
was due in Durham in connection with the Ryton and Blaydon

District Aged Miners' Homes Scheme.[16] In the event, neither was able to attend.[17]

Whilst the Lloyd Georges were in Scotland, JTR and his wife may also have been looking after Olwen's daughter Margaret:

Dear Mr Rhys

I expect I shall be back by the 27th. My husband has left Port Said – so he ought to be here the end of this week, and we shall probably come home on Monday in heaps of time for the garden party, and for the concert too I hope. I suppose you are looking after Margaret – as no news is good news. Tell Mother please that I shall ring her up one morning on the phone. If you see a small parcel arriving for me looking like my glasses, would you please send them on – as I left them in the train – and have asked the man to send them on. I am sure the people on that line are sick of the sound of my name – second time I've lost something.

Kind regards Olwen Carey Evans[18]

On 9th October it was time for Mrs Lloyd George to welcome home Olwen and Eluned, the granddaughter who had yet to make the acquaintance of her famous grandparents. The reliable private secretary was called into action:

Dear Mr Rhys

I enclose 2 things for you. Will you find out when boat is due at Marseilles & when at Boulogne. It is supposed to be at Marseilles on Saturday. Mr JTD or you must go to Boulogne by the time train arrives & wire me in Downing St from Folkestone when train is due at Victoria. Am coming up Saturday. Yrs in haste M Ll G[19]

It was JTR (or 'Little JT' as he was sometimes referred to in No. 10) not JTD (Davies), who did the honours, meeting the train at Calais rather than Boulogne.

Mr and Mrs Lloyd George, with Miss Megan Lloyd George, motored up to town on Sunday evening from Chequers, in order to meet the Prime Minister's daughter, Mrs Carey Evans, on her return from India, where her husband, Major Carey Evans, is serving. Mrs Evans was expected to arrive by an early train, and the Premier intended to take her back with him to Chequers, but she did not arrive until about 8.15 p.m., and in these circumstances Mr Lloyd George determined to remain for the night in town. Mrs Evans brought with her her youngest baby, Elunyd [*sic*]. Mr Rees, Mrs Lloyd George's private secretary, went to Calais to meet Mrs Evans, and escorted her to London. Mother and baby were accompanied by Miss Ries. A nurse brought to the station Mrs Evans' elder daughter, Margaret, to meet the train.

The voyage from India was a good one, and the baby became a great favourite on board. On arrival at Victoria mother and baby were affectionately greeted by Mr and Mrs Lloyd George and Miss Megan Lloyd George.[20]

On 14th October there was a small luncheon party at No.10, attended by Eleftherios Venizelos, the former PM of Greece, and his wife (both then in self-imposed exile).[21]

On 18th October Mrs Lloyd George and Megan attended a ceremony presenting the US Congressional Medal of Honour to the Unknown Soldier, and in the evening they were at Covent Garden for a performance of *Samson and Delilah*.[22] On the 20th she presented the awards at the London Academy of Music, at the Aeolian Hall.[23]

On Friday 21st Mrs Lloyd George attended another dinner at the Prince's Restaurant, Piccadilly, this time honouring Dame Adelaide Anderson, former HM Principal Lady Inspector of Factories, and attended by close to 400 prominent women, including Lady Astor, and chaired by Viscountess (Margaret) Rhondda.[24]

The work of rallying Coalition Liberals continued with a visit on 24th October to Leicester, and opening the Saxon fair heralded earlier in the month. Ernest Evans joined her. She was the guest of Dame Lucy Markham.[25]

Her speech notes were relatively brief and, as usual, succinct and to the point:

Very glad to meet here so many Coalition Liberals.

Very important we should keep together & be prepared for any emergency.

Those who have attacked the Coalition Government have done so on two grounds. They have objected to the principle of a Coalition Government, & they have objected to the policy of this Government.

The attack on the principle of a Coalition Government has completely failed. Sir William Harcourt used to say: 'We are all Socialists now.' We can say that 'We are all Coalitionists now.'

The Independent Liberals have done their best to effect an alliance with the Liberals; & now Earl Grey & Lord Robert Cecil are talking of an alliance. The only trouble is that in neither case can a Coalition be effected. The Independent Labour [Party] will not unite with the Independent Liberals, & Earl Grey is a wee bit shy of uniting with Lord Robert Cecil. There is therefore no longer any need of defending the principle of Coalition.

They are now attacking the policy of this Govt.

Well, let us see. The three great subjects now engaging the attention of this Government are Disarmament, Ireland & Unemployment. In regard to these three the Government is doing more than any former government to deal with these problems. No alternative Government could do more or do better.

What other Government would carry such weight at the Washington Conference as this Government?

Would any other Government go further than this Government in going to effect a settlement with Ireland.

Has any other Government in this country or any other gone so far to deal with unemployment?

It is because we believe that this Government is so essentially & courageously Liberal that we support it, & ask you to help it in every possible way.[26]

Her Leicester hosts wrote back with a letter of appreciation, enclosing some newspaper clippings. On one clipping JTR had pencilled 'Written by a Wee Free' – which marks it as a very genuine appreciation of Mrs Lloyd George's character, unbiased by political affiliation, being written by an Asquithian.

Whatever may be the political views of the many people who saw and heard Dame Margaret Lloyd George yesterday afternoon, there can only be one view of her as a woman, and if one may express the opinion heard on all hands it is that never did a women less desire publicity, nor did ever any woman shoulder it more nobly.

Her quiet unassuming manner, her thoughts of common sense, and her earnest desire for the good of mankind, were things that won the heart of every woman who heard her. Dame Margaret is so obviously what we all may desire to be, a real good woman doing her utmost to tread worthily the path in which the fates have placed her.

She certainly must have carried away with her a very warm and happy sense of the loyalty of Leicester to her husband and his cause. The Reception organised by the Coalition Liberals at the Edward Wood Hall was an unqualified success, excellently organised and a social as well as a political event.

Dame Margaret also carried away with her a very practical proof of Leicester's loyalty, for she was presented by Miss Skevington and little Miss Jessie Parsons with a handsome silk scarf and a little knitted suit and big box of hazel cakes – the latter two gifts she smilingly held in reserve for her grandchildren. Little Miss Olwen Roberts shyly added to the gifts with a beautiful bouquet.[27]

Once again Mrs Lloyd George had overdone it. November was spent recuperating at Chequers, London and Bournemouth, followed by a low-key December. She would be back on the campaign trail in 1922, but with a much lighter schedule and increasingly focused on managing Lloyd George's health.

In October, at a by-election in Westhoughton, Lancashire, Labour successfully defended the seat against a Coalition Liberal. That Mrs Lloyd George did not get involved might be due to her need for a rest, or because the Labour candidate was a Welsh temperance campaigner.

Nearer home, in Hornsey, north London, there was another relatively close contest, a Unionist defending against an Asquithian Liberal, which she might have avoided, even if well enough, rather than campaign against a Liberal, at a time when all kinds of alliances were being discussed. Mrs Lloyd George was by then recuperating in Bournemouth.

The postbag also included a typed letter from Robert Cecil, writing with his League of Nations hat on, sending a complimentary ticket for the Women's Demonstration on Armistice Night, 11th November, in support of the British Delegation ahead of the Washington Conference on disarmament.[28]

Though the event was attended by a galaxy of leading women, Mrs Lloyd George spent the upcoming Armistice period in bed.

An early postbag in November included two letters from Thelma Cazalet, one addressed playfully to 'My dearest aunt Margaret, OBE!!!'

In the first, Thelma, thanking Mrs Lloyd George for a very happy weekend, noted that she heard the PM's speech on Monday after all (much thanks to Mr Rhys for getting her a seat 'he took no end of trouble'), and 'hoped that Mrs Lloyd George and Olwen could come next weekend (provided the rest of your family go to the USA). Otherwise we shan't see you for ages when once you spin off to Wild Woolly Wales'.[29]

Mrs Lloyd George's cold doubtless killed off the weekend visit, though perhaps Olwen went. The family did not go to the USA for the Washington Naval Disarmament Conference, and nor did Lloyd George, staying at home for the Irish negotiations; he delegated the Washington role to Arthur Balfour (who performed well).

The second letter from Thelma Cazalet was for JTR, thanking him a thousand times for getting her the seat – noting she stayed 'for nearly four hours!'[30] The seat was most likely for the notable Irish debate of that time.

The next day, 2nd November, Olwen accompanied her mother to a wedding reception for the Ellis-Griffith family of north Wales.[31]

The family then retired to Chequers for the weekend.

It was stated in official circles to-day that Mr Lloyd George is very tired after an exhausting week and will rest as much as possible during his week-end stay at Chequers. The Premier will be accompanied by Mrs Lloyd George, Major General [*sic*] Lloyd George, Mrs Carey Evans, with her two children, and Miss Megan Lloyd George.[32]

(Major Gwilym Lloyd George: mis-transcribed.)
The papers kept a regular bulletin on her health too:

Mrs Lloyd George is suffering from a severe chill. She has been confined to her room for two or three days, and cannot be at the Guildhall with the Prime Minister to-night.[33]

Still indisposed on Saturday 12th, with a nod to her workload:

Mrs Lloyd George's indisposition is, happily, nothing worse than a severe cold, but the cancellation of all her engagements for the immediate future has been considered advisable. Very few people realise how busy a life the wife of the Prime Minister leads and the amount of travelling involved in carrying out her voluntary tasks.[34]

It did mean she could not unveil a war memorial in Wrexham.[35]

By Wednesday 16th, Mrs Lloyd George was sufficiently recovered to travel to Bournemouth, for a seaside rest, accompanied by her husband, Olwen, Gwilym, and Miss Ries, 'a friend of the family'.[36]

The party stayed at the Branksome Tower Hotel, a grand hotel on the cliff (now replaced with apartment buildings). Mrs Lloyd George kept in regular communication with her private secretary at No. 10.

JTR also held the fort in Wethersfield, Essex, and seemed to have got himself a new job, though you can't believe all you read in the press:

The Rev. J. H. Rhys [*sic*] Downing Street, London, private secretary to the Premier [*sic*], Mr Lloyd George, preached at morning and afternoon services at Wethersfield Congregational Church on Sunday [27th]. There were large congregations, and the sermons proved helpful. The Rev. J. H. Rhys is staying over the week-end as the guest of Sir Fortescue Flannery, Bart., MP, and Lady Flannery, at Wethersfield Manor. Mrs Lloyd George, wife of the Premier, was expected to visit Wethersfield, but was prevented from travelling by a cold.

The Rev. gentleman announced from the pulpit that Dame Margaret Lloyd George promised to attend Wethersfield Chapel at some future date, and expressed her regret at being prevented by illness from coming on this occasion, but she expressed an interest in the village chapel, and would visit it when able.[37]

At the beginning of December Mrs Lloyd George was well enough to return to London, where she attended some light opera with the 'Welsh Wizard' (as the PM was known) and his Chief Whip:

The chief Coalition-Liberal Whip, Mr McCurdy and Mrs McCurdy, dined with the Premier last evening, and then accompanied the Prime Minister and Mrs Lloyd George to the Prince's Theatre to witness the performance of the Gilbert and Sullivan opera, *The Sorcerer*.[38]

Whilst Mrs Lloyd George was recuperating, Olwen helped out before returning to India, offering to go to Southport and Bolton to attend a meeting of Liberals hosted by Lord Leverhulme.[39] Letters in the postbag, arranging accommodation at one of Leverhulme's 'bungalows', suggests this offer may have been taken up.

On 6th December, the fifth anniversary of Lloyd George becoming Premier, the historic Irish treaty was signed at Downing Street.

During Mrs Lloyd George's recuperation, Mary FitzAlan, wife of the Lord Lieutenant of Ireland, called on No. 10:

Dear Mrs Lloyd George.
I shall be delighted to come to tea on *Monday* next and see your
grandchildren before they go to India.
   I did not come in yesterday because a very nice gentleman
[JTR?] came out of your house and told me that you might *not*
want to talk because it brought on a fit of coughing, so I did
not feel that I ought to bother you, any how we shall meet on
Monday.[40]

On 7th December Olwen stepped in again, opening a bazaar
and Christmas fair at Roulpell Park Wesleyan Church, West
Norwood.[41]

On Friday, 9th December, Mrs Lloyd George ventured
down to Croydon to open a bazaar at the George Street
Congregational Church, Croydon.[42] Signed photographs of the
PM were proving good money spinners, as this letter to JTR
indicates:

Monday 12th December 1921
Dear Mr Rees [*sic*]
You suggested to me that if we had a second bidder for the signed
photograph of the Premier, you might be able to get a second one.
Well, I am in a position to say that the first went for fourteen ½
guineas & we have a second offer for the same amount. In the
hope that you will help us, we are sending another photograph
with this letter...
With kind regards, Yours faithfully, Frank Y. Leggatt[43]

Frank Leggatt was regarded as one of the great preachers
of his day.

On 16th December there was Welsh music at No. 10,
with a lecture by Dr Walford Davies under the auspices of
the Cymmrodorion Society, entitled 'Our Mother Tongue:
Suggested Musical Policy for Wales' – and thanks to JTR's
squirreling tendencies, we have the programme of music for
that evening. After some singing, in which Lloyd George joined
in, Dr Davies proposed a threefold policy:

(1) That there should be a national songbook in the hands every child in the schools of Wales, and that there should be ten minutes' singing a day in every school, the whole school assembled:
(2) That ten minutes should be allotted once a week (Fridays preferably) for a school concert of forty minutes;
and (3) That the children should have certain period each week set aside, when, instead of learning crotchets and quavers and so on let them get at their work at once, and the result would be assured. At the end of the lecture Mrs Lloyd George remarked upon the great interest of Dr Walford Davies's remarks; but said she was glad the Premier was not present when the doctor had commented upon his singing. [Laughter][44]

Also attending were Olwen and Megan, with some 400 ladies and gentlemen invited.[45]

The *Pall Mall Gazette* noted the presence of two Welsh Liberal politicians (both at the time without a seat): Lloyd George's great opponent Llewelyn Williams, and Sir Ellis Jones Ellis-Griffith of Anglesey, and added a little of the history of No. 10's dining room:

> This took place in the dining-room where Pitt was wont to drink his three bottles of port each night, and when Mr Lloyd George was asked if the custom was still kept up he laughingly said it was not. Mr Llewelyn Williams, one of the Prime Minister's strongest opponents in Wales, and Sir Ellis Griffith [*sic*] were among those present. Mrs Lloyd George, Miss Megan Lloyd George, and Mrs Carey Evans were with the Prime Minister, who had to leave during the lecture to meet M. Briand.[46]

One absentee was Margaret Wintringham, the relatively newly elected MP for Louth, the first British-born (Yorkshire-born) woman MP, the first woman Liberal MP, the second woman to take her seat in the Commons (after Nancy Astor) and the third woman to be elected. Like Nancy Astor, she fought the seat vacated by her husband (her husband died in office). She wrote in January from The Grand Continental

Hotel, Cairo, expressing her regret that she had not been able to attend the concert, suggesting: 'I wish you could stand on a magic carpet and find yourself out here in this lovely climate and gorgeous sun. It would soon banish the colds you suffer from.'[47]

The hotel, a favourite with foreign visitors, albeit where Howard Carter, discoverer of Tutankhamun, breathed his last, was finally demolished in January 2018, after a long campaign to preserve it.

For entertainment before Christmas, on 21st December Mrs Lloyd George, Miss Megan and Major Richard Lloyd George occupied the royal box at Olympia for the International Circus.[48]

The next day, 22nd December, she and Megan were the guests of the Strand Theatre manager, Arthur Bourchier, in the royal box, for the latest play, *The Thing That Matters*, by Britten Austin.[49] The *Daily Herald* reviewer couldn't work out what mattered in this 'bewildering' play, though that may have been the idea, all players having a differing viewpoint.[50]

After celebrating Christmas Eve at No. 10, the PM left for the South of France to meet the French and other allies. For Mrs Lloyd George, her first priority was to look after his health:

> Lloyd George nowadays – as is shown by his visit to Cannes – is far more ready to follow medical advice than was the case. In his first days at Downing street (says a London writer) Mrs Lloyd George was compelled to use wifely strategy. 'David,' she would say, entering his study at No. 11 when he was Chancellor, 'there's the doctor here and I want him to see your throat.' 'I'm all right, I won't see him,' protested Mr Lloyd George. And it was only when he had been literally driven into a corner of the room whence escape was impossible, that he submitted himself to the doctor's surprise visit.[51]

Christmas was spent at No. 10; it would be the family's last at Downing Street:

No. 10 Downing-street took on a less serious aspect on Saturday, when Mr and Mrs Lloyd George entertained at their Christmas party about thirty children belonging to the servants and messengers of the department. The guests, brought along by their mothers and nurses, appeared to enjoy themselves immensely. The youngest member of the party was only six months old, the baby of one of Mrs Lloyd George's former cooks. The child came in for much praise from the company, and Mrs Lloyd George was nursing it most of the time. When the party opened the Premier was the first to take advantage of the mistletoe. He seized hold of his youngest grand-daughter and gave her a big kiss.[52]

Sophie Ries, who was to succeed JTR in 1922, was in attendance, and if the *Observer* is correct, her brother, Captain Howard Ries, helped to serve the cake at the party.[53] (illustration 36)

Mrs Lloyd George concluded a note to JTR with seasonal greetings:

*Cofion & Nadolig Llawen i chi a'r teulu* (Regards and Merry Christmas to you and the family) Yours sincerely M. Lloyd George[54]

On the 27th Mrs Lloyd George and her daughters left for Wales;[55] and as the year reached its close, the old question as to Mrs Lloyd George's political ambitions for Westminster was raised, and duly dismissed:

So Mrs Lloyd George has decided not to stand for Parliament. Though she is ever interested in political affairs, she feels she can assist her husband as well outside Parliament than inside. No one is quicker to sense the Premier's standing in the country.[56]

JTR's notes included some cryptic references to Margaret saying:

> Often asked why not stand myself. Invited formally and informally. Mother of Parliaments and Parliament of Mothers. My ambitions limited to Criccieth Council.

The year concluded with two letters written on New Year's Eve and sent to JTR, in reference to the equivalent of a traditional royal telegram for the 100th birthday of an upstanding Welsh citizen. The first royal telegram to a centenarian was sent in 1917.[57]

Change was now in the air. As the editor of *Lord Riddell's Diaries* put it: 'The last ten months of the coalition ministry were one long diminuendo, occasionally punctured by arresting bursts of sound.'[58]

CHAPTER 16

# Changing of the Guard
## (January to June 1922)

MRS LLOYD GEORGE began 1922 by cutting back on her public engagements in order to focus on her husband's health. The year began in north Wales:

> Major and Mrs Richard Lloyd George have arrived at Criccieth from London to join the home party at Brynawelon, which includes Mrs Lloyd George, Mrs Carey Evans, Miss Megan Lloyd George, Major and Mrs Gwilym Lloyd George.[1]

The PM was in Cannes, and Tom Carey Evans in India. The JP had a new responsibility:

> Mrs Lloyd George was appointed one of the visiting justices to Caernarvon Prison.[2]

But for now was taking it easy.

> Mrs Lloyd George is better, but she will be unable to fulfil any engagements for the present.[3]

By the third week of January it was back to London, with Olwen, Margaret and Eluned, and nurse Miss Thomas, preparing to return to India. Sophie Ries would be staying behind. Mrs Lloyd George had last-minute games with Margaret:

Welsh is spoken constantly in the Prime Minister's household, and I noticed the other day that his example is being followed by his descendants. Mrs Lloyd George was leaving Downing-street with her little granddaughter, Miss Carey Evans. The tiny toddler, playing hide-and-seek, had concealed herself behind one of the corridor doors. Noticing that Mrs Lloyd George had missed her, she sleepily announced from her hiding place, *Wele fi, nain*.[4] [Here I am, grandmother.]

Until it was time to go:

Mrs Carey Evans, elder daughter of the Prime Minister and Mrs Lloyd George, concluded her visit to her parents yesterday, and left the Premier's official residence at a quarter-past ten yesterday morning for her return journey to India, where she will rejoin her husband. Mrs Carey Evans was accompanied by her two little girls, Margaret and Elunyd [*sic*], and their nurse. She bade farewell to her parents at 10 Downing Street, and both the Prime Minister and Mrs Lloyd George were much affected at the parting with their daughter and grandchildren.

Mr Rees [*sic*] private secretary to Mrs Lloyd George, and Miss Megan Lloyd George accompanied the travellers to Fenchurch Street Station, where they caught the boat train for Tilbury.[5]

The day of Olwen's departure coincided with the first day of the two-day great National Liberal Conference at Central Hall, Westminster – where the Coalition Liberals set up their National Liberal Council, followed by a reception at Devonshire House, tagged the 'Great Crush' or 'Social Fiasco' – attended by both Mr and Mrs Lloyd George and up to 6,000 guests.

Those in morning dress suffered least, but some of those ladies of whose evening dresses the upper part consisted mainly of a couple of small straps, looked considerably dishevelled when they made their exit. One burly gentleman with a rich Northern accent, remarked, 'I have been at football matches and fights and other queer gatherings, but I don't remember seeing the like of this.' From the point of view of numbers the Coalition Liberals' reception was an unqualified success.[6]

Prior to the reception, Mrs Lloyd George and a number of political leaders and their wives were entertained to dinner by Sir Arthur Crosfield, at Claridge's. Unavoidably the PM could not attend.

Winifred Coombe Tennant wrote in her diary:

> On to Devonshire House – huge crush. Found Megan and PM just about to flee into private rooms, and the Prime Minister drew me in with him. In a small room hung with tapestry he and I, Megan, McCurdy, Mrs Lloyd George, and one or two others talked...[7]

The 'Talk of the Town' gossip column by 'Damaris' observed:

> The Prime Minister and Mrs Lloyd George seemed to have recovered from Friday's hustling when they brought Miss Megan Lloyd George to Claridge's on Saturday, this time for the dinner and dance Lucy Lady Markham and Sir Herbert Morgan were giving. Sir William and Lady Sutherland were there – they had a small luncheon party of their own that day – and, of course, Lord Leverhulme and Mr Davies, Lord and Lady Rathcreedan, and many others, with men slightly preponderating. Miss F. L. Stevenson, who is still the chief, though not any longer the only woman secretary attached to the PM, was also present.[8]

A 'pea soup' fog prevented driving out to Chequers that weekend. Winifred Coombe Tennant stayed as a guest at No. 10.

The diary was being kept light. On 27th January Mrs Lloyd George met with the Dean of Lincoln and Alfred Davies MP, planning a drawing room meeting in aid of the Restoration Fund for Lincoln Cathedral.[9]

The country's sailors still needed safe havens around the world, and a meeting was being planned for 23rd February, to be chaired by Mrs Lloyd George, to organise a bazaar in

May at the Mansion House. Again Alfred T. Davies MP was assisting.[10] By May Mrs Lloyd George was in Genoa, and Lady Beatty stood in for her at the bazaar, Mrs Alfred T. Davies manning the Welsh stall, with her two children dressed in Welsh costume.

Meanwhile, Mrs Lloyd George's potential power was being recognised by some of her opponents. Not all women were temperance advocates and the Licensed Victuallers Centre Protection Society had a 'women's movement', with 'lady licensees' and wives and daughters of retailers organised to protect the drink trade. Mrs Marshall, the Chair of its London arm, the Women's Auxiliary League, warned that the teetotal party's hostility to the trade was shared by the Prime Minister, and, though he perhaps did not voice his opinion, Mrs Lloyd George was most energetic in exhorting the teetotal party to organise. 'We women in the Trade may, I think, learn something from her activity. We have the vote and we must use it.'[11]

As part of Mrs Lloyd George's political activities there were Coalition supporters to encourage:

> I am told that the Prime Minister and Mrs Lloyd George are
> to hold several receptions for supporters of the Coalition and
> their wives in the course of the next few weeks at 10 Downing-
> street. Mrs Lloyd George is very busy making the necessary
> arrangements.[12]

Mrs Lloyd George could still support good causes – by letting others use No. 10 for their own events. Mrs W. M. Cazalet, mother of Thelma, held her own 'At Home' there in aid of the Day Servants' Hostels, with music and short presentations.[13]

And bookings were being taken for March:

> The Prime Minister and Mrs Lloyd George have given permission
> for an invitation meeting in aid of the YWCA to be held on

Thursday afternoon, March 2, at 10, Downing-street. Lady Astor
and the Vicar of St Martins-in-the-Fields will speak, and Mr H. A.
L. Fisher will preside.[14]

And Mrs Lloyd George continued to support others'
functions:

Brilliant was the scene at Viscountess Farquhar's reception
in Grosvenor Square to-night for supporters in Parliament of
the Government. Mrs Lloyd George assisted Lady Farquhar in
receiving the guests, and there was a full attendance of Ministers,
including the Prime Minister.[15]

On 7th February there was the opening of Parliament to
attend, with the return of brilliant fashions, where 'Mrs Lloyd
George favoured black relieved with gold tissue while Miss
Megan Lloyd George wore simple white and silver, with a filet
of silver leaves in her fair hair.'[16]

There then followed a series of weddings and dinners.
On 8th February, Mrs Lloyd George and Megan attended
the wedding reception in London of Miss Gladys (Sadie)
Hamar Greenwood, the sister of the Secretary for Ireland.[17]
That evening there was a dinner party with Lady Mond at 35
Lowndes-square, which included the Countess of Onslow,
Viscountess Birkenhead, Lady Worthington, Lady FitzRoy,
Mrs Munro, Mrs Macnamara, and Miss Mary Mond.[18]

On 25th February Mrs Lloyd George and Megan signed the
register at a 'Welsh wedding' in Bloomsbury, at St George's
Church, of Mr Rowland Bartholomew and Miss Mary Lewis.
The bride's father was prominent in insurance and her brother,
Sir Alfred Lewis, General Manager of the National Provincial
Bank of England.[19]

The month closed with a glittering royal wedding at
Westminster Abbey, when Princess Mary married Viscount
Lascelles:

Mrs Lloyd George wore a grey hat with a dark dress, and Mr Lloyd George was in blue-and-gold uniform. Miss Megan Lloyd George was in grey with a demure grey fur-hemmed cloak and a May-like hat.[20]

In their braided uniforms it was the male peacocks who showed their feathers that day. That evening Lady Astor hosted a dinner at her home at 4 St James's Square, followed by a reception, for 700 guests, to meet the former PM and former Foreign Secretary Arthur Balfour.[21]

In the last week of the month, Mrs Lloyd George's private secretary was stepping down:

Mr J. T. Rees [sic], for some years private secretary to Mrs Lloyd George, concluded his services in that capacity to-day, having decided to undertake a political life. During his association with Mrs Lloyd George he has been indefatigable in watching her public interests and the course of the various philanthropic and charitable movements in which she has been interested. He has proved himself to be extremely popular in London Welsh circles. Mr Rees, who years ago was a minister, first at Pontycymmer, and then at Swansea, is mentioned as a possible candidate for a Welsh constituency.[22]

But he would not be lost to Downing Street in this final year of Lloyd George's premiership, as we shall see. His successor, Sophie Ries, well known to Olwen and the Lloyd George family, would be announced in June.

March began in the traditional fashion, with the children of the Guild of Play of Southwark bringing gifts for the PM, Mrs Lloyd George and Megan, from the children of the Heritage Craft Schools at Chailey (illustration 29), including:

... miniature sets of stoolball, also made in the Craft Schools, as a reminder to Mrs Lloyd George of her game of stoolball on North Common in 1921. Mr Sydney Northcote, organist and Master of the Choristers, accompanied the little party, and, being a Welshman, sang folk songs in Welsh to the Prime Minister, who was delighted by this unexpected addition to the programme.[23]

That evening, Mrs Lloyd George, accompanied by Megan, and nearly 600 guests, attended the St David's Day banquet at the Hotel Cecil. Winston Churchill delivered a tribute to 'the greatest of living Welshmen'.[24]

Mrs Lloyd George attended an English-Speaking Union luncheon on Tuesday 7th March at the Hyde Park Hotel, on her table were Lord Lee of Fareham and Lady Lee, who had donated Chequers to the nation.[25] During the week she also addressed a meeting of Coalition Liberals with Lord Leverhulme, in Hampstead.[26]

On 10th March Mrs Lloyd George, the PM and Megan travelled to Cricieth.[27]

As always, the press found a story to write:

Following his week-end rest at Criccieth, the Premier yesterday assumed the role of a vigorous son of the soil. It is seed-time at Brynawelon, the planting of early potatoes being in full swing there. Mrs Lloyd George carried the seed on a wicker tray whilst the Premier planted them. In the flower garden mimosa and camelias are in full bloom; Mrs Lloyd George was personally attending the flowering borders, her husband watching.[28]

Mrs Lloyd George wasn't completely on holiday, popping down to Barmouth to support English churches in Wales:

Speaking at Barmouth, Dame Margaret Lloyd George said that at present the Premier was having rest at Criccieth. She also had been advised to take a rest from public functions until the end of March, but she had to ignore the advice and go to Barmouth to help the English Presbyterian bazaar. It was the duty of Welsh resorts to provide English churches for visitors to those places. It had been suggested lately that there was a danger of English churches getting stronger than Welsh churches, but she hoped the Welsh churches and the Welsh language would continue for generations.[29]

The Premier couldn't resist a chance to talk either (this time at his wife's chapel) on the loneliness of leadership:

The Prime Minister and Mrs Lloyd George attended an evening service at the Welsh Calvinistic Methodist Chapel at Criccieth.

At the close of the sermon Mr Lloyd George listened to children repeating portions of the Scriptures, and afterwards made a brief speech at a temperance demonstration.

'The Minister has referred to my having climbed the mountain of fame and responsibility. Let me warn all the young people who are here this evening that the mountain is not by any means an enviable spot. The higher you climb the colder it becomes, the lonelier you will find it. There you are open to the storm and every blast of wind. You are more exposed there to attacks of every kind. Often you will find yourself encompassed by mists with no beaten path. You must deny yourself of many comforts and the peace of home life.'[30]

For Mrs Lloyd George there was also local Council business on hand, not solely on local issues:

When Lloyd George has 'settled' Ireland, he will have a North and South Home Rule problem on his own doorstep. At a meeting of Criccieth District Council when Mrs Lloyd George was present, a letter was read asking for support for the Welsh self-government scheme. Mr Griffith Richards strongly opposed the idea. If the measure was adopted (he said), north Wales would be swamped by south Wales, and he preferred a thousand times to be governed from London to being governed from Cardiff. The Premier's wife voted in favour of the scheme, which was approved.[31]

Mrs Lloyd George was now setting out her priorities:

While politicians are speculating whether the Free Liberals or the Conservatives or the Centre Party are ultimately to capture the Prime Minister, it is Mrs Lloyd George who has stepped in during the last few days and taken complete charge of him. It was Mrs Lloyd George who got Lord Dawson of Penn to overhaul the Premier and when the physician prescribed 'complete rest for at least three weeks', she saw to it that her consort obeyed. Mrs Lloyd George has decided to cancel all her public work and devote herself to restoring him to complete health: 'My duty to my husband,' she said the other day, 'is to see that he husbands his strength.'

Hence when, on April 6, the Premier starts for Genoa, Mrs Lloyd George is going to accompany him. She has never attended any of the previous Conferences which have followed Versailles in such an unending series. She goes to Genoa because she realises that the Premier is staking his whole political future on the success of the first attempt to bring Russia and Germany into a general European Conference, and because she is determined that he shall be properly looked after while the deliberations last.[32]

In London, JTR was settling into his new role, rallying support at a luncheon he organised for 25 Nonconformist ministers, at the Hotel Metropole in London:

Politically, things are intensely lively, and there is much preparation in all parties. Twenty-five representative Nonconformist ministers lunched together to-day at the Hotel Metropole to discuss the present position of politics in this country. They included some of London's most famous preachers. This was the third conference of the kind held recently, the earlier ones having been at No. 10 Downing-street, the venue having to be changed this time owing to the Premier's absence from London ... The function was organised by Mr J. T. Rhys (formerly secretary to Mrs Lloyd George), who is now devoting himself to political work in connection with No. 12, Downing-street.[33]

For Mrs Lloyd George the show went on in a limited way, but planned visits to a sale of work in Nottingham for the Nottingham Day Nursery and Orphanage and a Congregational Church bazaar in Derby both had to be called off.[34] Perhaps it was the turn of her new secretary Sophie Ries to disappoint a minister in Derby, with other members of the Downing Street secretariat helping to find a stand-in.

The following letter from her secretary was received by the Rev. S. G. Long (secretary of the bazaar) on Saturday:

> Dame Margaret Lloyd George is exceedingly sorry that she is unable to come to Derby on Wednesday April 5th. She has a very bad cold, and unable to speak, and her doctor has advised complete rest before going to Genoa. Will you please convey Dame Margaret's regrets to the committee. She wishes you every success.

On receipt of the above, and through the good offices of Mr Shakespeare, one of Mr Lloyd George's secretaries, arrangements were made for Lady Sutherland, wife of Sir William Sutherland, to deputise for the Premier's wife.[35]

Mrs Lloyd George was well enough by 6th April to travel a short distance to to Crouch End, north-west London, to open a three-day bazaar at Ferme Park Baptist Church.[36]

Mrs Lloyd George was not abandoning all her commitments, being re-elected to the Cricieth Council, again playing second fiddle (with 404 votes) to the poll-topping Miss Leah Thomas (416 votes).[37]

On 8th April Mrs Lloyd George and Megan accompanied Lloyd George to Genoa. The conference, trying to plan economic reconstruction and peace in Europe, was not successful. But, in part due to the absence of the USA, in part due to Russia and Germany signing their own side-deal (The Treaty of Rapallo) in the first week, the lack of success was not enough to dislodge Lloyd George from power.

Ffion Hague has observed that this six-week conference was the longest continuous time for many years that Mr and Mrs Lloyd George had lived under the same roof. On the trip his relations with Megan were tense over her romance with Stephen McKenna, the 'playboy novelist', and nephew of political rival Reginald McKenna.[38]

There was some drama when an overtaking car smashed into the rear of theirs, but they suffered only shock, and a new car was provided.[39]

Megan and her mother picnicked in the hills with Lloyd George when he did have time off, played cards, and spent a day on Lord Birkenhead's yacht,[40] and Mrs Lloyd George visited the Sailors' Rest Home with Olwen and Megan.[41] But there would not have been a great deal for her to do – one reason why she rarely travelled with the PM. (illustration 39)

There was one lighter moment. Mrs Lloyd George wrote to Thelma Cazalet: 'I enclose specimens of how I am addressed here, so that you will not forget yourself when I return. I was actually called the Queen of England one day. So be on your guard.'[42]

In her absence in Genoa, on 3rd May Mrs Lloyd George was represented by her new secretary, Sophie Ries, at the Savoy dinner held for the Chailey Heritage Craft School.[43]

Meanwhile, back home:

Dame Margaret Lloyd George has written a foreword for a book entitled *Joy is My Name*, by Nicholas Fay, which Messrs. Cecil Palmer will publish next week. She says: 'If there is a more fascinating subject than the one treated by the author I have yet to hear of it. It is a new and beautiful experience to be introduced into an imaginary world of little people – a world that is an amusing travesty of our own, and to look at ourselves, so to speak, through their eyes. Politicians will find much to amuse them in the parts dealing with Parliament, and a general election in Babyland.'[44]

The Lloyd George party returned from Genoa on 20th May. Future political campaigning dates were being announced, notably a trip to the West Country, where she would be accompanied by Winifred Coombe Tennant:

Arrangements have been made by the Cornwall National Liberal Council, in conjunction with the Devon National Liberal Council, for Dame Margaret Lloyd George to visit the two counties in July. On Thursday, July 13, she will attend gatherings at Falmouth and Camborne. Mrs Lloyd George will be accompanied by Mrs Coombe

Tennant (prospective National Liberal candidate for Forest of Dean), and it is expected that a Minister will speak at the Camborne meeting in the evening. Dame Margaret will spend three days in the West, and attend other functions in Bristol and Exeter.[45]

'National Liberal' was the new designation of Lloyd George-supporting Liberals.

The July tour, though only three days in total, was the last sweeping electioneering tour by Mrs Lloyd George as the wife of the Prime Minister. It did have its moments, not least when visiting the discontented tin miners of Camborne. Such a visit had been mooted in 1921, but postponed, and JTR was doing some preparatory research on the ground himself, as we shall see.

On the evening of Sunday, 21st May, Mrs Lloyd George, the PM, Megan and Mrs William George attended chapel at the Castle Street Baptist Chapel in London where the PM had a warm reception, but did not speak.[46]

Three days later she chaired a meeting at No. 10 to review the project for a Welsh National Exhibition in Cardiff, which concluded: 'In view of the references to the present depression in south Wales it was decided that the matter be postponed for discussion till this time next year, for by then it is hoped the industrial conditions will have improved.'[47] The Exhibition never took place.

On 27th May there was a large luncheon at the Hotel Cecil for some 500 peers and MPs to 'signalise the work of the Prime Minister at the Genoa conference'. Mrs Lloyd George and Megan attended, as did Major Gwilym Lloyd George, by now 'throwing himself heart and soul into politics'.[48] Gwilym was seeking the Coalition Liberal candidature for the Pembrokeshire division, and would win the seat in November, joining his father in the House of Commons.

Finally, Mrs Lloyd George was signing up her husband to perform some ceremonies at home. Perhaps the prospect of a round of golf clinched it:

The Prime Minister, accompanied by Mrs Lloyd George, Miss Megan Lloyd George, and Mr J. T. Davies, his private secretary, will leave London at 10.45 to-morrow morning for Criccieth, where he will take a week's rest. On Friday afternoon he will be present at the opening by Lord Riddell of the extension to the golf course at Criccieth, and with the professional, Braid, will play in a foursome against Lord Riddell and Sir Edward Grigg.

Later in the afternoon Dame Margaret Lloyd George will present prizes won in a number of golf competitions which will take place during the day.

On Saturday afternoon the Prime Minister will unveil a tablet at the Memorial Hall, Criccieth, in memory of those who fell in the war.[49]

The professional golfer James Braid, a former Open Champion, had also played in a similar fund-raising contest during the war for Mrs Lloyd George's Troops Fund, at Llandrindod Wells.

The Cricieth schedule didn't go quite as planned: the PM missed the first day, 'detained in connection with the Irish situation', and disappointed the big crowds gathered for the big welcome that had been arranged for him and Mrs Lloyd George to celebrate his 'triumph' at Genoa. Gwilym stood in for his father and partnered the professional James Braid (and won) against Lord Riddell and the Cricieth professional Owen Owen. Mrs Lloyd George presented the prizes.

The Prime Minister did appear for the most important engagement, the laying of the foundation stone at the Cricieth Memorial Hall. It was now more than three years since the end of hostilities. On this occasion Mrs Lloyd George played the supporting consort and the opening speech was made by her colleague on the Council, Miss Leah Thomas. Memorial halls were another vehicle for creating a memorial that had a use:

The Prime Minister, accompanied by Dame Margaret Lloyd George and Lord Riddell, laid the foundation stone of the War Memorial Hall on Saturday afternoon. The hall will be capable of seating twelve hundred people, and the names of thirty-seven men of Criccieth who lost their lives in the war will be inscribed on panels in the inner hall. The ceremony took place in the presence of a great gathering of local people and visitors. A guard of honour of local ex-service men attended the Premier, who was enthusiastically received.

An excellent opening speech was made by the chairman, Miss Leah Thomas, who quoted Sir James Barrie on 'Courage', and said, 'These men who died had courage in battle.'

A silver trowel was presented to Mr Lloyd George, who, in laying the stone, deposited a number of records, including newspapers, coins, and a letter written by himself, which he read as follows:

> These young men died that the Dominion of Right and Reason should be more firmly established in the government of men. D. Lloyd George. June 3, 1922.[50]

The PM followed up with a speech in tribute to the fallen.

That Saturday evening the Lloyd Georges attended the Calvinistic Methodist Cymanfa Ganu (Singing Festival), and on the Sunday morning each to their own, Lloyd George attending the Berea Baptist Chapel, Mrs Lloyd George the Calvinistic Methodist Chapel. In the afternoon, accompanied by Lord Riddell and Mr J. T. Davies, they 'motored in beautiful weather' to Ffestiniog to hear the Rev. T. C. Williams at his evening service.[51]

Three and a half years since the Armistice, three years since the 'peace' of Versailles, attempts to further the peace in Europe faltering, Irish Home Rule agreed but on the brink of civil war, the reconstruction of Britain weak, and the Coalition struggling to stay afloat, it must have been quite a time to pause and reflect.

Duties remained light for Mrs Lloyd George. Possibly she was conserving energies for (as well as planning) her forthcoming electioneering visit to the West Country. Her impending presence was already prompting the prospective Liberal candidate for Exeter, Leonard Costello, to cause some ripples:

The second series of open-air meetings, addressed by Mr W. Llew Williams of London, was held Saturday night in Bedford Circus. Mr Walker King, who presided, emphasised the effectiveness of the Liberal wing of the Coalition Ministry.

Mr Williams said he had not come down to apologise for the Coalition, nor was he prepared to defend it by the use of personalities. But he had read a speech in the local Press made Friday night which he could not pass over in silence – a speech in which Mr Costello transgressed the bounds of decent criticism and debate.

Referring to the projected visit to the West of Dame Margaret Lloyd George, Mr Costello had said no doubt a certain number of snobbish people would be glad to receive an invitation to meet her. Why should these citizens of Exeter be stigmatised as 'snobbish': Mrs Lloyd George was the wife of the first Commoner of the Realm, a lady of infinite charm, and who took a deep and unaffected interest in politics. The Prime Minister had described her as his 'chief political asset'. Was it an offence against any code of morals or manners to desire to meet such a lady?

Mr Williams said that on a certain occasion in June 1914, which no doubt Mr Costello would vividly remember, he (Mr Williams) at Mr Costello's request introduced him to Mr Lloyd George. Why were Exeter citizens 'snobs' for seeking the very honour Mr Costello himself had sought? He owed an apology to the electors of Exeter, and ought to make it at the earliest moment.[52]

The above mentioned W. Llew Williams was not the former Welsh MP W. Llewelyn Williams, the opponent at Cardiganshire, who had died shortly before, in April.

In contrast to campaigning, Mrs Lloyd George was helping to rearrange the celebrations for the upcoming birthday (23rd June) of the Prince of Wales:

Dame Margaret Lloyd George presided over a further meeting of a committee comprising representatives of this country, the Colonies and Dominions, India, and Japan, for the purpose of considering a plan for the celebration of the Prince of Wales' birthday in conjunction with the flag day arranged for the same date by the

Veterans' Association. It was agreed to postpone the birthday demonstration till a later date, Mrs Lloyd George undertaking in the meantime to ascertain the Prince's wishes in the matter.[53]

The weather on 16th June caused another event, in Ealing, West London, for 'the wife of the Prime Minister of England', to be modified:

> The announcement that Dame Margaret Lloyd George, the wife of the Prime Minister of England [*sic*], was to take part in the opening ceremony of the Sisterhood brought a great throng to King's Hall on Thursday afternoon. The function was to have been a garden fête in the Manor House grounds, but owing to the rain of the morning and the still threatening aspect of the sky it was decided to transfer it to the Lecture Room of King's Hall.
>
> Mrs Lloyd George did attend, and after wishing them every success (they would at least have a sale that day), said that her words must be very short, as she had a deputation coming to her house at half past four.[54]

The former US President William Taft and his wife were coming to London and it was expected that Mrs Lloyd George, the PM and the King and Queen would attend a dinner hosted by the American Ambassador.[55]

Support for the children of Chailey continued:

> Dame Margaret Lloyd George has arranged for an exhibition of dances by pupils of the Heritage Craft School at Chailey, to be given on Wednesday, June 21, at 3 o'clock at 10, Downing-street, the object being to assist school funds.[56]

That morning, she and the PM welcomed the Prince of Wales back from his tour of the Empire, before they joined the children:

> An All-Welsh At Home: After cheering the Prince I looked in at 10, Downing-street. Although Dame Margaret Lloyd George went with the Premier to meet the Prince yesterday, she managed to

get back to her At Home in time to say a few words about the new hospital at Chailey, which is being equipped in connection with the Heritage Craft Cripples' Homes, and which benefited by the At Home. I just caught sight of the Premier looking so much taller in his full-dress uniform on his way upstairs, and he stopped to talk for a minute to the little child-dancers of the Children's Guild of Play who danced in during the afternoon. It was an all-Welsh programme, and we lustily sang 'God Bless the Prince of Wales', of course.[57]

On 22nd June, at a tense time in Ireland, Field Marshal Sir Henry Wilson was shot and killed by the IRA as he returned to his home in Eaton Square, London, after unveiling a war memorial in Liverpool Street. His funeral followed on 26th June at St Paul's Cathedral:

On the farther side with little ostentation the members of the Cabinet came in, and were shown to their places. They came in so quietly that only those on the side on which they were sitting observed them come. They were all in black frock coats. The Prime Minister and Dame Margaret Lloyd George seated themselves next the aisle on the first of the seats set apart for Ministers. Next to Mrs Lloyd George was Mr Fisher, and beyond him Mr and Mrs Austen Chamberlain. Then came the Earl of Balfour, who more than any of the others seemed to have his mind far away in some realm of its own. Beside him, Sir Robert Horne talked to Mr Shortt, on the other side of whom was Mr Churchill with his chin on his hand, the only clue to his thoughts being the frequent frowns that chased across his face. At the end of this first seat was Sir L. Worthington Evans, the Secretary for War, to whom several soldiers of high rank came up and talked briefly. A military band was playing Chopin's *Marche Funèbre*, and the sound entering the great door re-echoed in every corner.[58]

On 28th June, Mrs Lloyd George and Megan unveiled a tablet on the Lloyd George former house in Trinity Road, Wandsworth.[59] That afternoon the weather tried to rain on the YWCA parade:

The rain having suddenly decided to begin yesterday afternoon, and, what was worse, to stay, naturally prevented many people from attending the YWCA market which Dame Margaret Lloyd George opened at Lansdowne House. Everybody was very cheery, and quite a good trade was done in spite of all, especially in strawberries and cream, over which the Viscomtesse de Sibour presided, and many people didn't seem to mind a few raindrops falling through the big trees which, fortunately, sheltered the table.[60]

The Viscomtesse was the former Violette Selfridge, who had had flowers flown over from France for her wedding at the Brompton Oratory in May 1921, which Mrs Lloyd George had attended. The Viscomtesse and her husband Jacques were keen aviators. And now it was all coming up roses...

After Mrs Lloyd George had opened the Blue Fair and Produce Market in aid of the Young Women's Christian Association at Lansdowne House yesterday afternoon, Mrs Lall, an Indian lady, placed a long garland of red roses about her neck. This decoration was in accordance with the Indian custom of 'garlanding' and corresponds to our custom of presenting a bouquet.[61] (illustration 25)

That evening Mrs Lloyd George was one of several guests of the American Ambassador in his Albert Hall box at the Princess Mary Ball, otherwise known as the Hospital Ball, organised by the King Edward's Hospital Fund, a London hospitals' combined appeal to support voluntary hospitals.[62]

A busy day: a plaque, a fair and a hospital ball. More ominously, that day, in Dublin, the Civil War broke out in earnest.

Mrs Lloyd George's next main trip would be to the West Country. On 29th June the West Country (Somerset, Devon and Cornwall) schedule was published: quite an agenda of garden parties, Coalition meetings, lunches and dinners, starting in Bristol on Monday July 10th and closing in Camborne (not far from Land's End) on Wednesday 12th July: 18 events, six a day, as in Wales in 1918.

There was a 'cunning plan' afoot to make this tour a pioneer for the new technology of the age:

Fred Dimbleby to the Chief Whip, Charles McCurdy, 30.6.1922

The cunning plan was to equip the garden parties at Bristol, Exeter and Falmouth with loudspeakers and equip them so that a message from the Prime Minister could be transmitted from Marconi's offices in the Strand. And, if possible, for the PM to transmit one of the messages live. They also note that any such messages of course could be picked up anywhere in the country by anyone with a receiver. It would not be LlG oratory, as they were planning for messages for 150–200 words in length. It might alternatively be a message to Dame Margaret for delivery.[63]

In 1912 Lloyd George and Sir Rufus Isaacs (later Lord Reading) and other members of the Liberal Government had been accused of insider trading in Marconi shares. Reading's brother Geoffrey Isaacs was the Managing Director of Marconi. Their acquittal had saved their reputations, but the Marconi scandal nearly destroyed Lloyd George. Would it now make him a 'wizard' again?

June closed with a cruise on the McAlpine yacht, *Naida*, in Scotland, which included a return to Gairloch. Richard and Roberta Lloyd George joined the party. Back to business, there was the new private secretary to announce, the formal changing of the guard:

Mrs Lloyd George has appointed Miss Sophie Ries to be her private secretary, in succession to the Rev. J. T. Rhys, who has accepted another appointment.[64]

Very soon after this formal announcement, Miss Sophie Ries accompanied Mrs Lloyd George on the West Country political campaign tour.

It is time for a proper introduction to the new private secretary.

Sophie Ries was born in Hampstead on 24th February

1895, the eldest of the three children of Augustus Ries (1860–1927), merchant and banker, born in Württemburg, a naturalised British citizen, and Alice Hirschhorn (1872–1944), Hampstead-born daughter of jewellers from Hessen. During the First World War, Sophie nursed in London with the Red Cross Voluntary Aid Detachment (VAD).

Sophie had a short-lived, arranged marriage, celebrated on 30th April 1919 at the West London Synagogue to a Charles Gutman, whom she divorced via her petition for nullity in 1921. Gutman returned to Germany, married a Swedish woman in 1921 and then emigrated to the US: he worked for Ehrmann and Bahlsen, diamond traders, Sophie's mother being from the Ehrmann family.

In October 1920 Sophie travelled to India to accompany Olwen, who was then expecting her second child (daughter Margaret having been left at home with Mrs Lloyd George, partly in the care of JTR's wife Jane Rhys). Sophie might have been happy to get away to India, her divorce then still pending.

Later in life Sophie featured in two public dramas. In 1928 she went into hiding, triggering a big newspaper hunt, after her friend Elsie Mackay, also known as the actress Poppy Wyndham, daughter of Lord Inchcape, was lost in the sea to the west of Ireland when aiming to be the first woman to fly westwards across the Atlantic, with a professional pilot. Sophie eventually re-emerged, saying she didn't realise there was a public hunt for her. She was said to have been the last person to have seen Elsie, and she was in on the 'secret' flight attempt.

Sophie also featured in a fiction-based-on-fact book, *Crossing the Horizon*, on the race by four women to be the first to make the Atlantic crossing.[65] It is also reported that Sophie arranged a job for Emilie Hinchliffe, widow of the lost pilot, to work for Lloyd George.

Then, at the age of 70, Sophie made a brief press appearance, having witnessed the collapse of US diplomat Adlai Stevenson, in the street near the Dorchester Hotel, when he was walking with his assistant (who was also his mistress). He died of his heart attack. Sophie had been walking from her club, the International Sportsman Club, housed at the Dorchester.

Sophie died on 27th November 1976, leaving legacies to Olwen and members of her family.

CHAPTER 17

# The West Country Tour
## (July 1922)

THE THREE-DAY MOTOR car tour from Bristol to Land's End
was Mrs Lloyd George's last grand political tour of this nature.
En route to the tour, on 7th July Mrs Lloyd George attended
the annual meeting of the Welsh National Liberal Council in
Cardiff, moving the motion for Free Trade. Her speech notes,
retained in the NLW archives,[1] were written on the notepaper of
the home of Sir William Seager, her Cardiff host. She avoided
the complexities of this contentious policy issue by pitching it
as a means for getting nations to work together and to break
down barriers, both between nations and between classes in
nations, and for marking a difference between Liberals and
Socialists:

Lynwood, Newport Road, Cardiff
    There are two words in the middle of this resolution which
describe its purpose very well. They are the words 'better relations'.
Each part of the resolution has to do with the promotion of better
relations. First there is the maintenance of Free Trade that is,
we all know, an economic necessity for us, but it is something
more: it is a great help in breaking down the walls of prejudice, of
ignorance & of selfishness around nations. When these walls are
broken down, or even when a fairly big breach is made in them,
nations get together, understand each other better, respect each
other, & realise their common interest in the great cause of peace.
Nothing will help to promote better relations in the world than the
fullest measure of commercial intercourse between nations.

In Industry, as in other walks of life, we want to get away from the idea of separating classes & considering interests apart from the general welfare of the community. In some of our greater industries masters & men got together to work out a solution of their common problems. Well, if masters will think of their workers not as pieces of machinery for the mere production of profits, & if workers will think of employers not as mere exploiters, they will soon understand each other's point of view & ensure peaceful, just & progressive conditions for the good of all. Better relations in industry are an urgent necessity & we as Liberals want betterment to come by co-operation & not by conflict.

There has been a great quickening of the social conscience since the war. Socialists talk as if they are the only people, & the Labour party as the only party, that care for the poor, that hate oppression & injustice, & that strive for better times. Why, there isn't a decent Christian man or women in Britain who does not feel very strongly about these things. We differ from the Socialists because we believe in improving the present system by instalments. The Socialists, on the other hand, say the existing system must be destroyed. We Liberals think that class war, and all that makes for hatred, distrust and suspicion in life is bad, and as you cannot advocate Socialism without stirring up strife, we say Socialism is a menace.

Compared to her other speeches, this comes across more carefully worded, more politically sensitive. Of course, it was in support of a formal resolution, rather than rallying support to a 'cause'.

The motion was passed. Mrs Lloyd George then entertained the delegates to tea at the Park Hotel, Cardiff. The Welsh National Liberal Council had been set up by Lloyd George in 1898 to bring together the North and South Wales sections of the Liberal Party, but it had limited power.

From Cardiff Mrs Lloyd George took the train to Bristol. The West Country tour, from Bristol to Camborne, was Mrs Lloyd George's most notable political intervention in 1922, apart from supporting her son Gwilym in December in Pembrokeshire. She was accompanied by her new private secretary, Sophie Ries, and by Winifred Coombe Tennant, Lloyd George's candidate for the Gloucestershire constituency of the Forest of Dean. Whilst Mrs Lloyd George received the usual strong reception (in most places), the tour also yielded a good example of the reality that, though she had the ear of the Prime Minister, her political power was limited.

JTR's country-wide meetings with Free Church Ministers showed there was work to be done to regain support for Lloyd George and his Coalition, Cornwall being one area singled out. The General Secretary of the National Liberal Organisation, Col. Scovell, had recently reported to the Chief Whip on JTR's surveys:[2]

3rd May 1922
Memo to Rt. Hon. C. A. McCurdy, KC, MP.
Visits of the Rev. J. T. Rhys.

Mr Rhys found that few Ministers in Cornwall were supporters of the Government, and he is of the opinion that this is due in great measure to the result of the Bodmin election and to the vigorous campaign that the Independent Liberals have been carrying on ever since. He was fortunate, however, to meet the Rev. Captain Frank Edwards, Wesleyan Minister, Newquay, who is a strong supporter of the Prime Minister and has offered his assistance. Captain Edwards is in charge of 39 churches in Cornwall, is personally known to every Methodist Minister, and on account of his popularity wields great influence throughout Cornwall.

The letter continued with reports on visits to Sheffield, Leeds and Hull, concluding:

Mr Rhys's experiences confirm our impression that we have lost considerable ground in Cornwall and that special efforts will have to be made to regain it.
12 Downing Street, SW1
Initialled by C.S. Scovell.

Mrs Lloyd George's trip was part of the 'special efforts'.

In the Bodmin by-election in February, Isaac Foot (the Liberal defeated by Nancy Astor in Plymouth) had stolen the seat from the Unionists in what some called a landslide, marking the Asquithian Independent Liberals out as the radical party for the region, and was a blow for Lloyd George's Liberals. In one sense, defeating Foot could only be achieved by a Unionist candidate, but it was important to try and stop a resurgence of belief in Independent Liberals elsewhere.

After Mrs Lloyd George's arrival at Bristol Station, the day started with a private lunch with Coalition supporters, followed by a visit to Clifton Zoo, thronged with people in the sunshine, and featuring a radio display by Marconi:

> During the afternoon Dame Lloyd George visited the tent in which Mr E. T. Chapman of Poole (late of the RFA and a radio engineer) demonstrated broadcasting wireless telephony upon a Burndept (ultra4) receiving set. The weather report, sent in Morse code from the Eiffel Tower, was plainly heard, then followed messages from Croydon aerodrome, and from aeroplanes in flight, and at a time fixed General Fernier, who is in charge of radio in Paris, transmitted from the Eiffel Tower a concert proceeding in Paris. This included vocal items and instrumental selections, including a violin solo.[3] (illustration 14)

The plan for Lloyd George to address the gathered multitude by radio doesn't seem to have been realised.

The day's proceedings culminated with a meeting at the Colston Hall, which was packed. After a short concert and a number of speeches Mrs Lloyd George addressed the meeting, with a focus on peace, followed by a strong statement of how Britain was leading the pack:

> The great need of the present moment was peace; they wanted to see the nations living in friendly concord and not regarding themselves as enemies. [Hear, hear] It was a deplorable fact that after a great war that had caused so much destruction and trouble to the whole world, that nations were still devising new machinery

to renew the conflict. One would have thought that their Christianity would have been enough to restrain them, and if their Christianity were not strong enough, their common sense ought to do it. [Hear, hear] They had only to look at Russia, Germany, and Austria. Those great countries were bankrupt and their people were starving. Coming nearer home, let them look at the exchanges of Italy and France, the unemployment in our country, and the crushing burden of taxation everywhere. The world was too poor to buy and millions were weeping for their dead. Surely those things ought to teach the blessing of peace, even to war-loving madmen. The peace and stability of the world depended upon this old country of ours.

In spite of all the ills of the Coalition Government the people of the Continent were looking to Great Britain to help them. So let them keep steady and not lose their heads. She thought the Coalition Government was doing so with true British calm and steadfastness. They only had to look at their credit; how it was rising while every other European power was losing its credit. The British credit was going up in spite of bad trade, unemployment, and in spite of the world's disturbances. That was due to the increased belief in British steadiness and the very sound policy of the Coalition Government. [Hear, hear] They had avoided extremes on both sides, they had kept a middle course.

She had a verse on the subject; but it was in Welsh and she could not translate it into English. Mrs Lloyd George repeated the verse in the Welsh language, and, proceeding, she said by means of keeping to the middle course they had offended extreme men and women on both sides. When women became extreme they were much worse than men. [Laughter]

The extreme revolutionists attacked the Government, and so did the extreme reactionaries; but the Government had kept a middle course: it had avoided the ditches and precipices of both sides.

If they had not done so she would not have been there that night to support the Government, in spite of her husband being at the head of the Government. They also wanted industrial peace in the country, and she thought from the speech of Mr J. H. Thomas they were on the high road to get it. She hoped the railway companies would answer Mr Thomas in the right spirit, and she hoped all other industries would follow. If they did, this country would be on the right road to be the best country in the world. [Hear, hear][4]

A letter written on the trip to Olwen provides Mrs Lloyd George's perspective:

Woodville, Sneyd Park, Bristol
On one of my pilgrimages, Sophie is here too but she is not staying here but we meet tomorrow to motor through Devonshire, many little meetings on the road side and a public meeting at Exeter tomorrow evening. Then the next day we go to Cornwall, another similar day ending in the evening public meeting. We go home on Thursday. There was a meeting tonight of 5,000 people. Think of poor Mamie having to speak 5 minutes to them. And *ysgwyd llaw hefo canoedd*. [Shaking hands with hundreds.] However, I am now writing in a most comfy bed, and now going to lie down to sleep. I have no campaign after this. I am staying with Mr Gange MP. He tells me he has a sister in Delhi. She is a mistress of a school there. Mrs Gange put it down in your notebook.
... Tuesday, we are now near Torquay after a strenuous day. Tomorrow is bigger still. Then we go home.
... I must try to sleep and before doing so think of a few notes for tomorrow.[5]

Stanley Gange was the current Coalition Liberal MP, merchant and son of a Baptist minister, who did not stand at the next election.

The next two days involved a motor tour to Taunton and then almost to Land's End, accompanied by the local MPs, organisers, and Sophie Ries:

Taunton was the first stopping place. Having acknowledged the welcome, Mrs Lloyd George recalled that just a year previously she had visited Taunton to assist the candidature of Sir Arthur Griffith-Boscawen, whom the electors returned with a majority to the House of Commons. Then came one of those quiet touches of humour greatly relished by the crowd who pressed closer and closer around her car. 'We are having such splendid weather now,' she remarked, glancing up at the blue skies, 'and I really think I can claim to have brought it with me.'[6] (illustrations: book cover, 10, 16, 32)

In her more serious remarks, Mrs Lloyd George would talk of the efforts being made to keep the peace at home and abroad.

The day's closing event was in Exeter's Theatre Royal for a mass meeting of the faithful, where Mrs Lloyd George gave probably the fullest version of her speeches of the day, and where Freddie Guest, now Secretary of State for Air, for whom she had spoken in Poole, delivered a longer speech. This was an important meeting for the Devon National Liberal Council, part of the organisation that the Coalition Liberals had been developing since the split with the Free Liberals had become open. Both Winifred Coombe Tennant and Sophie Ries attended. At the meeting Mrs Lloyd George gave a sample of what had been referred to in an earlier report as her 'taking a tilt at Independent Liberalism'. The press report is close to Mrs Lloyd George's handwritten speech notes, on record at the National Library of Wales:

> The Theatre Royal at Exeter was packed last evening, when Dame Lloyd George addressed a mass meeting. Admission had to be limited to ticket holders, and the accommodation of the Theatre, large as it is, was quite inadequate to admit all who wished to be present. For half an hour before the commencement of the meeting, the Band of the Depot Devon Regiment played sections of music.

Dame Margaret Lloyd George, having paid tribute to the beauty of Devonshire, countered the view that supporting the Coalition meant a bartering of principles, referring to:

> a recent Free Liberal meeting in that City. Mr Costello, at that meeting said he could not support the Coalition Government because a union of Liberals with Conservatives meant a bartering

of principles. She could not see that. Some people had a funny idea of what a Liberal should be. He apparently must be a very exclusive person. He might be an Englishman, Scotsman, a Welshman, but he must not co-operate with his fellow-countrymen. He could work with Germans, Russians, Bulgarians, any other nation, but he was not to work with that dangerous type who fought side by side with him during the war, or who sent their sons to fight, for common cause of the country. There were a great many real Liberals after the war who felt it their duty to join with all men of goodwill in the very difficult task of constructing a solid peace. Had they given up their Liberal principles on that account? She did not think so.

They were not ashamed of the achievements of the Coalition Government. She thought it would stand comparison with any Government that had gone before. The problems it had to deal with were much more baffling and complex than the problems before the war. They passed a sweeping measure of electoral reform; they had given the votes to women, and made it possible for them to sit in the House of Commons and on the Bench, and to become members of professions that were not open to them before. The Government also made wise provision for unemployment. They were not ashamed, either, of the work done at Washington, where we were so ably represented by Lord Balfour. And yet Liberals were told it was wicked to work with him because he was a Conservative.

She defended the efforts being made over Ireland, attacking the Free Liberals:

Then, as to the Irish question, they hoped that long feud was drawing to a close. The Government had offered to the Irish people a more generous measure of Home Rule than had ever been offered. The Free Liberals approved of it, but said it ought to have been done before. Why did not Mr Asquith do it during his eight years of office as Prime Minister, during six of which there was peace? It was the union of the two great political parties that had made a settlement of the Irish question possible. Mr F. D. Acland also said at a Free Liberal meeting that many lives were lost, and millions in money wasted because the Government would not see that the only of settling the Irish question was trust, and not violence and hatred. That was a very unfair criticism, because Mr Lloyd George, more than a dozen times on behalf of the Government, offered to treat with anyone who could speak for Ireland and the Irish people. No one came forward; if they had, perhaps Home Rule would have been settled long ago.

And she concluded with a defence of the lack of progress in Genoa, underling her husband's determination to achieve peace:

At the same Free Liberal meeting, Lord Beauchamp said a British policy was wanted, and British policy must always be one peace; that we also wanted the new method of the League of Nations, and needed someone to conduct our foreign affairs in whom the people of this country and the nations of Europe had confidence. All agreed to the need for peace, and the Coalition took credit for the League of Nations, which was really an outcome of the much abused Treaty of Versailles. Mr Lloyd George was partly responsible for that. Genoa was very much criticised, too, because America was not there. That, at least, was not the fault of the Coalition Government, who would have been very glad to see America represented there. It was, however, a great achievement to get nations sitting round a table to discuss peace. Mr Lloyd George was as keen on peace as anyone in the British Empire and meant to do all in his power to secure it for this country, for Europe, and for the world.[7]

Further south in Cornwall, there were rumblings in Redruth:

There was a division of opinion at Monday evening's meeting of Redruth Urban Council as to accompanying the chairman (Mr W. T. Hart) to the public reception to Dame Margaret Lloyd George in the town this afternoon.[8]

A year earlier, whilst Mrs Lloyd George was on 'holiday' with LlG and the Cabinet in Flowerdale House in Scotland, a letter to the Cornish press indicated that whilst Cornwall would give a civilised welcome to 'his estimable lady', there was no point her coming if there was to be nothing done to aid the Cornish miners, whose industry had been hit by a collapse in the price of tin.

Dear Prime Minister, It was announced as a great forthcoming political event that Mrs Lloyd George was coming to the Camborne Division to address the Electors. I have heard since that the visit has to be deferred. In saying that this will give time both for reflection and action, I wish to make clear that I write in no spirit of hostility to your estimable lady; and that if I do not wear the label of a Coalitionist, I wear no other party label. I only wish, as a Cornish publicist, to remind you that grave industrial crisis exists in Cornwall; that the circumstances are exceptional; that while our industrial population – particularly our Cornish tin miners – have distinguished themselves alike by their bravery in war and by restraint and loyalty during a long period of distress and injustice, they are in no mood to listen to political harangues, even from the wife of a Prime Minister.

So, my dear Prime Minister, you will see, if you read these lines, that if Mrs Lloyd George comes to us with a financial olive branch, she will be welcomed as a harbinger of Hope. I do not think that our splendid fellows would in any case be rude to a lady, but distressed people, smarting under a real grievance, do not want to hear political platitudes, even from the wife of a Prime Minister.[9]

Mrs Lloyd George's motorcade entered Cornwall by a different route than advertised (perhaps simply to avoid Plymouth), taking her across the moors on a wonderful day. The tour proceeded well enough, through Liskeard, Bodmin and Truro (lunch), and Falmouth (garden party) with Mrs Lloyd George drawing attention to the cultural links between Wales and Cornwall, until the moment for some answers began to arrive, first in the afternoon in Redruth: (illustrations 20, 37, 44)

Half an hour after the scheduled time the party reached Redruth, to find several thousand people awaiting them on Station Hill. Mr W. T. Hart, chairman of the Urban Council, supported by some of his colleagues, was there to voice the town's welcome, and Mrs Lloyd George was instantly brought into touch with the industrial privations of the neighbourhood. Having received a bouquet from Miss Joan Chegwidden, grand-daughter of Mr W. L. Chegwidden, Mrs Lloyd George, speaking from her car, returned thanks for the welcome. 'I assure you,' she said, 'that when I go back to London I shall put your case to the Government. I do not say I can do much, but I will present it with the best of hearts.' Cheers were given for Mrs Lloyd George and the Prime Minister, and a man among the crowd called for cheers for the unemployed.[10]

And so on to Camborne, where the locals were still expecting more than 'political platitudes'.

The *Cornishman and Cornish Telegraph* published its summary of the lively exchange:

Dame Margaret then motored to St George's Hall, Camborne, where a public meeting was held.

The chairman, Mr George M. Bray, said, 'If it had not been for Mr Lloyd George, the Germans would have been here now.'

A voice: What about the troops?

Reference by the chairman to the many thousands of pounds raised through the Camborne and Redruth Unemployment Relief Committee for the benefit of miners out of work provoked the emphatic retort: 'We don't want charity.'

'What has the Government of Mr Lloyd George done for the working men?' ventured Mr Bray.

The hall immediately rang with cries of 'Nothing'.

'You tell me nothing,' replied Mr Bray. 'May I read to you from the published...' The rest of the sentence was lost in confusion, and continuance of the uproar caused a temporary stop to the opening speech.

When the opposition had cooled a little, Mr Bray managed to get in a few figures, the substance of which was that the Government had laid out something like £25,000,000 for the working men alone. No other Government, ancient or modem, had spent anything like that sum for such a purpose, proceeded Mr Bray, amid prolonged interruption.

In the ensuing din the chairman made a gallant effort to conclude his speech, but was eventually obliged to resume his seat.

Mrs Coombe Tennant and Major-General Sir Frederick Poole were accorded a hearing.

After receiving a bouquet from Miss Rachael Luke, Mrs Lloyd George reiterated her promise to do her very best to place the case of the Cornwall tin mining industry before the Prime Minister.

Mr G. Hay Morgan KC was subjected to interruption. Mr Lloyd George, he asserted, had real interest and sympathy with the workers.

A voice from the gallery: 'What has he done for the Cornish workers?'

Mr Hay Morgan: 'He was the head of a Government which passed the most democratic Education Bill ever passed through any Parliament in the world.'

The voice: 'We don't want education, old man.'

Mr Morgan: 'You ought to want it.'

The voice: 'We want work.'

Another man in the gallery rose to explain his grievance, asking: 'What's a chap going to do for a living?'

Mr Hay Morgan: 'We all have the deepest sympathy with men out of work. [Cries of "rot"] But, deep as our sympathy is, it is not within the power of every one of us to give complete satisfaction to everybody out of work.'[11]

Winifred Coombe Tennant wrote scathingly in her diary, 'On to Camborne, a fine meeting of very intelligent people, spoilt by a half-drunken fool of a chairman.'[12]

A fortnight later, on 26th July 1922, Col. Scovell, the General Secretary of the Coalition Liberal Organisation, wrote to Charles McCurdy, the Chief Whip, to urge a response to what was dubbed elsewhere the Camborne Commitment:[13]

I understand that at a large meeting held at Redruth at which Dame Margaret spoke, she used the following words in connection with the terrible unemployment distress in the tin industry in Camborne and Redruth:

'I can assure you that when I go back to London after all I have heard here, I shall put your case before the Government. I do not say I can do much, but I will present it with the best of hearts.'

It has been represented to me today by one of our leading supporters in the County of Cornwall that the result of her talk with the Prime Minister on the subject should be sent down to Cornwall. Perhaps you would like to consider the matter and take such steps in connection therewith as you think desirable.

G. J. SCOVELL

On the same day, the *Cornishman* paper was relaying the discussions taking place at the meeting of the Camborne/ Redruth Unemployment Committee: should they follow up with a letter to Dame Margaret?

Mrs H. Dungey referred to the recent visit to the district of Dame Margaret Lloyd George, and said she endeavoured to place all the facts relative to the distress and unemployment prevalent before Dame Margaret, who was deeply interested, and promised as she stated publicly to bring the matter to the notice of the Prime Minister. The serious position confronting the district had 'got the ear' of Dame Margaret. If the secretary of the committee would write to Dame Margaret confirming officially the position as told her, that the suggestion that the matter should be placed before the Prime Minister, she (Mrs Dungey) was quite sure some good would result.

Mr W. Nicholas inquired what was suggested the secretary should write about.

The Chairman (Mr W. T. Hart): 'We are anxious that the facts of the situation shall come before the Prime Minister. He is a busy man, and I question if he has had time to properly think of the circumstances existing here.'

Mr W. Uglow suggested that the best course to adopt would be to ask the Prime Minister to receive a deputation respecting the resuscitation of the staple industry of the district, was by far the most important matter as far as the future welfare of the area was concerned. Ultimately it was decided to instruct the secretary to write to Dame Margaret asking her to use her influence with the Prime Minister to receive a deputation with the object of discussing with him the whole of the economic problem in the mining area.[14]

The answer, which came in August, may seem as predictable as (perhaps) disappointing:

In answer to the committee's resolution to Dame Margaret Lloyd George, sent at the last meeting, the following reply was received from the Prime Minister's secretary:

With reference to your letter and enclosed resolution of the 22nd July, addressed to Dame Margaret Lloyd George, I am desired by the Prime Minister to say that much as he regrets the present state of affairs in Cornwall, the Government cannot see their way, at a time when nearly every industry is in difficulties, to pick out one for special favourable treatment. Mr Lloyd George wishes me to add that he hopes some of the companies may be able to secure grants from the Trade Facilities committee to tide over their present difficulties and that a revival in trade and rise in the price of tin may shortly help to restart the mines. Should you and your relief committee have anything in your mind as regards relief measures, the Prime Minister asks to suggest to you that you communicate straight with the Ministry of Health or the Ministry of Labour on the matter.

The Chairman observed that some of them knew what it was to apply to the Ministry of Health and the Ministry of Labour but, unless the Government departments could grant them something different to their present terms, it was no use.[15]

There was a varied response in the Cornish press. A writer from St Ives called for a peaceful constitutional response, suggesting that they should help the PM gain time to find a more favourable moment, and adding:

Too much should not be made of the alleged failure of Dame Margaret Lloyd George to understand the situation or the method by which it could be relieved. There were several reasons why Dame Margaret was disappointed. The arrangements were faulty,

and the 'platform' often unsuitable. The visit failed rather because it was neither wholly humanitarian, political, nor social. We are always for the straight issue. Hence what Cornwall thinks to-day Britain thinks to-morrow. Cornish choirs have been singing through the hills of Wales, and an echo of their tale of woe may have been heard at Pontypridd. Voices crying in the wilderness have been heard in strange places before now.
Reginald T. Reynolds, St Ives.[16]

And Mrs Lloyd George's efforts *were* recognised in the *Cornubian and Redruth Times*, albeit with the buck being passed more aggressively to the PM:

It is unfortunate that Dame Margaret Lloyd George's intervention with the Prime Minister on behalf of the Cornish miners has been unsuccessful. Nevertheless, she can be credited with womanly sympathy for the suffering unemployed.

Mr Lloyd George's letter is a true example of the attitude which makes him the worst peace Minister the country has known...[17]

The 'tale of woe' in Pontypridd, noted by Reginald Reynolds of St Ives, referred to the recent by-election defeat, at the hands of Labour, of Coalition Liberal T. A. Lewis, for whom Mrs Lloyd George had campaigned in 1918. He lost when seeking re-election after being appointed as a Junior Lord of the Treasury. This would prove to be the last time an MP lost their seat through promotion, that convention being abolished in 1926. Lewis returned to Parliament as MP for the University of Wales, but, of uncertain health, died in 1923.

Despite the disappointments, the Cornish mining crisis was about to abate, 1922 proving to be the nadir of tin production, though the later 1931 crash brought it almost as low. The Treasury started providing loans to tin mining in 1922 and in November Camborne re-elected a Coalition Liberal, Col. Algernon Moreing, a Lloyd George-supporting Australian-born civil and mining engineer, who had been appointed the first chairman of a Joint Industrial Council for tin mining formed in January 1919.[18]

Perhaps the final political tour of the wife of the Prime Minister had at least nudged things in the right direction. An Oxfordshire paper looked ahead:

> The western tour of Dame Margaret Lloyd George has been such a success that suggestions have already been made to headquarters that she should follow other itineraries elsewhere. But such a tour, with its long motor drives, receptions, and speech-making, means hard and exhausting labour, and friends in other parts of Britain who wish to be heartened by a visit from the Prime Minister's wife must 'wait and see'. Her western tour will long be remembered.[19]

It would prove to be her final major tour, one which reflected not only the limits to her influence in the harsh world of politics, but also the fact that the clock was running down on her husband's Coalition.

CHAPTER 18

# The Secret Missioner

## (July 1922)

MEANWHILE, 'THE URBANE' JTR hit the front page of the *Daily Herald*, when touring the country, on behalf of the Coalition Liberal Chief Whip's Office, drumming up support amongst the Free Church community.

From Our Own Correspondent, NORWICH, Thursday.—
The Rev. J. T. Rhys, a prominent Free Church minister, stated to be the emissary of Mr Lloyd George, yesterday visited Norwich and addressed a secret meeting of local Free Church ministers, and it is understood that a series of similar meetings are being called.

Not only was the meeting secret, but sacred, according to the chairman, Ald. J. H. Copeman, a prominent local Coalition Liberal.

It is presumed that he meant that the meeting, like all that are of any significance in connection with the Coalition, was sacredly secret.

Despite the secrecy, however, the weight of opinion is that the mission of the Rev. J. T. Rhys is not spiritual, but for the material purpose of securing the support of Free Church ministers for Mr Lloyd George at the next Election. His formidable task is to justify the Premier's past policy and ask for their views on current questions.

This early request for views is no doubt intended to give Mr Lloyd George ample time to think of the answers.

The 'secret and sacred' meeting called forth some strong criticism. Temperance and education were amongst the matters discussed.

Speakers pointed to the intemperance of Coalition legislation, and remarked upon the incongruity of ministers being called together by one of the authors of the unhappy and unchristian Treaty of Versailles. On education the Geddes proposals were vehemently challenged.

But Mr Rhys was urbanity itself, refused to be downed, and rather diplomatically invited the discontented to call at 10, Downing-street – the home of the super-diplomat.[1]

JTR's handwritten notes on his tours provide a first-hand analysis of the attitudes of Nonconformists around the country as confidence in Lloyd George weakened:

> During the past four months I have attended 10 Conferences attended by Free Church Ministers at centres as far apart as Newcastle & Camborne, and as different in their social complexion as Leeds, Hull, Portsmouth & Norwich. In addition I have personally interviewed practically all the Ministers in such constituencies as South Derbyshire & Forest of Dean.
>
> At each Conference & at each interview the first object has been to elicit the views of the Ministers themselves on politics in general & on the work of the Government in particular.
>
> Speaking generally it may be said that Free Church Ministers take a less active part in politics than at some periods in the history of the Free Churches. This is not to say that they are less interested. Two causes may be suggested as explaining this inactivity. First, the uncertainty as to what is to be the future policies of the two historic parties; and secondly, the growth of the Labour movement within the Churches which would make it difficult in very many ways for a Minister to take sides without rending his Church in twain.
>
> The questions asked at Conferences and interviews may roughly be divided into two categories: those in which some men or some localities are interested & those which have universal approval & excite passionate enthusiasm.
>
> In the first category I would include Religious Equality, Education, Land Reform, relation of Capital & Labour, Emigration, Housing & questions relating to Sunday and Liberal Reunion. (In no single instance has a Free Church Minister raised the question of Taxation!)

There are two & only two questions that might be said
to belong to the second category. They are the questions of
Temperance Reform & questions relation to World Peace.

In the regard to Temperance, interest is nationwide. It has
come up for consideration at every Conference & at practically
every interview. Interest, however, varies in intensity. Interest in
the Drink problem is least keen in agricultural areas & most keen
in industrial areas. In the North of England Ministers who have
a national reputation for social work have stated that they will
follow that political leader who offers the best hope of solving
this problem. They state as their reason for that attitude that a
considerable portion of their religious work is stultified by alcohol
& that their social efforts are frustrated by the influence of the
Drinking Clubs.

There are three [*sic*] observations that should be made in this
connection.

1. There is fairly general admission that a mistake was made in not
supporting the PM when he attempted to carry his scheme of State
Purchase & Local Option.

2. When it is pointed out that the Government, in spite of the
supposed power of Sir George Younger, has (a) passed the
Licensing Act of 1921 (b) sanctioned Temperance teaching in
schools & (c) refused to reduce taxation on beer & spirits, it is
conceded that Mr Lloyd George has not forfeited the confidence of
Temperance Reformers.

3. The Rev J. S. Sharp, President of the Wesleyan Conference, is
devoting the whole of his year of office to the task of arousing
the Wesleyan Church & also others to the imperative need of
Temperance Reform. Mr Sharp is meeting with considerable
success. An intimation that the PM is watching the movement
closely meets with cordial approval.

4. The vast majority of those to whom I have spoken realise that
in view of the fact that a Bill was passed last year, & that there
are so many other urgent & vital problems, it is unreasonable
to expect any Licensing legislation in the immediate future.[2]
(illustration 46)


An ardent temperance campaigner, it is not surprising that
JTR gives the subject prominence, including the view that it

had been a mistake not to support State Purchase & Local Option (Lloyd George's 'compromise' legislation that both JTR and Mrs Lloyd George backed).

The second group of questions which excite general enthusiasm are those connected with Peace. It is not too much to say that this problem overshadows every other & that the party which gives this its first place in its programme will rally to its support the Free Churches absolutely & enthusiastically. A study of the speeches of candidates at by-elections would confirm this.

Nothing has so contributed to alienate the Free Churches from the Prime Minister as the fear that he holds less firmly than formerly his Peace Principles. This fear was, I think, inspired by his political enemies who based their suggestions on three alleged facts: that he was determined to make Germany pay the whole cost of the War; that the Versailles Treaty was based on a French revenge; & that the League of Nations does not enjoy his support.

It has, of course, not been difficult to show that these alleged facts are fictions.

It was, however, the policy & efforts of Genoa that rallied & stabilised Free Church sentiment. It removed every doubt as to his loyalty to Peace principles and I am assured that so long as he champions that policy he will have the whole of the Free Churches with him.

Though one hears considerable criticism of the PM, yet he enjoys in a remarkable & rare degree the confidence and affection of the Free Church Ministers. This actually happened at a recent Conference. An Asquithian having offered some critical observations concluded: 'What I want to see is a reunion of the Liberal forces under Mr Lloyd George that will secure Liberalism for a generation to come.' He was followed by a member of the Labour Party who having offered some caustic criticism concluded by saying, 'Why does not Mr Lloyd George effect a Coalition with the Moderate Labour Leaders & so guarantee to the nation sane social progress?'

One may say that this is no less true of all the Free Church laymen who have acted as hosts at the Conferences e.g. Mr Carter Firth of Bradford, Alderman Copeman of Norwich.

The Asquithian suggestion had to be faced: coalition between Liberals and Unionists was unlikely to offer a convincing platform around which the Free Churches could rally, whilst some greater cohesion on the left might stand a chance of an alternative.

CHAPTER 19

# The Last 100 Days
## (July to October 1922)

As the West Country tour finished, Lloyd George's premiership had entered its last 100 days, but no one knew that then. Some may have predicted it. Some will have wondered how it had held on so long.

After the West Country tour, the usual summer social round included the wedding of Lord Louis Mountbatten at St Margaret's, Westminster, on 18th July: 'Miss Megan Lloyd George, in coffee-coloured georgette with a red bead girdle and red hat, came with Mrs Lloyd George.'[1] That evening, 'Mrs Lloyd George gave a dance for her daughter, Miss Megan, at 10 Downing Street, when there were about 150 guests, mostly young people.'[2] No sooner was it over than Mrs Lloyd George was preparing to make an early start to support her husband in Wales.

The following day Lloyd George received the Freedom of the Borough of Aberystwyth, an invitation which had taken two years to schedule. Although Mrs Lloyd George was not mentioned in any of the press comments beforehand, she did attend, as the *Western Mail* (which had the scoop) reported:

> Everyone appreciated the effort which Mrs Lloyd George had made to be present. Punctilious in her engagements, she had remained in London on Tuesday, and travelled alone in the early morning hours in order to be an eye-witness to the great reception that was assured to her husband in the collegiate town.
>
> The exclusive information in the *Western Mail* that Mrs Lloyd

George was expected had spread with astonishing quickness throughout the town, and when she appeared on the dais the acclamations of the audience were wonderfully cordial and demonstrative. She immediately preceded the mayor (Mr J. Barclay Jenkins), and took a seat alongside of Mrs Evan Evans, mother of Capt. Ernest Evans MP, who also had a splendid reception. Mrs Lloyd George was presented with a bouquet of carnations by Miss Lilys Jenkins, the little niece of the mayor.[3]

At the weekend, she travelled up from Chequers to Rushden, Northamptonshire, for lunch at Rushden Hall, before attending a fête at Higham Ferrers in aid of the Blind and Crippled Children's Fund. In the early evening she addressed a meeting at Rushden before returning to Chequers for dinner. Her speech at the meeting was a re-run of the West Country stump speech.

On her way from Rushden Hall, to the fête, she stopped off at the Rushden war memorial, and laid upon it a wreath, with the dedication: 'To the men of Rushden who gave their lives in the great war, from Dame Margaret Lloyd George, 22nd July 1922.'[4]

The dinner at Chequers was one for the inner circle, including Sir Auckland and Lady Geddes, Sir Eric Geddes, Sir Alfred and Lady Mond, Lord Riddell, and Lord and Lady Dawson.[5]

Back in London on 24th July there was more political entertaining at No. 10 for Coalition MPs, for representatives of the Yorkshire and West Country Coalition Liberals, and for a number of Nonconformist ministers (perhaps attended by JTR). Welsh singing was the chief part of the music programme and a photo album of the West Country tour was presented to Mrs Lloyd George.[6] (illustrations: book cover, 10, 14, 16, 20, 32, 37, 44)

The month closed amongst familiar campaigners, as Mrs Lloyd George again visited the Lynn-Thomases in south Wales to open the Cardigan and District War Memorial Hospital, another practical memorial to the fallen. Like the Cardiff Prince of Wales Hospital for the Limbless, the new hospital was using an existing building, this time the old Priory on the banks of the Teifi. 'There was a large influx of people into the town from over a wide area, and the old borough was gaily decorated with flags and bunting', and she and the Lynn-Thomases were accorded a civic welcome.

> Dame Margaret then inspected the ex-service men of the town and district, who had formed up along the road, and a procession followed from the public buildings to the hospital grounds.
>
> There was a touching incident at the opening of the proceedings when Private Tom Jones, of Blaenffos, who lost both legs in the war, mounted the platform and presented a bouquet to Dame Margaret Lloyd George, who shook hands with him heartily amid loud cheers.
>
> Dame Margaret Lloyd George congratulated Cardigan and district upon having such a practical war memorial. They wanted such hospitals in Wales, she said, and she was glad to see that they were springing up everywhere. She thought it was the war that had showed to them the need of those hospitals. Before that patients from Wales had to go to London, Liverpool, or Cardiff, and other places a long way off in order to be operated upon, when, perhaps, they could not stand the strain of the journey, and to have a hospital of their own would be a great blessing to that district. There could be no more practical object as a memorial to the brave men who lost their lives in the war than a hospital of that kind. Concluding in Welsh, she wished the institution every success and a beneficent career. [Applause]
>
> The Chairman announced that Sir John Lynn-Thomas was presenting to the institution radium which, in pre-war days, would have been worth over £200. [Applause]
>
> Responding to a vote of thanks, Dame Margaret said that she had a personal and motherly interest in that hospital. Her son was passing along there one day and he became the first out-patient at the hospital. He had a septic hand, and finding there was a hospital there he turned in and had it dressed. [Applause]
>
> The gathering sang the Welsh and English National Anthems, and then Dame Margaret, amid loud cheering, proceeded to

open the hospital. In the hall the medical and nursing staff were presented to her, and she then signed the visitors' book and visited the wards.[7]

Sir John Lynn-Thomas retired from the medical profession in 1921 and lived at Stradmore House, Cenarth, Carmarthenshire. In December he had written to JTR about obtaining a De Soutter leg, presumably for the Cardiff Hospital. Marcel and Charles Desoutter's company designed and manufactured artificial limbs and tools – initially a duralumin leg for Marcel after his had been amputated below the knee in 1913 following an accident flying a Bleriot plane.[8]

On 5th August, in Cricieth, Mrs Lloyd George hosted a meeting of ladies at Brynawelon, when 50 of them associated with four local lifeboat stations were enrolled as members of the Ladies' Guild established in connection with the Royal National Lifeboat Institution (one of her lifelong causes).[9]

A few days later the St John Hospitallers honoured her as a Lady of Grace of the Order of the Hospital of St John of Jerusalem in England.[10]

On 10th August she then 'signified her intention' to attend the Harlech Castle pageant to play a family scene with Gwilym and Megan (which she did). 'The PM hopes to attend on the day his family acts.'[11] (illustration 21)

September began with another promise: 'Mrs Lloyd George has consented to lay the foundation stone of a new Baptist church at Little Kimble, near Chequers.'[12] But on the day, Megan had to step in.

On 7th September, in 'delightful weather', the holder of the Cricieth annual bowling tournament's silver challenge cup, presented by Mrs Lloyd George in 1921, was surprisingly defeated in the first round.[13] A week later, on 14th September, in 'inclement weather', she presented the prizes at the International Sheep Dog Trials Society at Cricieth Golf Links. Lloyd George had recently become the first Welsh Patron of the Society.[14]

There was a positive update from Witham, where the Nurses' Bungalow Home she had opened in July 1921 was 'now quite free from debt, and is proving a great benefit to the inhabitants of Witham'.[15]

A report in the *Sheffield Daily Telegraph* listed Dame Margaret as one of the Patrons of 'The Cedars College Fund', supporting a college for blind girls at Chorleywood, Herts, which continues today.[16]

The *Illustrated London News* carried photographs of Mrs Lloyd George examining the remains of the old Roman fort of Segontium near Caernarfon.[17]

In Llandudno Megan again had to step in for her mother, at an event Mrs Lloyd George would have liked to attend, allotments being one of her causes.

> Miss Megan Lloyd George opened the annual show of the Llandudno Allotment Holders' Association on Saturday, and apologised for the absence of her mother, who had been called to London. The exhibits were greatly admired, the entries being a record. Miss Megan Lloyd George had a great reception from the large crowd of visitors who witnessed her arrival and departure.[18]

This was all good exposure for the young lady who one day would become the first Welsh woman to take a seat in the House of Commons. Mrs Lloyd George was meanwhile entertaining Cabinet ministers at Chequers, a social gathering with politics on the menu.

And if you can't be everywhere at once, you can send a telegram:

> Mme Clara Novello Davies, who has been celebrating her golden jubilee, was the recipient of many further tributes last night at the Castle-street Chapel, where Sir Vincent Evans presided over a 'full house'. A telegram from Dame Margaret Lloyd George was received, and many bouquets were presented to Mme Davies, who herself contributed to the evening's entertainment by conducting the 'Hallelujah'. She is sailing today for America in the *Aquitania*.[19]

Clara Novello Davies was a well-known Welsh singer, teacher and conductor (named after the famous soprano Clara Novello). She used the bardic name 'Pencerddes Morgannwg'. Her son, Ivor Novello, was the actor, composer, dramatist and director, once termed as 'the master of the musical' – one of his greatest songwriting successes was the October 1914 First World War song 'Keep the Home Fires Burning'.[20]

Another way of reducing the travelling is to get everyone to come to you, this time hosting an event at her Welsh home in the last week of September: a conference of the south Carnarvonshire branches of the North Wales Temperance Union at Brynawelon.[21]

On Wednesday, 5th October, she opened the new Girls' County School in Ruabon, noting that boys for years had had secondary schools, and now, as in other walks of life, the girls had been given their chance. The school had been built near Offa's Dyke, and she saw this proximity as an opportunity to stimulate the children to study the history of their own country, which she held to be of prime importance, 'though much neglected in these days'.[22]

On Thursday, 5th October, she was unable 'owing to a business engagement in North Wales' to keep a date in Newport to open a bazaar. Lady Sybil Rhondda, who took her place, noted that 'Mrs Lloyd George did enough work for ten women'.[23]

The next day, Mrs Lloyd George did get to Birmingham to open a bazaar, assuring her audience that 'the Prime Minister has made up his mind that for the rest of his life he is going to devote himself to securing peace.'[24]

In fact, peace was threatened, some would say by Lloyd George. The Chanak crisis, a conflict between Turkey and Greece, was under way, and Lloyd George was risking bringing the country, and the Empire, into the turmoil. His stance resulted in him to this day being hailed as a national hero in Greece, but it would also help to trigger his fall from power at home.

There were changes happening literally underfoot at No. 10 and No. 11:

The basements of 10 and 11 Downing Street are undergoing reconstruction. It goes deeper than the basements, indeed, for the foundations the houses have required attention of the kind known as 'underpinning' and workmen have been busy since the rise of Parliament.

All basements are to some decree abominable: dark, chilly, gloomy, labour-making abodes for the fostering of domestic discontent, and those of the great Ministers in Downing-Street are worse than any.

Mrs Lloyd George used to tell stories of what she found there when she went – airless, blackness, unhygienic inconvenience. She seems to have been one the first practical housekeepers to find her way to Downing Street. It may not have occurred to ladies brought up in the grand manner to penetrate below stairs, and promptly she set herself to have alterations and improvements made. She discovered that was easier said than done when she had Government departments to deal with, but she persevered.

There is an advantage in having a furnished residence to step into with the assumption of office, and of having necessary expenses connected with the dwelling paid for by the State. There are drawbacks also, and these the housewife soon discovers. Before she can have a cup and saucer all kinds of machinery have to be set in motion, and the chances are that she renews the articles herself long before red tape would permit her to have them.[25]

Politics and elections were now back on the agenda and on 11th October Mrs Lloyd George made two political speeches in East London. The first was at an afternoon reception and meeting at Burghley Hall, High Road, Leytonstone, chaired by Sir Walter Gibbons, Coalition candidate for the East Leyton Division. The second was an evening meeting in Romford with Tom Macnamara, now Minister of Health, as the chief speaker.[26]

Her key message was that the PM was now free to speak his

mind (a trailer for his coming Manchester speech), and that there might be an election soon. She delivered her full-throttle defence of her husband and of his government:

Dame Margaret George [*sic*], wife of the Premier, addressed a crowded and enthusiastic meeting of Coalitionists in Romford Corn Exchange last night. A large number of people were unable to obtain admission. Mrs Lloyd George, arriving with Dr Macnamara, Minister of Labour, was given a tremendous welcome. Mr W. Edwards, JP, presiding, said that was a unique occasion Romford had never before been so favoured. The Coalition parties were now banded together in common cause. He preferred to call it the Unity of Parties. In its dark days the country required a man of push and go, and the Premier was that man. [Cheers] He stepped into the breach, and his new methods won. [Cheers] All through his labours he had had the unstinted support of his wife. [Cheers]

Mrs Lloyd George, loudly cheered on rising, was presented with a bouquet by Miss Isobel Gerrard. She said it was the first time she had addressed a Romford meeting, but she had passed through their ancient town on many occasions, and had taken some pride in it. She felt as one of them, for her eldest son had come to live in Essex (at Springfield, Chelmsford).

We were living in times of great changes and many more had yet to come before life would be worth living for a good many of our fellow men and women. Home politics were overshadowed by foreign affairs and the Near East question. At times people were inclined to be a little impatient. The war was over, but its effect was not. The firm stand made by Great Britain had prevented war in the Near East. [Applause] They should thankful that the work of the Government had been successful, for the outcome of the trouble, anxiety, and labour of the past few weeks had been a great success. [Applause]

She was glad from another and a personal view, and felt that it left Mr Lloyd George free to speak his mind. [Hear, hear] He had been severely criticised in the newspapers. Some of the criticisms had been really abominable. Criticism was inevitable, and she was not adverse to it if it was fair. 'But I can assure you,' proceeded Mrs Lloyd George, 'that in his next speech Mr Lloyd George will answer that criticism, and that you who have been looking

forward to and anticipating a reply will not be disappointed.'
[Cheers]

Dr Macnamara said it was the portion of Dame Margaret
Lloyd George's day-by-day help to clear the burdens of care and
anxiety, more weighty surely than ever before, rested upon human
shoulders. All who knew her knew how loyally and how bravely
that duty was performed. He had never admired the Premier more
during the quarter of a century in which he had been his supporter
than he had during the last few anxious weeks. Faced with
misunderstanding, misrepresentation, and denunciation, he had
held patiently and steadfastly to his cause, seeking to secure for the
support and assistance of our Allies the freedom of the Straits.

Referring to the devastation caused by the war, Dr Macnamara
said the Government was doing its utmost to bring the labour
market round ... Much of the taxation of the day was necessary to
meet war obligations, one of the chief of which was the repayment
of war debts and pensions. Industrial depression was world-
wide in its incidence. The only true and permanent remedy was
to get the Wheels of trade going round again. Alluding to the
unemployment 'dole', Dr Macnamara said it was not a dole; neither
was it a grant – men were drawing back what they had paid in.
[Applause][27]

On Friday 13th she joined the Premier on the Macclesfield
train from Euston, en route for his speech in Manchester.
Megan stepped in at the unveiling of the foundation stone at
the church at Kimble, near Chequers:

... there was a notable gathering at this ceremony, with only one
disappointment. Dame Margaret Lloyd George was to have been
present and show the sympathy of herself and the Prime Minister
to the little place beneath the shadow of their trees, but the Prime
Minister was going north and it was the wifely duty to be with
him, and so she did not appear at Kimble. But in her stead sweet-
faced Miss Megan Lloyd George appeared, a happy little lady who
smilingly carried through all her duties and showed the keenest
interest in them all, and all about – especially in a golden half
sovereign tendered as one of the gifts to the church.[28]

While in the north, Lloyd George finally accepted the Freedom of Salford and of Blackpool. He had been unable to receive these honours in 1918 when he fell dangerously ill with the 'Spanish Flu'. His wife had cared for him for ten days in Manchester Town Hall. For a while he was on a ventilator. That was a battle he had come close to losing.

Now, in October 1922, he was battling for his political life. Having delivered his speech in Manchester, the Prime Minister returned to London. Mrs Lloyd George went to Colwyn Bay, where she attended a service with Gwilym and his wife Edna on the Sunday, and then stayed overnight with them at Rhos-on-Sea, before going on the next morning to sit on the Grand Jury at the Caernarfon Assizes.[29] It would not be long before Gwilym and Edna's first son, David, would be born.

The final by-election under the Coalition was in Newport, Monmouthshire, on 18th October. It was seen as a test of the Coalition, but Mrs Lloyd George did not campaign: the Unionists took the formerly Coalition Liberal seat, Labour coming second and the 'reunited Liberalism' Liberal candidate third. It is often debated as the election that finally broke the Coalition, though the end was probably already nigh.

On Thursday, 19th October, Mrs Lloyd George travelled down to Reigate to open, in the afternoon, an 'Olde Ryegate Fayre' at the Public Hall, in support of the town's Congregational Church.

At lunchtime, at the meeting of Conservatives at their Carlton Club, Pall Mall, Lloyd George's coalition partners voted to withdraw their support for the Coalition and to set up a government under Andrew Bonar Law, who surprisingly returned to the front line, having been in virtual retirement due to ill-health. That afternoon Lloyd George went to Buckingham Palace to offer the King his resignation. Unusually, the transition of power would take four days, though in reality Lloyd George's premiership was at an end.

In Reigate, Dame Margaret, in what was perhaps her last

such engagement as wife of the Prime Minister, offered her favourite line that a little debt was an incentive for people to keep busy – at the same time hoping the event would make more than their target. She also slipped in a word for the men:

> Some people said it was not a very good thing to clear off the whole of a debt, that there ought to be still some left in order to make people work. Her own Minister used to say that if he were to pay off the whole of the debt of the church, he must find something else in order to keep the congregation at work. She was sure that they of that congregation would find something to do in Reigate, probably in helping others, which was much better than helping themselves entirely.
>
> No doubt the ladies had had a lot to do with that Fair, for it generally fell on the shoulders of the ladies to prepare work of this kind, and she was glad, wherever she went, she always found a stall for the men. Men selling at a store were a great help, and showed that they were taking a real and keen interest in the sales. They knew that men did a great deal, behind the scenes, but now they were coming forward.[30]

Was she making sure of the male vote?

It fell to little Dorothy Jutson, the parson's daughter, to be one of the last to present a bouquet to Dame Margaret Lloyd George, 'wife of the Prime Minister'.

That evening, Dame Margaret went on the offensive again in East Ham:

> Speaking at East Ham last night, Mrs Lloyd George said her husband loved a fight. His spirit goes up and his health improves, and I am very pleased there is a fight going on, for then he gives me far less trouble. I know a fight is like a tonic to him, that he thoroughly enjoys it.[31]

She then motored to Barking where the Romford Coalition Party had arranged a meeting at the public baths (also a setting for concerts). When she rose to speak she had a mixed reception – loud booing mixed with cheers. She delivered her customary attack on unfair criticism and asked the audience to vote for the National Liberal candidate Captain Martin. He won the seat comfortably in the upcoming general election.[32]

This may well have been her final speech as wife of the PM, the transition from power having started that afternoon.

On 21st October, London's *Evening Standard* reported her reaction:

> Dame Margaret declares that though Thursday was so dramatic she was more or less 'out of it'. She had been out of town and then went down to the East End to speak at a women's meeting, not getting back to Downing Street until ten o'clock, when all was over, to find the ex-Premier calm and cheerful, and about to retire for the sound night's sleep which he can always depend on even in crises.[33]

CHAPTER 20

# Departure from Downing Street

## (November to December 1922)

LLOYD GEORGE TENDERED his resignation to the King on 19th
October. Bonar Law was to succeed him, but waited until he
had been elected leader of the Conservative Party, in succession
to Austen Chamberlain, who had resigned on the fall of the
Coalition. Lloyd George continued his planned schedule with
a trip to Leeds to receive the freedom of the city. He formally
handed over the seals of office to the King on 23rd October.
Mrs Lloyd George and the family had four days to move out of
Downing Street. (illustration 42)

On the 20th Mrs Lloyd George gave an interview to Edith
Shackleton, for the *Daily Sketch*:

> 'It is a long time we have been here,' went on Dame Margaret,
> looking out through the long windows to the yellowing trees
> across the Horse Guards Parade. 'My daughter Megan can scarcely
> remember any other London home than a Downing Street one.
> I suppose it is the busiest term of office any Prime Minister has
> ever had.' 'Or any Prime Minister's wife,' I suggested, for Dame
> Margaret shouldered countless dull duties and reigned during a
> period when glitter and gaiety were rare.[1]

On the afternoon of Friday, 20th October, Mr and Mrs
Lloyd George and a party of 100 left London for Leeds in a
special train. They were met with great shows of support at all

the stops. Back in 1918 it had been opposition from Labour in the local council that had stopped Leeds from offering Lloyd George, then 'the man who had won the war', the Freedom of the City. He now arrived, as ex-Premier, to collect his civic tribute.

Whilst in Leeds they stayed at Farnley Hall, with Leeds Central Liberal MP Robert Armitage and his wife, accompanied by the cameras. A former Lord Mayor of Leeds, Armitage would lose his seat to the Conservatives at the upcoming election, coming in third, just behind the Labour candidate.

Someone was keeping a close eye on Mrs Lloyd George's reactions when her husband was speaking in London to his supporters:

> Mr Lloyd George learns quickly. He was a day in Leeds, and he learnt the word 'jannock', which he worked off on his audience this morning. His bouts with M. Briand and M. Poincare have taught him to shrug his shoulders in thoroughly French fashion. He did so today when elaborating his metaphor about Unionists dismissing him from the citadel when the danger had diminished. He used every trick he ever learned. He employed a full dozen ornate metaphors or images, ranging from company promoting to whale fishing. His gestures never ceased, and must have given him more physical exercise than a round of golf.

Yet the speech did not sweep his audience off its feet. Dame Margaret Lloyd George, a good judge, never smiled or applauded once during its delivery, and, though he drew much applause from his imagery and quips, it was only once that the hero-worshippers before him, shouted 'Hooray!' That was when he threatened to 'assail Unionism all along the line, a thing he cannot do successfully, and does not desire to attempt'.[2]

On 23rd October Mrs Lloyd George followed her husband out of Downing Street for the last time.

Some of the moving wasn't going to be too hard, logistically at least:

Dame Margaret Lloyd George is going through one of the rough bits of a politician's wife's career, hustling out of Downing Street, and she is a thorough enough housewife to realise all its difficulties; but 'moving' from Chequers is merely an official affair, as no Prime Minister, in the domestic sense, can ever 'move in'! Chequers is furnished with appropriately historic and rare things, which must remain in their appointed places. All the rooms were photographed and catalogued when the house was handed over by Lord and Lady Lee, and according to these records the furnishings must remain. No Prime Minister's wife will be able to go down to Chequers, bundle its furniture into corners, and set out her own characteristic possessions. 'Removing' from there is, for the ladies of the family at least, only like removing from a week-end hotel.[3]

There was now a general election to fight. As many times before, the name of Mrs Lloyd George came up:

The name of Dame Margaret Lloyd George, Criccieth, wife of the ex-Premier, is freely discussed as a likely Liberal candidate for Merioneth. A meeting of the Women's Liberal Association is to be held to-day (Tuesday) at Barmouth.[4]

The *Sheffield Daily Telegraph* noted that the rumour was incorrect.[5] The Merioneth seat had been firmly held by Henry Haydn Jones, a Liberal, since 1910, who retained the seat until he stepped down in 1945, at the age of 81. Having supported and owned the local Talyllyn slate railway (now a Heritage Railway), he is immortalised as 'Sir Handel Brown' in the Rev. W. W. Awdry's *Thomas the Tank Engine* books. Haydn Jones was the brother of the Rev. J. D. Jones, the Bournemouth pastor collecting money at Milton Mount College.

But if Mrs Lloyd George wasn't standing for election, perhaps JTR, her former private secretary, could join the fray.

The *Western Mail* of Saturday, 4th November, reported that Lloyd George had decided, at the eleventh hour before nominations were due in, to field at least another 15 candidates to the 170 already selected, in retaliation against Conservatives for raiding National Liberal Seats. JTR was one of the eleventh-hour candidates:

> The full list of candidates will be available tomorrow afternoon
> after the nominations take place, but it is possible to announce a
> few of them tonight: in London it has been resolved to oppose one
> Minister, viz., Sir William Joynson-Hicks, Parliamentary Secretary
> of the Overseas Department, who is contesting Twickenham
> and was hitherto unopposed. Mr J. T. Rhys, formerly Mrs Lloyd
> George's private secretary, and lately associated with the National
> Liberal headquarters as an organiser, has been put forward in
> the National Liberal interest. Mr Rhys was formerly a minister
> at Pontycymmer and Swansea. He is a well-known temperance
> reformer.[6]

Johnson-Hicks, a prominent target, was going to be very hard to dislodge, especially with a local Labour candidate, Charles Joseph Clements, also in the ring.

Prior to this announcement, JTR had been in Bedford, supporting the outgoing Postmaster General F. G. Kellaway (who had been re-elected in 1921 when Labour objected to Mrs Lloyd George being serenaded by the school children).

> Queen's Park: The Rev. J. T. Rhys (who is one Mr Lloyd George's
> secretaries) [sic] said that he could remember every election since
> 1880, but the present was most peculiar. People did not know what
> they were fighting about. If the present Prime Minister did not
> know, how could they?
> Ampthill Road School: Pending Mr Kellaway's arrival, addresses
> were given by the Rev. J. T. Rhys from London; Colonel E. C.
> Complin, a Canadian, and Mrs Merry.[7]

In this four-way fight, the Unionist Party won the seat back from Kellaway, with 50.3 per cent of the vote, having not contested it during the Coalition days (Kellaway had been awarded the Coupon in 1918).

JTR's own campaign was short-lived:

The expected National Liberal opposition in the Twickenham Division of Middlesex to Sir William Joynson-Hicks, Parliamentary Secretary to the Overseas Trade Department, did not materialise. Mr J. T. Rhys, a former private secretary to Mr Lloyd George [*sic*] who was to have fought the seat, telegraphed early in the morning that he was too ill to undertake the contest.[8]

The *Western Mail* also reported:

The formation of the new Parliament began yesterday by the return of unopposed candidates. In many cases it would have been an almost impossible task to unseat ex-members, though in this election the number of uncontested seats is smaller than in 1918. The nominations provided one or two surprises. Only twelve of the eleventh-hour 'retaliation' candidates, the phrase officially adopted by the Lloyd George Liberals, appeared. At Twickenham, where Sir Joynson-Hicks had an unopposed return, Mr J. T. Rhys, a former secretary to Mrs Lloyd George, withdrew on account of illness. Co-operation between Conservatives and National Liberals in certain constituencies may still be sought before polling day.[9]

The Labour candidate had also failed to stand.

It is very possible that ill-health was an excuse to bow out with grace as the 'retaliation' candidates withdrew. In 1938, all JTR's obituaries cited the sudden illness, though his local paper, *The Richmond and Twickenham Times,* noted that 'when funds were low and the chances of success so remote that the party was in danger of losing its deposit, Mr Rhys, with his Radical tendencies, urged that the party should officially support the Labour candidate rather than the Conservative.'[10]

Also on the list of withdrawing 'retaliation' candidates was the Welshman Richard Morris, the former MP for North Battersea, one of the few attendees at the House of Commons dinner to celebrate Mrs Lloyd George's 1918 'Coupon' election campaign – but for whom she had not campaigned.

Meanwhile, Mrs Lloyd George had a husband and a son to get into Parliament. It meant that she had to disappoint the annual meeting of the British & Foreign Bible Society to be held at the Victoria Hall, Sheffield. This she would have regretted, the Bible Society being important to her.

> The secretaries of the Sheffield Auxiliary of the British and Foreign Bible Society received a wire last evening from Dame Margaret Lloyd George regretting that she will be unable to fulfil her promise to come to Sheffield on Thursday for the annual meetings of the society. She states that she infinitely regrets this decision, but is working in the Carnarvon Boroughs, and is unable to leave the constituency. The Lord Mayor has regretfully cancelled the reception he had arranged at the Town Hall on Thursday evening, when the friends of the Bible Society were to meet the wife of the ex-Premier.[11]

A trip to Bath with Lloyd George and Megan was also cancelled. Lloyd George was to have received the Freedom of the City; the cancellation was due to his having a winter cold.[12]

On 4th November Mrs Lloyd George's 56th birthday coincided with the arrival of her first grandson:

> Mrs Gwilym Lloyd George, wife of the ex-Prime Minister's second son, who is Liberal candidate for Pembroke, gave birth to a son, on Saturday, at her home at Rhos-on-Sea. Mother and son are doing well. Dame Margaret Lloyd George celebrated her own birthday on Saturday.[13]

The same day she signed her husband onto the nomination lists for the election, with the satisfaction that for the first time he would be unopposed:

> Mrs Lloyd George appeared to be in excellent spirits when representing her husband at the nomination on Saturday, and when one o'clock arrived and all fear of opposition dissipated (a last-minute candidate had been rumoured) she remarked, 'To-day is my birthday, and my husband is returned unopposed for the first time – a birthday present.' In the nomination paper, under the

heading of 'Rank, profession, or occupation,' Mr Lloyd George is described as Privy Councillor.[14]

Lloyd George could rely on some long-standing support:

Mrs Lloyd George handed in at Carnarvon a nomination paper on behalf of her husband, signed by twelve men who were schoolfellows at his father's school in Pwllheli. Another of Mr Lloyd George's nomination papers was signed wholly by old-age pensioners.[15]

When nominated by the Carnarvon Boroughs Liberal Association, the ex-PM also had the support of Mrs Lloyd George's fellow Councillor Leah Thomas, backing him on behalf of the Women's Liberal Association.[16]

In the second week of November, with the Carnarvon Boroughs secure, south Wales was the target, Lloyd George also campaigning on behalf of Gwilym:

On 9th November in Pembroke Dock, 'Mr Lloyd George was about to put the vote [of thanks to the Chairman] to the meeting, but there were loud cries for a speech from Mrs Lloyd George, who in seconding, said. 'I thank you for receiving us so kindly as a family. [Cheers and laughter] I am looking forward to your support from now till Wednesday for my son, and if you will trust him I am sure he will serve you faithfully in the House of Commons.' [Loud applause][17]

The next day she accompanied her campaigning husband at a large meeting at Swansea's new Albert Hall Cinema, attended by all the local National Liberal candidates, where he made his pitch for national unity. The mayoress and her daughter presented bouquets to Mrs Lloyd George and Megan respectively.[18]

Shortly before Remembrance Day, Dame Margaret sent a message to the women electors of Scotland:

I would like to convey my heartiest good wishes to the women of Scotland who will, I know, exercise their votes in the coming election. There never was a time in the history of this country when moderate counsels, such as women are preeminently fitted to give, were so necessary. Appeals to party, of selfishness, of reaction are the wrong appeals to make to women, whose interests – the interests of home, children, and peace – are the first consideration. My husband has fought strenuously all his life for peace, for better industrial conditions for the workers, and for equality of opportunity between man and man and man and woman. The women of Scotland will, I am sure, not fail to record their votes for those candidates who stand by him now.[19]

On Saturday, 11th November, the family tour continued through western Wales, arriving home in Cricieth, and processed home by torchlight. On Monday, 13th November, Lloyd George made a one-day tour by train, through north Wales, Mrs Lloyd George accompanying him as far as Flint. While Lloyd George went on to Lancashire, Mrs Lloyd George, and their son Richard, travelled to south Wales to rally support for Gwilym, who would be elected to join his father on the back benches.

The *Western Mail* of 11th November also featured a number of those awarded honours by Lloyd George in the Dissolution Honours List, including his private secretary J. T. Davies KCB, retiring MP Herbert Lewis GBE, and Sir Vincent Evans CH.[20]

The ex-PM was conserving his strength for the last lap of the election, even on Remembrance Sunday: In Caernarfon, 'Amongst the hundreds of beautiful wreaths deposited at the foot of the monument was one by Dame Margaret Lloyd George, on behalf of the ex-Premier'.[21]

The election saw a heavy defeat for the Liberal Party. The combined total of seats, Asquithian and for Lloyd George's party, came below the total for the Labour Party for the first time. However, the Lloyd George family doubled their tally of seats in Parliament. Seven years later they would be joined by Megan.

On 17th November there were still prizes to present for an essay competition on 'Safety First' run by the Kingsbury County Schools, Roe Green, north London, contested by 846 scholars, with 130,000 essays written.[22]

On 22nd November, a distinguished assembly drew a sad conclusion to the past decade's events:

> There were many moist eyes at Westminster yesterday, when the Prince unveiled the monument to members and sons of members who died the war. Mr Bonar Law and Mr Asquith stood in a row together, with Mr Lloyd George between. The monument contains the names of two sons of Mr Bonar Law and one of Mr Asquith, and both these parents were touched almost to the point of breaking down during the ceremony. Mr Bonar Law looked a tired old man. Elsewhere, Mrs Asquith had realised that Mrs Lloyd George was standing beside her, and the two conversed before the ceremony began, Mr Chamberlain being also of the group.[23]

On the evening of the 23rd she attended an 'At Home' hosted by Lady Astor at 4 St James' Square, where an assembly of peers and members of Parliament, and other notables, met the representatives of the International Council of Women and the Women's Suffrage Alliance.[24]

On 24th November, there was a bazaar to open at St Michael's Church Hall, Cricklewood, in aid of church funds.[25]

The next evening Mrs Lloyd George presided at the Castle Street Welsh Baptist Chapel, as President of the Young Wales Association, where Sir Walford Davies lectured and proposed the establishment of a choral union for the Welsh in London.[26]

On 6th December 1922, precisely six years since becoming wife of the Premier, Mrs Lloyd George, attired 'in black velvet with bands of moleskin and gold and black quills in her tricorne hat' attended a Commons 'At Home' hosted for members of the Society of Women Journalists by their Chairman, Lady Brittain, to meet leading MPs and to have 'the rare opportunity of visiting the Press Gallery'.[27]

On Friday, 8th December, she went down to Upper Norwood in support of peace:

No. 10 Downing-street had never known a nobler woman than Mrs Lloyd George, whose simplicity of life and character had been unchanging and untouched.

That was the graceful compliment paid to Mrs Lloyd George at Upper Norwood, last Friday, when she presided at a meeting in support of the League of Nations, at the Wesleyan Church. The speaker was Mr J. Hugh Edwards MP, a fluent, persuasive orator, who also has written a biography of the ex-Premier.

Mrs Lloyd George spoke for a few minutes as 'opener' of the proceedings.

She was sure, she said, they all wanted to know whether the League would succeed in persuading all the nations to join. 'We want peace,' she continued. 'We want the nations to have peace, and not to regard each other as potential enemies. No one wants another war. They knew what the world suffered in the last war. They wanted the League to stop war.' She was sure that every peace loving man and woman was anxious for the success of the League'.[28]

J. Hugh Edwards, one of Mrs Lloyd George's successful candidates on her 1918 south Wales campaign, had just lost his Neath seat, in a 24 per cent swing to Labour.

In the fortnight before Christmas she opened a sale of work at the Baptist Church in Mitcham, where she expressed sympathy with Sunday school work, which, she claimed, 'was more thorough in Wales than anywhere'.

On 19th December St Margaret's, Westminster, was 'filled to overflowing... for bride and bridegroom are immensely popular'. Megan was a bridesmaid for her long-time friend from Paris days, Ursula Norton-Griffith, who was marrying J. H. Thorpe MP – as noted earlier, their future son would become Liberal leader Jeremy Thorpe. The event was attended by familiar names: Griffith-Boscawen, Mond, and Ellis-Griffith. Ursula was also known as 'the 'monocled bride' for she did not discard the single eyeglass which she had worn since childhood, even on her wedding day.[29]

There was a new house to be warmed, with a party at their new home at Churt, near Farnham, Surrey, before celebrating Christmas in Algeçiras, Spain.[30]

And what did the immediate future hold for No. 10?

During the past week Mr Bonar Law has taken up his residence at No. 10, and for the time being his house at Onslow Gardens has been closed. It is extremely unlikely that activities, politically or socially at Downing-street, during the regime of the Prime Minister, will be comparable to those of Mr Lloyd George.

For one thing there will be no official hostess at No. 10, without which the social side of the Prime Minister's life must of necessity suffer. Bonar Law is accompanied by his younger daughter, who has hardly reached the age of fulfilling the duties of political hostess. If there should be functions needing the presence of an official hostess, Lady Sykes will support her father.

Very little renovation and practically no alterations have been found necessary to suit the homely tastes of the Prime Minister, and the domestic staff at No. 10 is the smallest known there for many years. Mrs Asquith, when at No. 10, required a round dozen, and Mrs Lloyd George found nine or ten none too many. Mr Bonar Law finds four or five sufficient to carry out the household duties of the establishment.[31]

In a friendly letter, back in May 1920, Bonar Law's daughter Isabel had addressed Mrs Lloyd George as 'Dear Mrs Weinidog', in reference to the Welsh for 'Minister', admonishing Mrs Lloyd George for not addressing her as Isabel: 'I do think it was horrid of you to call me 'Miss Law'. You generally remember that my name is Isabel!' Isabel, now Lady Sykes, had now replaced 'Mrs Weinidog' as the hostess of No. 10, helping her widowed father.[32] (illustration 43)

JTR would no longer be roaming the corridors of No. 10, able to rescue the mail sent to 'Prif Weinidog' which in 1921 had been sent back to the Post Office for forwarding (incorrectly) to a visiting Russian Trade delegation, leading him to exclaim to his colleagues that, 'You don't apparently know anything about the only pure language in existence. "Prif Weinidog" is "Principal Minister"'.[33]

Sophie Ries continued to work with Mrs Lloyd George at least until 1924, and, like her predecessor, sometimes struggling to get the post to the right place.[34]

# CHAPTER 21

# An Insider's View
## (October 1922)

THE DAY AFTER the formal handover of power JTR wrote to his eldest daughter Margaret, my aunt, then just turned 19, who had asked for his views on what was happening:[1]

61 Sydenham Park SE 26
24.10.22

My dear Pegs

To give you an exhaustive & accurate account of the dramatic movements in the political world of the last few days is beyond my power & beyond the power indeed of any human being, for a complete account would involve a knowledge not only of party intrigue, but of the varying & various motives which activate men in crises of this nature. Still, I will very gladly give you some of my own impressions.

To begin, we whose work it was to defend the Lloyd George Coalition felt that a change was both inevitable and desirable. It was inevitable because the position of the Government had been very greatly weakened in the Country as has been abundantly proved by the by-elections. Governments generally lose by-elections, and Ll.G's government was no exception. Indeed when one remembers that most contests were three-cornered ones the wonder is that our people did so well. Besides, the intrigues within the Tory Party, & by the Tory party in the Government added immensely to Ll.G's difficulties. In a sense, therefore, the fall of the Govt. brought immense relief.

I also think a change was desirable. The effect of the attacks on the Govt. had been to weaken the efforts of our representatives abroad & so made a Settlement of European problems difficult if not impossible. That has its bearing on Home affairs: for lives of nations are today so international that we can't make progress here commercially & industrially [?] unless & until Europe is on its feet. If Ll.G. had been loyally supported by the Nation, settlement would have been effected long ago, but it was the interest of some parties to thwart him. In passing I might say that in Germany Ll.G. is a great hero & they had every confidence in him, but it is not so in France because he is opposed to French militarism.

Though we all felt a change was coming & wished it to come, still none of us expected it to come so soon nor in the way it came. Most of us expected the Government would last until the Spring & that then the two wings would dissolve by mutual consent. But we knew little of the intriguing that had been going on behind the scenes. Even Chamberlain & his Tory friends were in the dark. People here are rather severe on Bonar Law. They say he did not play the game either with Lloyd George or with Chamberlain. It is fairly certain if he had been loyal, the Fall would have been postponed. What motives actuated him I know not.

Not being a prophet I can say nothing regarding the future. Whatever happens nothing will surprise me. The problems much discussed now are: Will Chamberlain & his party stand by Ll.G? or will they return to the Tory fold? I think, & in a way I hope they will. What about the Liberals? Will the two sections always unite? That is being discussed. I hope they will, but my faith is weak for the Independent Liberals are very bitter and vindictive. My own view is that prior to the election some kind of understanding will be arrived at, & that after the election the two sections will be practically but not formally united. A quarrel does not take long to make but to restore friendship is a slower business. That is true of politics, but not of politics only.

Meanwhile Ll.G's supporters are full of fight & of hope. I think that for him 'the best is yet to be'. He is in the prime of life, is admittedly the most brilliant living statesman, & those who know him best believe in him most.

Heaps of love, your affectionate Dad

Like Mrs Lloyd George, JTR didn't think it was the end of the game for Lloyd George. But then, he was close to the scene, and an admirer. A year later, JTR observed, in one of his public lectures:

> British public life did not furnish a parallel to the political friendship that existed between the late Mr Bonar Law and Mr Lloyd George. During the years they were colleagues, their mutual confidence was unique, and when Mr Bonar Law resigned the blow was almost the heaviest Mr Lloyd George had received during his public life.[2]

In 1923 JTR did find a seat in Twickenham, but as pastor of the Twickenham Congregational Chapel. It was probably as political a seat as the one in Westminster, the congregation being at war with itself. He continued to write on politics, contributing to the *Western Mail* and the *Welsh Gazette*, toured the country with his 'lantern talks' on 'Lloyd George As I Knew Him', or on 'Downing Street from Within', and in 1923 tried to arrange an American tour of lectures on that basis. Trying that, in the same year as Mr and Mrs Lloyd George were also in the USA, was either good timing, or bad timing.

In October 1923, a year after the fall of the Coalition, when lecturing on '10, Downing-street', JTR commented thus on Lloyd George:

> He had a gift amounting almost to genius for profiting by failures without brooding over them. His mind was on the task to be accomplished, leaving the dead past to bury its load. So he was always full of hope and faith.[3]

JTR continued to be an active member of the Welsh political and Nonconformist community.

At the end of 1923, with friends still urging him to run for Parliament, JTR resisted and wrote to his daughter with his reasons:

> I am keenly interested in politics which rightly interpreted means the application of the teaching of the New Testament to the

problems of the day. But I am not very anxious to enter Parliament as the atmosphere would not suit me. It is a world of great intrigue and I would not be happy in that I could take no part in that kind of thing.

Mrs Lloyd George perhaps shared similar sentiments.

During the short-lived Labour Government of 1924, JTR contributed a strong critique of Ramsay MacDonald's administration, for his weekly 'Janitor' column (possibly a play on 'JTR) for the *Welsh Gazette* – the Rees/Rhys brothers sought to get along despite their different views over Lloyd George.

In June 1924 he spoke for Howard Williams (son of a Congregational Minister and former private secretary of Sir John Simon) at the Lewes by-election – Williams, however, came third behind the Unionist winner, and Labour. At the general election that October, on the fall of the Labour Government, JTR worked the South Hackney election for Capt. Garro Jones, former private secretary of Sir Hamar Greenwood, and again son of a Congregationalist Minister (who had trained at Brecon College, like JTR). Garro Jones won the seat, defeating Labour's Herbert Morrison in one of the surprise wins for the Liberals.

In 1927 JTR did not please some fellow Liberals by writing to *The Times* arguing that Nancy Astor should still be unopposed in her Plymouth constituency, despite Coalition days being over. She appreciated his gesture.

In 1929 JTR was back in South Hackney, the election agent for Miss Muriel Morgan Gibbon, again a daughter of a Congregational Minister, but this time she came third, Morrison winning the seat. In the 1931 election Muriel spoke in support of Herbert Morrison and joined the Labour Party that November, as would Garro Jones.

Campaigning for private secretaries and children of Congregationalist Ministers seemed to be a speciality. JTR campaigned for road safety, even from the pulpit, and stood in for fellow-pastors when they took Sabbaticals.

He continued to network within the Free Church community and led cruises for the Free Church Touring Guild. In 1937, the tour on the SS *Richmond* to Palestine and Greece was eventful, the 1,000 passengers, including a party of 65 pilgrims from Wales, having to stay a little longer when the ship lost its moorings in a storm off Tel Aviv. The party included the Rev. Elvet Lewis, albeit blind by this time, ministers from Lampeter, and Mrs Lloyd George's fellow councillors Leah Thomas and D. Williams from Cricieth.

On 9th July 1937 there was a reunion for JTR and his wife Jane Rhys with Dame Margaret and her granddaughter Margaret Carey Evans (who had been looked after by my grandmother some 17 years earlier), when they all attended the opening by Queen Mary of a new medical wing of the King George V Building of St Bartholomew's Hospital. JTR was then a Governor and Chairman of the Finance Committee.

After JTR's death in 1938, David and Margaret Lloyd George headed the subscription list for the tribute carved for him in the first church he had built, in Pontycymer in the Garw mining valley in Glamorganshire. She wrote:

> Mr Rhys devoted a great deal of his time to the work of a Secretary for me during the war. He was very careful of my interests in every way, and a great help in that very trying and anxious time. He took some of the burden and a great deal of the work off my shoulders. I always think of him and the work he did with gratitude.

With the generous annotation: 'Do you need more money?'

A kind reflection on a warm working relationship, amidst a challenging, changing world of stress and intrigue, of great human loss and hard-to-meet new expectations.

In his lecture notes, JTR wrote:

> No one [was] more easily managed. My main task was to restrain her from overdoing herself in doing good. No PM [was] more fortunate in [his] wife. No-one has added more lustre to [the] position.[4]

# Postscript

DAME MARGARET SERVED on the Cricieth Urban District Council for the rest of her life, and was Chairman from 1931 to 1934. Whilst she stood by her commitment not to stand for Parliament, she remained a JP and a Councillor; a decade later she campaigned for Megan, who became the Member for Anglesey in 1929. Both Mr and Mrs Lloyd George also stood by their commitment to always be Liberal, though their children went in divergent ways, Megan to the left, to the Labour Party, and Gwilym to the right, to the Conservatives.

JTR's Notes recorded some of her reflections:

> Electioneering: No ground of personal complaint seeing Husband, son & daughter and only one defeat in – contests. My experience must be unique. All my work unpaid. Taken for granted I should do it. Why wives of some people should work hard and no pay I don't know – curates, ministers, doctors, lawyers, grocers... Curious.
>
> And on speaking after 40 years' experience: give people good stuff – help them to find a sound verdict. Public appreciates good food esp. when well-cooked and well-served.[1]

Margaret and David Lloyd George then mainly lived apart, he in London and at the new house Bron-y-de in Churt, Surrey (with Frances Stevenson), where he also engaged quite profitably in farming; she at Brynawelon, Cricieth.

Margaret Lloyd George died on 20th January 1941, after breaking her hip in a fall at home, which led to a period of illness. Heavy snows prevented Lloyd George from arriving in time to say his goodbyes.

It is perhaps fitting that our narrative should be closed, first, with more from the tribute written by Ernie Evans in October 1922, when Margaret Lloyd George left Downing Street:

> Mr Lloyd George's departure from No. 10 Downing-street is an event of great political significance; Mrs Lloyd George's is an event of great social interest.
>
> I have written 'social' with a small 's' for, in regard to the more limited and exclusive meaning which attaches to the word when spelt with a capital letter, it may be said that Mrs Lloyd George was in Society, but not of it. Her interests lay elsewhere.
>
> In many ways her career is not less remarkable than that of her husband. Though a member of an old and honoured family, her early life was spent in the solitude of the countryside, where no calls of a public nature interfered with the routine of her home life on her father's farm, and no social gaieties disturbed its quietude.

Ernie Evans then expounded on her talent as a public speaker:

> It has truly been said of Mrs Lloyd George that she was able to turn an official residence into a home – a gift not commonly disposed. Mrs Lloyd George has truly been described as a second Mrs Gladstone on account of the care she has taken in watching over the health of her husband.
>
> Coupled with those qualities is a pretty wit. 'She is just like one of us' is a comment often heard. She would probably regard the comment as a compliment. Some people seek popularity by being unnatural; Mrs Lloyd George has achieved it by remaining natural.
>
> She leaves Downing-street with as much unconcern as she entered it. During the full period of her residence there, she has thrown open the doors to innumerable charities, and has acted as hostess on countless occasions of both private and public character. It was in recognition of her outstanding services, particularly to war charities, that the King in 1920 conferred upon her the honour which now makes it incumbent on us to refer to her officially as 'Dame Margaret Lloyd George'.[2]

Yet, after all the furious debates and conflicts, dividing

nations, political allies, families, it would be appropriate to remember the words of the Wee Free writer in a Leicester newspaper (quoted earlier):

> Dame Margaret is so obviously what we may all desire to be, a real good woman doing her utmost to tread worthily the path in which the fates have placed her.

# Endnotes

## The Inspiration

1 My grandfather was generally referred to as JT, but for this work I have used JTR to avoid confusion with J. T. Davies, private secretary to Lloyd George, generally referred to in letters, in notes and in the literature as JT. My grandfather was known at No. 10 as the 'other JT', or 'Little JT'.

2 *Daily Mirror*, 18.11.1916, p.10.

3 *The Sketch*, 28.7.1915, p.14.

4 JTR Notes for a possible autobiography of Dame Margaret Lloyd George, GBE, JP, henceforth JTR Notes. JTR Private Collection.

5 Richard Lloyd George/Viscount Gwynedd, *Dame Margaret*, p.184.

## Chapter 1: Margaret Lloyd George: The Story So Far

1 JTR Notes.

2 Ibid.

3 Ffion Hague, *The Pain and the Privilege* (Harper Perennial, London 2008), pp.55–6.

4 DLG to MLG, 19.11.1895. Cited in Kenneth O. Morgan, *Lloyd George Family Letters 1885–1936* (University of Wales Press and Oxford University Press), p.91; and Ffion Hague, *The Pain and the Privilege* (Harper Perennial, 2009 edition) p.270.

5 *Carmarthen Weekly Reporter*, 30.1.1915, p.4.

6 JTR, 'Lloyd George As I Knew Him', lecture notes, JTR Private Collection.

7 *The Richmond and Twickenham Times*, 9.7.1938.

8 *Chart and Compass*, BFSS, June 1917, pp.109–110. With thanks to the Society's archivists.

## Chapter 2: Peace and the 'Coupon Election'

1 Margaret Lloyd George, 'How do you help your husband?', typed draft A. J. Sylvester Papers, C25, NLW.

2 JTR Notes.

3 Since 1912 the Tory party had been named the Conservative and Unionist Party.

4 In May 1918 Field Marshal General Sir Frederick Maurice alleged that the War Cabinet had misled the Parliament over troop strengths,

at a time when Lloyd George was seeking to gain more control over the conduct of the war. Asquith attacked Lloyd George, dividing the Liberal Party. Whatever the truth in the allegations, they were not proven, Maurice broke military protocol by writing to *The Times*, and Lloyd George survived the vote, strengthening his arm in prosecuting the war. But it did lasting damage to the Liberal Party by exposing the Asquith–Lloyd George divide. In an unpublished letter to Mrs Lloyd George, in the JTR Private Collection, Lloyd George wrote 'I mean to go down fighting'.

5   Dame Margaret Lloyd George, 'What it means to be the wife of the Prime Minister of England', Sixth Instalment, 20472C LG Papers, 1, NLW. This passage was not included in the published version of the article in *Sunday News*, 4.9.1927.

6   *Newcastle Journal*, 16.11.1918, p.4.

7   Margaret Holborn, Women's Suffrage – February 1918, *Guardian* online 5.2.2018, accessed 25.8.2021.

8   Margaret Lloyd George, interview, 'How do you help your husband?', typed draft A. J. Sylvester Papers, AJS C25, NLW.

9   Charles T. King, *The Asquith Parliament (1906–1909)* (Hutchinson & Co., 1910), p.319.

10  Ernest Evans, 'Homely Chatelaine of 10, Downing Street, powerful influence of the ex-premier's wife', *Daily Mirror*, 27.10.1922, p.8.

11  Olwen Carey Evans, *Lloyd George Was My Father* (Gomer Press 1985), p.103.

12  *Sheffield Daily Telegraph*, 21.11.1918, p.6.

13  *Aberdeen Daily Journal*, 29.11.1918, p.2.

14  *Western Mail*, 9.12.1918, p.3.

15  *Cambria Daily Leader*, 9.12.1918, p.7.

16  *Western Mail*, 9.12.1918, p.3.

17  *Sheffield Independent*, 13.12.1918, p.7.

18  *Daily Mirror*, 9.12.1918, p.2.

19  *Western Mail*, 9.12.1918, p.3.

20  *Amman Valley Chronicle and East Carmarthen News*, 12.12.1918, p.4.

21  *Western Mail*, 7.12.1918, p.5.

22  Ibid.

23  John M. McEwen (Ed.), *The Riddell Diaries: a selection, 1908-1923* (Athlone Press, 1986), p.352.

24  *Hartlepool Northern Daily Mail*, 9.12.1918, p.3.

25  *Western Mail*, 9.12.1918, p.3.

26  JTR Notes.

27  *Western Mail*, 9.12.1918, p.3.

28  *Liverpool Daily Post and Mercury*, 11.12.1918, p.8.

29  *Chester Chronicle*, Saturday 14.12.1918, p.3.

30  *North Wales Chronicle*, 13.12.1918, p.5.

31  *The Sketch*, 18.12.18, pp.4–5.

32  *Carmarthen Journal*, 13.12.1918, p.1.

33  DLG to MLG, 13.12.1918. *Lloyd George Family Letters*, p.188.

34  *Dundee Evening Telegraph*, 27.2.1919, p.4.

35  *Western Mail*, 30.12.1918, p.3.
36  *Cambrian News*, 28.2.1919, p.5.
37  *Sheffield Evening Telegraph*, 27.12.1918, p.4.
38  *Pall Mall Gazette*, 30.12.1918, p.3.
39  Alice Balfour to Mrs Lloyd George, 2.2.1919, Letter 67, JTR Private Collection.
40  *Coventry Evening Telegraph*, 31.12.1918, p.1.

**Chapter 3: Settling the Peace.**

1   Ffion Hague, *The Pain and the Privilege*, p.347.
2   Based on letters from Megan to JTR in the JTR Private Collection.
3   Consuelo Marlborough to Mrs Lloyd George, 1.2.1919, Letter 109, JTR Private Collection.
4   *Glamorgan Gazette*, 14.2.19, p.3.
5   *North Wales Chronicle*, 14.2.1919, p.3.
6   Ibid.
7   Ibid.
8   Ibid.
9   *Daily Herald*, 22.2.1919, p.2.
10  From *How do you help your husband?*, A. J. Sylvester papers, page 4, AJS C25, NLW.
11  *The Times*, 26.2.1914, p11.
12  *Derby Daily Telegraph*, 13.2.1919, p.2.
13  Mrs Lloyd George to JTR, 30.1.1919, Letter MLG22, JTR Private Collection.
14  JTR MLG SP3 Derby, Rev. J. T. Rhys (Margaret Lloyd George) Papers, NLW.
15  The speech, in Mrs Lloyd George's hand, is one of the few in the NLW Collection from her time at No.10, aside from those from the JTR Collection. Lloyd George Papers 1, Speech to the Welsh Temperance Society, 20472C, 3019, NLW. Translation by J. Graham Jones.
16  *Sheffield Daily Telegraph*, 4.3.1919, p.6.
17  *Daily Telegraph*, 1.3.1919.
18  *The Landswoman*, 1.3.1919, p.8. Translation by Yvonne Davies, Drefach, Llanwenog, Ceredigion.
19  *Yorkshire Herald*, 12.3.1919.
20  Ibid.
21  *Western Times*, 15.3.1919, p.2.
22  *The Scotsman* 17.3.1919, p.7.
23  JTR MLG SP6 Royal Sanitary Institute, Rev. J. T. Rhys (Margaret Lloyd George) Papers, NLW.
24  *Pall Mall Gazette* 18.3.1919, p.2.
25  *Grantham Journal*, 29.3.1919, p.7.
26  *Hull Daily Mail*, 4.4.1919, p.4.
27  *Western Mail*, 24.3.1919, p.4.
28  *Heywood Advertiser*, 4.4.1919, p.2.
29  *Cambria Daily Leader*, 9.4.1919, p.3.
30  *Carnarvon and Denbigh Herald*, 2.5.1919, p.7.

31  *Labour Leader*, 10.4.1919, p.7.
32  *The Millgate Monthly: A Popular Magazine Devoted to Association, Education, Literature & General Advancement*, published by the Cooperative Newspaper Society Ltd., Manchester. Reported in the *Leicester Daily Post*, 25.3.1919, p.3.
33  Dame Margaret Lloyd George, *Petticoats behind Politics*, 12.6.1927, NLW.
34  *Pall Mall Gazette*, 1.4.1919, p.9.
35  *Cambrian News*, 11.4.1919, p.5.
36  *Le Journal*, 7.4.19, pp.1,2.
37  *Liverpool Echo*, 7.4.1919, p.6.
38  Ibid.
39  *The Bioscope*, 17.4.1919, p.99.
40  *Carmarthen Journal*, 18.4.1919, p.1.
41  *Yorkshire Post*, 8.5.1919, p.6.
42  *Western Mail*, 10.5.1919, p.5.
43  *The Rhondda Leader*, 24.5.1919, p.5.
44  *Western Mail*, 16.5.1919, p.4.
45  *Pall Mall Gazette*, 19.5.1919, p.3.
46  'The London Letter', *Aberdeen Press and Journal*, 22.5.1919, p.4.
47  *Western Mail*, 23.5.1919, p.5.
48  *Pall Mall Gazette*, 29.5.1919, p.1.

## Chapter 4: The 'Lampeter Incident' and Peace Day

1  *Cambrian News*, 6.6.1919. p.5.
2  Notes from her speech in JTR MLGSP4 Garreglwyd, Holyhead, Rev. J. T. Rhys (Margaret Lloyd George) Papers, NLW. The *North Wales Chronicle*, 20.6.1919, p.8, carried a full report.
3  *Cambrian News*, 11.4.1919, p.8.
4  Matthew Cragoe, 'The Anatomy of an Eviction Campaign: the General Election in 1868 in Wales and its Aftermath', *Rural History*, Vol. 9, Issue 2, October 1998, pp.173–193, published online by Cambridge University Press, 31.10.2008.
5  *Welsh Gazette Jubilee, 1899–1949*, 'Recollections of Half a Century' by Mr James Rees, 1949, ABY/X/115 Archifdy Ceredigion Archives
6  *Cambrian News*, 20.6.1919, p.6.
7  *Cambrian News*, 20.6.1919, p.5.
8  A copy of her speech, in JTR's handwriting, is at the NLW: JTR MLG SP5 Lampeter Cardiganshire Liberals, Rev. J. T. Rhys (Margaret Lloyd George) Papers, NLW.
9  *Western Mail*, 19.6.1919, p.4.
10 MLG to JTR, undated note. MLG30, JTR Private Collection.
11 For a fuller account see Richard Rhys O'Brien, *Mrs Lloyd George Comes to Lampeter*, published June 2019, Museum of Lampeter.
12 *North Wales Chronicle*, 27.6.1919, p.4.
13 *Yr Herald Cymraeg*, 1.7.1919, p.4.
14 Marie Corelli to Mrs Lloyd George, 23.6.1919. Letter 113, JTR Private Collection.

15    Dame Clara Butt to Mrs Lloyd George,19.5.1919. Letter 83, JTR
      Private Collection.
16    *Westminster Gazette*, 7.6.1919, p.4.
17    *Cambria Daily Leader*, 30.6.1919, p.4.
18    *Daily Graphic*, reported in *Yorkshire Post*, 26.6.1919, p.10.
19    *Pall Mall Gazette*, 24.6.1919, p.3.
20    *Common Cause*, 4.7.1919, p.1.
21    The article appeared at least in the *Liverpool Courier*, 30.6.1919
      (reported in the *Derby Daily Telegraph*, 30.6.1919, in *Pall Mall Gazette*,
      30.6.1919, p.2). A typescript has survived in the JTR archive: JTR
      MLG SP8 'Women and Peace on Earth', Rev. J. T. Rhys (Margaret
      Lloyd George) Papers, NLW.
22    *South Wales Weekly Post*, 12.7.1919, p.3.
23    *Western Mail*, 7.7.1919, p.4.
24    *Staffordshire Sentinel*, 14.7.1919, p.4.
25    *Sheffield Daily Telegraph*, 19.7.1919 p.8.
26    *Cambrian News*, 25.7.1919, p.8.
27    *Pall Mall Gazette*, 30.7.1919, p.1.
28    *Richmond and Twickenham Times*, 9.7.1938.
29    *Western Daily Press*, 1.8.1919, p.6.
30    *Western Mail*, 28.7.1919, p.4.
31    *Dundee Evening Telegraph*, 4.8.1919, p.10.

## Chapter 5: From the Normandy Coast to the Spen Valley

1     *Western Mail*, 7.8.1919, p.5. The successful bard was Cledlyn (D. R.
      Davies) of Cardiganshire, whose own 1939 history of his parish of
      Llanwenog, close to Lampeter, makes particular reference to JTR's
      siblings and his father.
2     *North Wales Chronicle*, 15.8.1919, p.8.
3     *Pall Mall Gazette*, 19.9.1919, p.2.
4     *Hull Daily Mail*, 22.9.1919, p.7.
5     *Sheffield Evening Telegraph*, 20.9.1919, p.3.
6     *Aberdeen Daily Journal*, 14.10.1919, p.4.
7     JTR MLG SP9 Bangor, Normal College , Rev. J. T. Rhys (Margaret
      Lloyd George) Papers, NLW.
8     *Daily Telegraph*, 27.10.1919.
9     *The Scotsman*, 1.11.1919, p.9.
10    Richard O'Brien, 'The Missing Mahogany WW1 Memorial, Mrs
      Lloyd George and the Royal Dental Hospital Twenty-Nine', *Dental
      Historian*, Vol. 67 (2), July 2022; and 'Mrs Lloyd George and the first
      Women Students at the Royal School of Dentists, 1916 to 1926',
      *Dental Historian*, Vol. 65 (1), January 2020; and speech in MLG SP10,
      Rev. J. T. Rhys (Margaret Lloyd George) Papers, NLW.
11    *East London Observer*, 15.11.1919, p.3. Written here as reported.
12    'Petticoats behind Politics' by Dame Margaret Lloyd George DBE,
      typescript for release in the *Sunday Herald*, 12.6.1927, NLW.
13    *Hamilton Daily Times*, 15.11.1919, p.7.
14    JTR, MLG, SP11 Plymouth, Rev. J. T. Rhys (Margaret Lloyd George)
      Papers, NLW.

15   *Daily Telegraph*, 13.11.1919. The ILP (Independent Labour Party) was the political party founded by Keir Hardie in 1893.
16   JTR, MLG, SP11 Plymouth, Rev. J. T. Rhys (Margaret Lloyd George) Papers, NLW.
17   Lady Astor to Mrs Lloyd George, Letter 3, JTR Private Collection.
18   Lord Astor to Mrs Lloyd George, Letter 5, JTR Private Collection.
19   *Caerphilly Journal*, 7.2.1920, p.2.
20   *Pall Mall Gazette*, 19.11.1919, p.11.
21   *The Tatler*, 19.11.1919, p.4.
22   *The Scotsman*,21.11.1919, p.6.
23   *Western Mail*, 20.11.1919, p.7.
24   Helena, Princess Christian to Mrs Lloyd George, 18.11.1919. Letter 11, JTR Private Collection.
25   *Western Mail*, 22.11.1919, p.6.
26   Ibid.
27   *Llangollen Advertiser*, 5.12.1919, p.5.
28   JTR MLG SP12 YWCA Bazaar, Rev. J. T. Rhys (Margaret Lloyd George) Papers, NLW.
29   *Y Llan*, 12.12.1919, p.3.
30   *Yorkshire Post*, 12.12.1919, p.5.
31   *Daily Telegraph*, 6.12.1919.
32   *Western Mail*, 12.12.1919, p.6.
33   Ibid.
34   *Dundee Evening Telegraph*, 2.2.1920, p.2.
35   MLG to JTR, 12.4.1920, Postcard, Letter MLG33, JTR Private Collection.
36   *Caernarvon & Denbigh Herald*, 2.1.1920, p.7.

## Chapter 6: Campaigning from North to South

1    *Common Cause*, 16.1.1920, p.11.
2    *Daily Telegraph*, 9.1.1920.
3    *The Women's Leader* and *The Common Cause*.
4    *Common Cause*, 23.7.1920, p.2.
5    *Nottingham Journal*, 7.1.1920, p.8; *Daily Telegraph*, 7.1.1920.
6    Lord Astor to Mrs Lloyd George, 8.12.1919. Letter 5, JTR Private Collection.
7    *Dundee Courier*, 16.1.1920, p.8.
8    *London Letter, The Devon and Exeter Gazette*, 29.1.1920, p.4.
9    *The Bystander*, 17.3.1920, p.9.
10   *Edinburgh Evening News*, 20.1.1920, p.3.
11   Frances Stevenson (ed.), A. J. P. Taylor, 'Lloyd George: A Diary', 17.1.1920, page 196 (uncorrected proof edition), (Hutchinson, 1971).
12   *Daily Herald*, 4.2.1920, p.4.
13   *Aberdeen Press and Journal*, 6.2.1920, p.5.
14   *Pall Mall Gazette*, 7.2.1920, p.7.
15   Olwen Carey Evans, *Lloyd George was my Father*, pp.105–108.
16   *Western Mail*, 13.2.1920, p.6.
17   For an excellent recent review of Edith's life see 'The Good Life of

Edith Picton-Turbervill' in *Rocking the Boat, Welsh Women Who Championed Equality 1840–1990*, by Angela V. John (Parthian, 2018).
18 *Hendon & Finchley Times*, 27.2.1920, p.5.
19 *Western Mail*, 2.3.1920, p.7.
20 *The Globe*, 28.2.1920, p.4.
21 Princess Alice to Mrs Lloyd George, 8.3.1920. Letter 13, JTR Private Collection.
22 Princess Alice, Countess of Athlone, to Mrs Lloyd George, 6.10.1920. Letter 14, JTR Collection.
23 JTR MLG SP13 'On Temperance', Rev. J. T. Rhys (Margaret Lloyd George) Papers, NLW.
24 *Western Daily Press*, 5.3.1920, p.10.
25 *Bournemouth Guardian*, 13.3.1920, p.9.
26 *Western Gazette*, 12.3.1920, p.10.
27 *News Chronicle*, 12.1.1938, cited in Ffion Hague, p.499.
28 *Cambria Daily Leader*, 5.12.1913, p.8.
29 *Daily Telegraph*, 15.3.1920; 17.3.1920.
30 *Ealing Gazette and West Middlesex Observer*, 20.3.1920, p.5.
31 *Pall Mall Gazette*, 19.3.1920, p.11.
32 *Cambridge Daily News*, 24.3.1920, p.3.
33 *Pall Mall Gazette*, 18.3.1920, p.9.
34 *Western Evening Herald*, 26.3.1920, p.3.
35 JTR MLG SP14 Stockport Women's Groups, Rev. J. T. Rhys (Margaret Lloyd George) Papers, NLW. In JTR's hand.
36 *The Yorkshire Post*, 26.3.1920, p.10.
37 *Daily Telegraph*, 22.3.1920; 23.3.1920; 26.3.1920.
38 JTR MLG SP15 Camberwell Women's Rally, Rev. J. T. Rhys (Margaret Lloyd George) Papers, NLW. In JTR's hand.
39 Dame Margaret Lloyd George DBE, 'Petticoats behind Politics', typescript for release in the *Sunday Herald*, 12.6.1927, NLW.
40 *Kensington Post*, 26.3.1920, p.9.
41 Dame Margaret Lloyd George DBE, 'Petticoats behind Politics', typescript for release in the *Sunday Herald*, 12.6.1927, NLW.
42 *Pall Mall Gazette*, 23.4.1920, p.4.
43 *Clifton and Redland Free Press*, 27.5.1920, p.2.
44 *The Globe*, 8.4.1920, p.3.

## Chapter 7: Mid-year Miscellany
1 *Lancashire Evening Post*, 3.4.1920, p.3.
2 *Exeter and Plymouth Gazette*, 5.4.1920, p.1.
3 *Leeds Mercury* 12.4.1920, p.10.
4 *The Scotsman*, 14.4.1920, p.11.
5 *The Globe*, 16.4.1920, p.4.
6 *Montrose Standard*, 16.4.1920, p.6.
7 *Western Mail*, 26.4.1920, p.5.
8 *The Globe*, 27.4.1920, p.4.
9 *Liverpool Echo*, 30.4.1920, p.8.
10 *The Globe*, 5.5.1920, p.4.

11   Ffion Hague, *The Pain and the Privilege*, p.367.
12   *Framlingham Weekly News*, 1.5.1920, p.1.
13   *Daily Telegraph*, 18.5.1920.
14   *The Scotsman*, 18.5.1920, p.4.
15   Mary Drew to MLG, 19.5.1920. Letter 25, JTR Private Collection.
16   *Dundee Evening Telegraph*, 1.6.1920, p.7.
17   *Cheshire Observer*, 14.8.1920, p.6.
18   Ibid.
19   *Daily Telegraph*, 4.6.1920.
20   MLG to JTR, Letter MLG 15 JTR Private Collection. It was the first presentation at Court for Megan.
21   *Dundee Evening Telegraph*, 8.6.1920, p.1.
22   *Western Gazette*, 18.6.1920, p.12.
23   *Daily Telegraph*, 12.6.1920.
24   Christopher Addison to Mrs Lloyd George, 11.6.1920. Letter 33, JTR Private Collection.
25   *The Scotsman* 14.6.1920, p.6.
26   *Aberdeen Press and Journal*, 18.6.1920, p.4.
27   *The Globe*, 18.6.1920, p.7.
28   *The Scotsman* 19.6.1920, p.8.
29   *Birmingham Gazette*, 28.6.1920, p.5.
30   *Daily Telegraph*, 2.7.1920.
31   *Acton Gazette*, 9.7.1920, p.3.
32   *Western Mail*, 3.7.1920, p.8.
33   *Western Mail*, 15.7.1920 p.4.
34   *Hull Daily Mail*, 17.7.1920 p.1.
35   *Pall Mall Gazette*, 24.6.1920, p.9.
36   Letters 52,45,44,42,38 in the JTR Private Collection, plus *Pall Mall Gazette*, 19.7.1920, and *Western Mail*, 22.7.1920, p.5.
37   *Belfast News-Letter*, 27.7.1920, p.8.
38   *Western Mail*, 27.7.1920, p.5.
39   *Western Mail*, 6.8.1920, p.4.
40   *Banbury Advertiser*, 12.8.1920, p.3.

## Chapter 8: Dame Margaret

1   *Western Mail*, 23.8.1920, p.4.
2   *Belfast News-Letter*, 23.9.1920, p.6.
3   *Daily Telegraph*, 25.8.1920.
4   MLG to JTR. Letter MLG 6, JTR Private Collection.
5   Peter Lord (ed.), *Between Two Worlds: The Diary of Winifred Coombe Tennant, 1909–1924* (National Library of Wales, 2011), p.294.
6   *Aberdeen Press and Journal*, 20.10.1920, p.4.
7   http://www.londonwelsh.org/about-us/history-of-the-centre/
8   *Western Mail*, 22.10.1920, p.6.
9   JTR, MLG, SP17 Brown's, Chester, Rev. J. T. Rhys (Margaret Lloyd George) Papers, NLW.
10   *Cheshire Observer*, 30.10.1920, p.9.
11   Clementine Churchill to Mrs Lloyd George, 22.10.1920. Letter 1, JTR Private Collection

12   *Hull Daily Mail*, 4.11.1920, p.3.
13   *Essex Newsman*, 6.11.1920, p.4.
14   *Sheffield Independent*, 8.11.1920, p.8.
15   *Sunday Post*, 14.11.1920, p.11.
16   *Sheffield Independent*, 4.11.1920, p.5.
17   *Daily Telegraph*, 5.11.1920.
18   *Leeds Mercury*, 9.11.1920, p.9; *Pall Mall Gazette*, 8.11.1920, p.7; *Belfast News-Letter*, 10.11.1920, p.5.
19   *Pall Mall Gazette*, 9.11.1920, p.7.
20   *Coventry Evening Telegraph*, 12.11.1920, p.6.
21   *Leeds Mercury*, 13.11.1920, p.1.
22   *Falkirk Herald*, 14.1.1914, p.5 and *Forfar Herald*, 16.1.1914, p.3.
23   *Time and Tide*, 12.11.1920, pp.545–6.
24   *Pall Mall Gazette*, 10.11.1920, p.9.
25   *Pall Mall Gazette*, 24.11.1920, p.9.
26   *Sheffield Daily Telegraph*, 26.11.1920, p.4.
27   *Daily Telegraph*, 27.11.1920.
28   *Leicester Daily Post*, 29.11.1920, p.1.
29   *Daily Telegraph*, 1.12.1920.
30   *Western Mail*, 4.12.1920, p.7.
31   *Yorkshire Post*, 6.12.1920, p.5.
32   *Newcastle Daily Chronicle*, 10.12.1920, p.5.
33   *Western Gazette*, 10.12.1920, p.12.
34   Lettice Fisher to Mrs Lloyd George, 17.12.1920. Letter 103, JTR Private Collection.
35   *Daily Telegraph*, 17.12.1920.
36   *Aberdeen Press and Journal*, 29.12.1920, p.4.
37   Gwilym Lloyd George to JTR, 16.12.1920. Letter GLG2, JTR Private Collection.

## Chapter 9: From Chequers to Cardiganshire

1    From Olwen Carey Evans to JTR, 7.1.1921, OCE6, JTR Private Collection.
2    Olwen Carey Evans, *Lloyd George was my Father* (Gomer Press, 1985), pp.116–17.
3    *Berks and Oxon Advertiser*, 14.1.1921, p.3.
4    From 'Interview with Edith Shackleton', *The Sketch*, 21.10.1922.
5    *The Vote*, 14.1.1921, p.4.
6    *The Vote*, 21.1.1921, p.3.
7    *Liverpool Echo*, 20.1.1921, p.4.
8    *Western Mail*, 20.1.1921, p.7.
9    *Daily Telegraph*, 25.1.1921.
10   MLG to JTR, 4.1.1921. Letter 48, JTR Private Collection.
11   *Birmingham Gazette*, 5.2.1921, p.1.
12   *Nottingham Journal*, 8.2.1921, p.4.
13   MLG to JTR, Letter 17, JTR Private Collection.
14   *The Tatler*, 13.4.1921, p.38.
15   *Western Mail*, 27.1.1921, p.6.

16  *The Times*, 11.2.1921, p.10.
17  *Western Mail*, 27.1.1921, p.6.
18  *Western Mail*, 10.1.1921, p.6.
19  *Western Mail*, 27.1.1921, p.6.
20  *The Times*, 11.2.1921, p.10.
21  *Western Mail*, 8.3.1921, p.4.
22  *Western Mail*, 9.2.1921, p.5.
23  *Cambrian News*, 15.2.1921; cited by Dr J. Graham Jones in his comprehensive review of the election reprinted as Chapter 14, J. Graham Jones, *David Lloyd George and Welsh Liberalism*, first appearing in the *Journal of Liberal Democratic History*, 37 (Winter 2002–3).
24  *Western Mail*, 9.2.1921, pp5–6.
25  Cited in J. Graham Jones, 'Dame Margaret in Cardiganshire, Ceredigion', *Journal of the Cardiganshire Historical Society*, 2004, Vol XIV, No. 4, citing DLG letter to his wife: NLW MS 22,823C, ff. 74–75, DLG, 10 Downing Street, to MLG, 9.2.1921.
26  *Birmingham Gazette*, 28.1.1921, p.4.
27  *Western Mail*, 8.2.1921, p.6.
28  *Western Mail*, 9.2.1921, p.5.
29  *Western Mail*, 11.2.1921, p.7.
30  *The Times*, 11.2.1921, p.10.
31  Ibid.
32  *Western Mail*, 12.2.1921, p.8.
33  *The Times*, 12.2.1921, p.10.
34  *Welsh Gazette*, 10.2.1921, p.4.
35  *The Times*, 12.2.1921, p.10.
36  *Western Mail*, 12.2.1921, p.8.
37  *Western Mail*, 9.2.1921, p.5.
38  *Western Mail*, 3.2.1921, p.5.
39  *Western Mail*, 2.2.1921, p.5.
40  *Western Mail*, 9.2.1921, p.6.
41  *Welsh Gazette*, 10.2.1921, p.4.

## Chapter 10: Cardiganshire Decides

1   NLW MS 22,823C. f.76, DLG to MLG, 14.2.1921, in J. Graham Jones, *Dame Margaret in Cardiganshire*.
2   *The Scotsman*, 15.2.1921, p.5.
3   *The Times*, 16.2.1921, p.11.
4   J. Graham Jones, *Dame Margaret in Cardiganshire*.
5   *The Times*, 16.2.1921, p.11.
6   *Manchester Guardian*, 18.2.1921.
7   Peter Lord (ed.), *Between Two Worlds*, p.312.
8   *Western Mail*, 17.2.1921, p.5.
9   *The Times*, 17.2.1921, p.12.
10  *Western Mail*, 18.2.1921, p.7.
11  *Manchester Guardian*, 18.2.1921.
12  *Western Mail*, 17.2.1921, pp.5–6.

13  *Western Mail*, 17.2.1921, p. 6.
14  *The Times*, 17.2.1921, p.12.
15  *Hartlepool Northern Daily Mail*, 18.2.1921, p.8.
16  Peter Lord (ed.), *Between Two Worlds*, p.311.
17  *Manchester Evening News*, 17.2.1921, p.4.
18  *Aberdeen Press and Journal*, 16.2.1921, p.4.
19  *Dundee Evening Telegraph*, 1.3.1921, p.4. Corrected spellings would be Eglwysfach, Ysbyty Ystwyth, Llanfihangel y creuddyn.
20  *Western Daily Press*, 21.2.1921, p.5.
21  *Western Mail*, 23.2.1921, p.6.
22  *Western Gazette*, 25.2.1921, p.12.
23  *Flintshire County Herald*, 4.3.1921, p.6, and handwritten in JTR Collection.
24  *Sunday Post*, 27.2.1921, p.11.
25  David Lloyd George to Olwen Carey Evans, cited in J. Graham Jones, *Dame Margaret in Cardiganshire*, p.39.
26  *Birmingham Gazette*, 22.2.1921, p.4.
27  Mrs Lloyd George, in a speech after the Cardiganshire election, recalled by Ernest Evans in his 1922 tribute. *Daily Mirror*, 27.10.1922, p.8.
28  *Sunday Pictorial*, 27.2.1921, p.13.

## Chapter 11: The By-elections Continue

1   *Flintshire County Herald*, 4.3.1921, p.4.
2   *Western Mail*, 2.3.1921, p.8.
3   *Daily Telegraph*, 2.3.1921.
4   *Hull Daily Mail*, 3.3.1921, p.6.
5   Thelma Cazalet-Keir, *From the Wings* (Bodley Head, 1967), p.61.
6   *Sheffield Daily Telegraph*, 3.3.1921, p.6.
7   *Sheffield Daily Telegraph*, 4.3.1921, p.4.
8   *Sheffield Daily Telegraph*, 4.3.1921, p.6.
9   *Sheffield Daily Independent*, 4.3.1921, p.5.
10  *The Tatler*, 16.3.1921, p.5.
11  *Lancashire Evening Post*, 12.3.1921, p.2.
12  Thelma Cazalet-Keir, *From the Wings* (Bodley Head, 1967), p.57–8.
13  Peter Lord (ed.), *Between Two Worlds*, p.315.
14  *Daily Telegraph*, 12.3.1921.
15  *The Scotsman*, 17.3.1921, p.6.
16  *Western Mail*, 17.3.1921, p.4.
17  *Sheffield Independent*, 18.3.1921, p.1.
18  JTR MLG SP18 Llandudno Women's Liberal Association, Rev. J. T. Rhys (Margaret Lloyd George) Papers, NLW.
19  *North Wales Weekly News*, 7.4.1921, p.6.
20  *Taunton Courier*, 13.4.1921, p.7.
21  *Daily Herald*, 5.4.1921, p.5.
22  *Taunton Courier*, 13.4.1921, p.7.
23  Ibid.
24  *Daily Telegraph*, 18.4. 1921, 21.4.1921.

25 *Belfast News-Letter*, 20.4.1921, p.6.
26 *Biggleswade Chronicle*, 6.5.1921, p.5.
27 *Tewkesbury Register and Agricultural Gazette*, 23.4.1921, p.2.
28 *Dundee Evening Telegraph*, 22.4.1921, p.4.
29 *Western Mail*, 22.4.1921, p.5.
30 JTR MLG SP19 Baptist Women's League, Rev. J. T. Rhys (Margaret Lloyd George) Papers, NLW. This is one of the few instances where two handwritten copies of her speech still exist, one in her hand (in the original NLW Collection) and one in the hand of JTR.
31 *Western Mail*, 28.4.1921, p.4.
32 *Hendon and Finchley Times*, 29.4.1921, p.8.
33 *Belfast News-Letter*, 3.5.1921, p.2.
34 *Western Mail*, 28.4.1921, p.4.
35 *Montrose Standard*, 6.5.1921, p.6.
36 *Guardian*, 21.4.1921, p.7.
37 *Freeman's Journal*, 5.5.1921, p.4.
38 JTR MLG SP16 Women's Total Abstinence Union, Rev. J. T. Rhys (Margaret Lloyd George) Papers, NLW.

## Chapter 12: The Gloves Come Off

1 *Pall Mall Gazette*, 7.5.1921, p.3.
2 JTR MLG SP20 London Coalition Liberal Council Launch, Rev. J. T. Rhys (Margaret Lloyd George) Papers, NLW.
3 *Western Mail*, 12.11.1920, p.8.
4 *Western Mail*, 4.2.1921, p.6.
5 'London Letter', newspaper unknown 13.7.1938, JTR Private Collection.
6 *Evening Standard*, 7.5.1921, p.4.
7 *Mansfield Reporter*, 8.4.1921, p.5.
8 *Western Mail*, 9.5.1921, p.4.
9 JTR Notes.
10 JTR MLG SP23 Carnarvon Boroughs, Rev. J. T. Rhys (Margaret Lloyd George) Papers, NLW.
11 JTR MLG SP22 Llanfairfechan, Rev. J. T. Rhys (Margaret Lloyd George) Papers, NLW.
12 *Sunday News*, 4.9.1927, p.10.
13 Ernest Evans, 'Homely Chatelaine of 10, Downing Street: powerful influence of the ex-Premier's wife'. *Daily Mirror*, 27.10.1921, p.8.
14 Viscount Gwynedd, *Dame Margaret*, p.180.
15 *Nottingham Journal*, 3.5.1921, p.4.
16 JTR MLG SP21 Sunday School Bloomsbury Central Baptist Church, Rev. J. T. Rhys (Margaret Lloyd George) Papers, NLW.
17 From an appreciation of Mrs Lloyd George, quoting an anonymous observer, *Observer*, 15.5.1921.
18 *Yorkshire Post*, 28.5.1921, p.10, and *The Era*, 1.6.1921, p.8.
19 *Hastings and St Leonards Observer*, 4.6.1921, p.9.

## Chapter 13: Pure Milk, Pure Minds

1   *Hendon and Finchley Times*, 10.6.1921, p.6.
2   *Hull Daily Mail*, 2.6.1921, p.6.
3   Olwen Carey Evans to JTR, 3.6.1921, Letter OCE7 JTR Private Collection.
4   *Bucks Herald*, 4.6.1921, p.9.
5   *Bucks Examiner*, 10.6.1921, p.4.
6   *Sunday Post*, 5.6.1921, p.8.
7   Letter 1 MLG to JTR, JTR Private Collection.
8   *Worthing Herald*, 11.6.1921, p.3.
9   *Western Mail*, 14.6.1921, p.4.
10  JTR MLG SP24 'On Temperance, Purity and Religion', Porthmadog, Rev. J. T. Rhys (Margaret Lloyd George) Papers, NLW. Translation by Yvonne Davies.
11  'The Work of the Divorce Court', *The Times*, 2.6.1921, p.11.
12  JTR MLG SP25 Unveiling of Portrait, Dr John Morgan Jones, Porthmadog, Rev. J. T. Rhys (Margaret Lloyd George) Papers, NLW. The speech is in JTR's hand, on 9 sheets of small-size 10 Downing Street notepaper.
13  *Manchester Evening News*, 14.6.1921, p.4.
14  *Sunderland Daily Echo and Shipping Gazette*, 15.4.1921, p.3.
15  *Derby Daily Telegraph*, 15.6.1921, p.3.
16  JTR to Margaret Teify Rhys, 21.6.1921, JTR Private Collection.
17  Margaret Whitley to Mrs Lloyd George, 21.6.1921. Letter 101, JTR Private Collection.
18  Hilda Harwood, *The History of Milton Mount College* (Independent Press, London, 1959.
19  JTR MLG SP26 Milton Mount College, Rev. J. T. Rhys (Margaret Lloyd George) Papers, NLW.
20  JTR MLG SP28 Notes for Mrs Lloyd George on Education, Rev. J. T. Rhys (Margaret Lloyd George) Papers, NLW.
21  George M. Ll Davies to Mrs Lloyd George, 28.6.1921. Letter 107, JTR Private Collection. For an extensive discussion of Davies' efforts for the cause of peace in Ireland, see Dr Jen Llywelyn, *Pilgrim of Peace* (Y Lolfa, 2016).
22  *Hampshire Advertiser*, 2.7.1921, p.6.
23  *Western Morning News*, 28.6.1921, p.4.
24  *Liverpool Post*, 30.6.1921.
25  JTR MLG SP31 British & Foreign Bible Society, Rev. J. T. Rhys (Margaret Lloyd George) Papers, NLW. Translation by Yvonne Davies.
26  See also his entry in the *Dictionary of Welsh Biography* by Reverend John Edward Hughes, 1959.

## Chapter 14: The Summer Round

1   *Leeds Mercury*, 7.7.1921, p.7.
2   *Aberdeen Daily Journal*, 7.7.1921, p.5.
3   *Western Mail*, 4.7.1921, p.5.

4   JTR Notes.
5   *Luton Reporter*, 5.7.1921, p.6.
6   *Luton Reporter*, 12.7.1921, p.2.
7   Peter Lord (ed.), *Between Two Worlds*, p.328.
8   *The Scotsman*, 9.7.1921, p.10.
9   *Sunday Mirror*, 10.7.1921, p.13.
10  *The Bioscope*, 14.7.1921, p.10.
11  *Western Mail*, 12.7.1921, p.6.
12  *Daily Telegraph*, 14.7.1921.
13  *Western Mail*, 12.7.1921, p.6.
14  Ibid.
15  Evidence based solely on Marie Willingdon to Mrs Lloyd George,
    June 1921. Letters 39 and 40, JTR Private Collection.
16  *The Scotsman*, 13.7.1921, p.6.
17  *The Graphic*, 25.6.1921, p.10. Maharao is a variation on the term
    Maharaja.
18  *Belfast News-Letter*, 14.7.1921, p.4.
19  *Western Mail*, 15.7.1921, p.5.
20  *Sheffield Independent*, 16.7.1921, p.1.
21  *Daily Telegraph*, 20.7.1921.
22  *Chelmsford Chronicle*, 22.7.1921, p.5.
23  Ibid.
24  Ivy Chamberlain to Mrs Lloyd George, 28.6.1921. Letter 10, JTR
    Private Collection.
25  Ivy Chamberlain to Mrs Lloyd George, 21.6.1921 Letter 9, JTR Private
    Collection.
26  Almina Carnarvon to Mrs Lloyd George, 19.7.1921 Letter 102, JTR
    Private Collection.
27  *Northampton Daily Echo*, 15.7.1921, p.8.
28  Peter Lord (ed.), *Between Two Worlds*, p.328–9.
29  *Dundee Evening Telegraph*, 25.7.1921, p.9.
30  *Western Mail*, 5.8.1921, p.4.
31  Peter Lord (ed.), *Between Two Worlds*, p.329.
32  Herbert Lewis to JTR, 26.7.1921. Letter 105, JTR Private Collection.
33  *Western Mail*, 26.7.1921, p.4.
34  Ibid.
35  JTR MLG SP29 Bristol, Rev. J. T. Rhys (Margaret Lloyd George)
    Papers, NLW.

## Chapter 15: Time for a Break

1   *Western Mail*, 6.8.1921, p.7.
2   *Northampton Echo*, 8.8.1921, p.2.
3   Mrs Lloyd George to JTR, 18.8.1921. Letter MLG5, JTR Private
    Collection.
4   Olwen Carey Evans to JTR. Letter OCE9, JTR Private Collection.
5   John M. McEwen, *Riddell Diaries*, 15.8.1921, p.352.
6   *Yorkshire Post*, 8.9.1921, p.7.
7   Megan Lloyd George to JTR. Letter MeganLG8, JTR Private Collection.

8 Megan Lloyd George to JTR. Letter MeganLG9, JTR Private Collection.
9 Megan Lloyd George to JTR. Letter MeganLG10, JTR Private Collection.
10 Lloyd George to Megan, undated. Letter MeganLG12, JTR Private Collection.
11 JTR Notes.
12 *Dundee Evening Telegraph*, 7.10.1921, p.2.
13 *Western Mail*, 10.10.1921, p.5.
14 *Nottingham Journal*, 7.10.1921, p.4.
15 *Sheffield Daily Telegraph*, 10.10.1921, p.4.
16 *The Scotsman*, 1.10.1921, p.8.
17 *Newcastle Daily Chronicle*, 10.10.1921, p.5.
18 Olwen Carey Evans to JTR, undated. Letter OCE10, JTR Private Collection.
19 Mrs Lloyd George to JTR, undated. Letter MLG18, JTR Private Collection.
20 *Lincolnshire Echo*, 10.10.1921, p.3.
21 *Yorkshire Post*, 15.10.1921, p.12.
22 *Daily Telegraph*, 18.10.1921.
23 *Daily Telegraph*, 21.10.1921.
24 *Staffordshire Sentinel*, 24.10.1921, p.2.
25 *Nottingham Journal*, 21.10.1921, p.4. Not to be confused with Lady Violet Markham, aunt of Dame Lucy.
26 JTR MLG SP30 Coalition Liberals, Leicester, Rev. J. T. Rhys (Margaret Lloyd George) Papers, NLW.
27 Dora Burgess and L. Griffith-Jones to Mrs Lloyd George, 25.10.1921, Letter 55, JTR Private Collection.
28 Robert Cecil to Mrs Lloyd George, October 1921. Letter 18, JTR Private Collection.
29 Thelma Cazalet to Mrs Lloyd George, 1.11.1921. Letter 56, JTR Private Collection.
30 Thelma Cazalet to JTR, 1.11.1921. Letter 57, JTR Private Collection.
31 *Pall Mall Gazette*, 3.11.1921, p.9.
32 *Manchester Evening News*, 5.11.1921, p.3.
33 *Pall Mall Gazette*, 9.11.1921, p.7.
34 *Pall Mall Gazette*, 12.11.1921, p.3.
35 *Daily Telegraph*, 12.11.1921.
36 *Pall Mall Gazette*, 16.11.1921, p.1.
37 *Chelmsford Chronicle*, 2.12.1921, p.5.
38 *Nottingham Journal*, 1.12.1921, p.5.
39 Lord Leverhulme to Mrs Lloyd George, 5.12.1921 9.12.1921. Letters 77, 78, JTR Private Collection.
40 Mary FitzAlan to Mrs Lloyd George, 9.12.1921. Letter 97, JTR Private Collection.
41 *Daily News*, 8.12.1921, p.5.
42 *Western Mail*, 10.12.1921, p.8.
43 Frank Leggatt to JTR, 12.12.1921. Letter OJTR4 JTR Private Collection.

44 *Western Mail*, 20.12.1921, p.4.
45 *Sheffield Daily Telegraph*, 20.12.1921, p.5.
46 *Pall Mall Gazette*, 20.12.1921, p.4.
47 Margaret Wintringham to Mrs Lloyd George, 4.1.1922. Letter 80, JTR Private Collection.
48 *Pall Mall Gazette*, 22.12.1921, p.9.
49 Arthur Bourchier to Mrs Lloyd George, 6.12.1921. Letter 19, JTR Private Collection.
50 *Daily Herald*, 23.12.1921, p.5.
51 *Liverpool Echo*, 27.12.1921, p.2.
52 *Western Mail*, 27.12.1921, p.5.
53 *Observer*, 25.12.2921, p.7.
54 Mrs Lloyd George to JTR Christmas 1921 (albeit undated). Letter MLG11, JTR Private Collection.
55 *Yorkshire Evening Post*, 28.12.1921, p.4.
56 *Leeds Mercury*, 28.12.1921, p.5.
57 John Jones to JTR and to Lord Stamfordham, 31.12.1921. Letters 86 and 87, JTR Private Collection.
58 John M. McEwen, *Riddell Diaries*, p.358.

## Chapter 16: Changing the Guard

1 *Western Mail*, 3.1.1922, p.5.
2 *Western Mail*, 7.1.1922, p.7.
3 *Framlingham Weekly News*, 7.1.1922, p.2.
4 *Western Mail*, 21.1.1922, p.4.
5 *The Scotsman*, 21.1.1922, p.8.
6 *Western Mail*, 21.1.1922, p.5.
7 Peter Lord (ed.), *Between Two Worlds*, p.338.
8 *Pall Mall Gazette*, 23.1.1922, p.11.
9 *Pall Mall Gazette*, 28.1.1922, p.5.
10 *Pall Mall Gazette*, 3.2.1922, p.7.
11 *Common Cause*, 19.1.1922, p.7.
12 *Pall Mall Gazette*, 9.2.1922, p.6.
13 *Pall Mall Gazette*, 9.2.1922, p.11.
14 *Pall Mall Gazette*, 18.2.1922, p.7.
15 *Yorkshire Post*, 7.2.1922, p.6.
16 *Westminster Gazette*, 8.2.1922, p.1.
17 *Sheffield Daily Telegraph*, 8.2.1922, p.3.
18 *Western Mail*, 8.2.1922, p.5.
19 *Western Mail*, 27.2.1922, p.8.
20 *Belfast Telegraph*, 1.3.1921, p.8.
21 *Belfast News-Letter*, 2.3.1922, p.5.
22 *Western Mail*, 22.2.1922, p.7.
23 *Pall Mall Gazette*, 1.3.1922, p.12.
24 *Taunton Courier*, 8.3.1922, p.1.
25 *Irish Society (Dublin)*, 25.3.1922, p16.
26 *Daily Telegraph*, 14.3.1922.
27 *Pall Mall Gazette*, 10.3.1922, p.5.

28   *Westminster Gazette*, 14.3.1921, p.1.
29   *Gloucester Citizen*, 16.3.1922, p.3.
30   *Western Mail*, 21.3.1922, p.5.
31   *Shields Daily News*, 30.3.1922, p.5.
32   *Shields Daily News*, 24.3.1922, p.3..
33   *Western Mail*, 25.3.1922, p.7.
34   *Nottingham Evening Post*, 5.4.1922, p.5; *Derby Daily Telegraph*, 3.4.1922, p.2.
35   *Derby Daily Telegraph*, 3.4.1922, p.3.
36   *Western Daily Press*, 7.4.1922, p.5.
37   *Dundee Evening Telegraph*, 3.4.1922, p.6.
38   Ffion Hague, *The Pain and the Privilege*, pp.397–9, citing A. J. Sylvester.
39   *Daily Telegraph*, 4.5.1922.
40   Ffion Hague, *The Pain and the Privilege*, p.398.
41   *Daily Telegraph*, 9.5.1922.
42   Thelma Cazalet, *From the Wings* (Bodley Head, 1967), p.48.
43   *Daily Telegraph*, 4.5.1922.
44   *Hartlepool Northern Daily Mail*, 19.4.1922, p.1.
45   *Western Morning News*, 20.5.1922, p.4.
46   *Western Mail*, 22.5.1922, p.6.
47   *Western Mail*, 24.5.1922, p.7.
48   *Western Mail*, 27.5.1922, p.6.
49   *Pall Mall Gazette*, 31.5.1922, p.12.
50   *Yorkshire Post*, 5.6.1922, p.8.
51   Ibid.
52   *Western Times*, 13.6.1922, p.3.
53   *Yorkshire Post*, 17.6.1922, p.20.
54   *West Middlesex Gazette*, 17.6.1922, p.5.
55   *Westminster Gazette*, 17.6.1922, p.7.
56   *Pall Mall Gazette*, 16.6.1922, p.5.
57   *Pall Mall Gazette*, 22.6.1922, p.11.
58   *Sheffield Daily Telegraph*, 27.6.1922, p.7.
59   *Western Morning News*, 28.6.1922, p.4.
60   *Pall Mall Gazette*, 29.6.1922, p.11.
61   *Westminster Gazette*, 29.6.1922, p.7.
62   *Yorkshire Post*, 29.6.1922, p.6.
63   Fred Dimbleby to Charles McCurdy, 30.6.1922, Col. Scovell Collection, David Lloyd George (Coalition Organisation Papers), NLW.
64   *Western Daily Press*, 1.7.1922, p.4.
65   Laurie Notaro, *Crossing the Horizon*, (New York, Gallery Books, 2016).

## Chapter 17: The West Country Tour

1    Page 1 (the first 2–3 lines) from NLW MS 3045; the remainder from NLW MS 3023.
2    Col. Scovell to Charles McCurdy, 3.5.1922, Col. Scovell Collection, David Lloyd George (Coalition Organisation Papers), NLW.

3   *Western Daily Press*, 11.7.1922, pp.6–7.
4   Ibid. Her West Country speech notes are also in Lloyd George Papers MS 20472c, MS 3019 and MS 3045.3, NLW.
5   Mrs Lloyd George to Olwen Carey Evans. Letter, MS 3095i, NLW.
6   *Western Morning News and Mercury*, 12.7.1922, p.3.
7   *Western Times*, 12.7.1922, p.4.
8   *Western Morning News and Mercury*, 12.7.1922, p.3.
9   *Cornishman and Cornish Telegraph*, 7.9.1921, p.4.
10  *Western Morning News and Mercury*, 13.7.1922, p.3.
11  *Cornishman and Cornish Telegraph*, 12.7.1922, p.4.
12  Winifred Coombe Tennant, *Between two worlds, 1909–1924*, p.363.
13  Col. Scovell to Charles McCurdy, 26.7.1922, Col. Scovell Collection, David Lloyd George (Coalition Organisation Papers), NLW.
14  *Cornishman and Cornish Telegraph*, 26.7.1922, p.7.
15  *Cornishman and Cornish Telegraph*, 23.8.1922, p.7.
16  *Western Morning News and Mercury*, 23.8.1922, p.7.
17  *Cornubian and Redruth Times*, 24.8.1922, p.2.
18  For a recent review on the subject see Korikazu Kudo, 'Tin Mining in Cornwall 1918–38', *Keio Business Review* No. 50 (2015), p.25 (1)-53(29), Keio University Society of Business and Commerce, available online.
19  *Oxfordshire Weekly News*, 26.7.1922, p.7.

## Chapter 18: The Secret Missioner

1   *Daily Herald*, 7.7.1922, p.1.
2   JTR MLG SP33 JTR Report on the Meetings with Members of the Free Church Councils, Rev. J. T. Rhys (Margaret Lloyd George) Papers, NLW.

## Chapter 19: The Last 100 Days

1   *Sheffield Daily Telegraph*, 19.7.1922, p.7.
2   *Sheffield Daily Telegraph*, 19.7.1922, p.6.
3   *Western Mail*, 20.7.1922, p.7.
4   *Daily Echo, Northampton*, 24.7.1922, p.3.
5   *Yorkshire Post*, 24.7.1922, p.8.
6   *Pall Mall Gazette*, 24.7.1922, p.4.
7   *Western Mail*, 29.7.1922, p.8.
8   John King, 'Dessouter, André Marcel', *Oxford Dictionary of National Biography* (OUP, update May 2008). Sir John Lynn-Thomas to JTR, 17.12.1921. Letter OJTR5, JTR Collection.
9   *Yorkshire Post*, 7.8.1922, p.9.
10  *The Scotsman*, 9.8.1922, p.6.
11  *Western Mail*, 10.8.1922, p.6.
12  *Shields Daily News*, 1.9.1922, p.4.
13  *Western Mail*, 8.9.1922, p.10.
14  *The Scotsman*, 15.9.1922, p.8.
15  *Chelmsford Chronicle*, 1.9.1922, p.8.
16  *Sheffield Daily Telegraph*, 15.9.1922, p.4.

17    *Illustrated London News*, 16.9.1922, p.26.
18    *Western Mail*, 18.9.1922, p.6.
19    *Pall Mall Gazette*, 23.9.1922, p.7.
20    John Snelson, 'Novello, Ivor (David Ivor Davies)', *Oxford Dictionary of National Biography* (OUP, 2011).
21    *Liverpool Echo*, 28.9.1922, p.7.
22    *Western Mail*, 28.9.1922, p.7.
23    *Western Mail*, 6.10.1922, p.10.
24    *Western Gazette*, 6.10.1922, p.12.
25    *Aberdeen Press and Journal*, 6.10.1922, p.4.
26    *Sheffield Daily Telegraph*, 12.10.1922, p.6.
27    *Chelmsford Chronicle*, 13.10.1922, p.8.
28    *Buckinghamshire Examiner*, 20.10.1922, p.4
29    *North Wales Weekly News*, 19.10.1922, p.4.
30    *Surrey Mirror and County Post*, 20.10.1922 p5.
31    *Northern Whig*, 20.10.1922, p.5.
32    *Daily Telegraph*, 20.10.1922.
33    *Evening Standard*, 21.10.1922.

## Chapter 20: Departure from Downing Street

1     Interview with Edith Shackleton, for the *Daily Sketch*, 20.10.1922.
2     *Sheffield Daily Telegraph*, 26.10.1922, p.6.
3     *Dundee Evening Telegraph*, 26.10.1922, p.2.
4     *Western Mail*, 31.10.1922, p.9.
5     *Sheffield Daily Telegraph*, 2.11.1922, p.6.
6     *Western Mail*, 4.11.1922, p.7.
7     *Bedfordshire Times and Independent*, 3.11.1922, p.8.
8     *The Scotsman*, 6.11.1922, p.7.
9     *Western Mail*, 6.11.1922, p.6.
10    *The Richmond and Twickenham Times*, 9.7.1938.
11    *Sheffield Daily Telegraph*, 1.11.1922, p.4.
12    *Bath Chronicle*, 4.11.1922, p.15.
13    *Sheffield Independent*, 6.11.1922, p.1.
14    *Western Mail*, 6.11.1922, p.7.
15    *Linlithgowshire Gazette*, 10.11.1922, p.5.
16    *North Wales Weekly News*, 2.11.1922, p.6.
17    *Western Mail*, 10.11.1922, p.9.
18    *Western Mail*, 11.11.1922, p.8.
19    *Western Daily Press*, 10.11.1922, p.7.
20    *Western Mail*, 11.11.1922, p.8.
21    *Western Mail*, 13.11.1922, p.9.
22    *Hendon & Finchley Times*, 17.11.1922, p.10.
23    *Belfast Telegraph*, 23.11.1922, p.4.
24    *Western Evening Herald*, 24.11.1922, p.3.
25    *Western Mail*, 25.11.1922, p.8.
26    *Western Mail*, 25.11.1922, p.10.
27    *Sheffield Daily Telegraph*, 7.12.1922, p.6.
28    *Norwood News*, 15.12.1922, p.3.

29  *Sheffield Daily Telegraph*, 20.12.1922, p.6.
30  *Belfast News-Letter*, 22.12.1922, p.5.
31  *Hull Daily Mail*, 11.12.1922, p.6.
32  Isabel Law to Mrs Lloyd George. Letter 7, JTR Private Collection.
33  *Sheffield Daily Telegraph*, 27.1.1921, p.4.
34  Keith Middlemas (ed.), *Thomas Jones: Whitehall Diary, Vol. 1, 1916–1925* (OUP, 1969), p.277. Mrs Lloyd George to Olwen Carey Evans, NLW MS 3115i, NLW.

## Chapter 21: An Insider's View

1  JTR to Margaret Rhys, 24.10.1922, JTR Private Collection.
2  *Western Mail*, 7.11.1923, p.6.
3  *Western Mail*, 25.10.1923, p.8.
4  JTR Lantern Lecture Notes, JTR Private Collection.

## Postscript

1  JTR Notes.
2  Ernest Evans, 'Homely Chatelaine of 10, Downing Street: powerful influence of the ex Premier's Wife'. *Daily Mirror*, 27.10.1922, p.8.

# Bibliography

## Documents and Archives
### National Library of Wales (NLW)

Lloyd George papers; with thanks to the National Library of Wales and the Lloyd George family.

The Rev. J. T. Rhys (Margaret Lloyd George) Papers, copied from the JTR Private Collection. With thanks to the Lloyd George family.

Margaret Lloyd George: 'What it means to be the wife of the Prime Minister of England', Sixth Instalment, 20472C LG Papers 1, published in *Sunday News*, 4.9.1927, Document 3044; from Papers of Lady Olwen Carey Evans 84; Margaret Lloyd George, interview, 'How do you help your husband?', typed draft, A. J. Sylvester Papers, AJS C25; 'Petticoats behind Politics', Dame Margaret Lloyd George DBE, JP, typescript for release in the *Sunday Herald*, June 12th, 1927 Welsh Newspapers Online; and the *Welsh Gazette*.

### Other Archives

Online: British Newspaper Archive; *The Manchester Guardian* and *Observer*.

The British Library: *The Times, Daily Telegraph, Welsh Gazette, Daily Sketch, Daily Mail*.

The JTR Private Collection.

### Books

John Campbell, *If Love Were All, The Story of Frances Stevenson and David Lloyd George* (Jonathan Cape, London, 2006).

Olwen Carey Evans, *Lloyd George Was My Father* (Gomer Press, 1985).

Thelma Cazalet-Keir, *From the Wings* (Bodley Head, London, 1967).

Sir Alfred T. Davies KBE, CB, *The Lloyd George I Knew* (Henry E. Walter, London, 1948).

Viscount Gwynedd, *Dame Margaret, The Life Story of His Mother* (George Allen & Unwin, London, 1947).

Ffion Hague, *The Pain and the Privilege, The Women Who Loved Lloyd George* (Harper Perennial, London, 2008).

Glenys Harrison, *Sir John T Davies, PPS to Lloyd George* (South Books, Cheltenham, 2020).

J. Graham Jones, *David Lloyd George and Welsh Liberalism* (The Welsh Political Archive, NLW, 2010).

J. Graham Jones, 'Dame Margaret in Cardiganshire', *Ceredigion, Journal of the Cardiganshire Historical Society*, 2004 (Vol XIV, No 4).

J. Graham Jones, *Lloyd George papers at the National Library of Wales and Other Repositories* (NLW, Aberystwyth, 2001).

J. Graham Jones, 'Every Vote for Llewelyn Williams is a vote against Lloyd George', Chapter 14. *David Lloyd George and Welsh Liberalism*, p.232, *Welsh Political Archive*, NLW 2010, first appearing in the *Journal of Liberal Democratic History*, 37 (Winter 2002–3).

Mervyn Jones, *A Radical Life, The Biography of Megan Lloyd George* (Hutchinson, London, 1991).

Charles T. King, *The Asquith Parliament (1906–1909)* (Hutchinson, London, 1910).

Peter Lord (ed.) *Between Two Worlds: The Diary of Winifred Coombe Tennant, 1909–1924* (NLW, Aberystwyth, 2011).

Jen Llywelyn, *Pilgrim of Peace: a Life of George M. Ll. Davies* (Y Lolfa, 2016).

John M. McEwen (ed.), *The Riddell Diaries: A Selection, 1908-1923* (Athlone Press, 1986).

Keith Middlemas (ed.), *Thomas Jones, Whitehall Diary*, Vol. 1, 1916–1925 (Oxford University Press, 1969), p.277.

Kenneth O. Morgan (ed.), *Lloyd George, Family Letters 1885–*

*1936* (University of Wales Press, Cardiff, Oxford University Press, London 1973).

Richard Rhys O'Brien, Translation/Cyfiethiad Yvonne Davies, *A Lampeter Family Story / Hanes Teulu O Llambed 1870–1971* (Lampeter Museum, 2019).

Richard Rhys O'Brien, *Mrs Lloyd George Goes to Lampeter* (Lampeter Museum, June 2019).

Richard Rhys O'Brien, 'Margaret Lloyd George, Opening Up New Opportunities in 1919 / Yn Agor Cyfleon Newydd yn 1919', *Memories of Menai Bridge*, Volume 16 / *Atgofion Porthaethwy*, Cyfrol 17 (Menai Bridge and District Civic Society / Cymdeithas Ddinesig Bro Porthaethwy 2019).

Richard O'Brien, 'Mrs Lloyd George and the first Women Students at the Royal School of Dentists, 1916 to 1926', *Dental Historian*, Vol. 65 (1), January 2020.

Richard O'Brien, 'The Missing Mahogany WW1 Memorial, Mrs Lloyd George and the Royal Dental Hospital Twenty-Nine', *Dental Historian*, Vol. 67 (2), July 2022.

A. J. P. Taylor (ed.), *Lloyd George, A Diary by Frances Stevenson* (Hutchinson, London, 1971).

\* \* \*

Place names have generally been given their modern Welsh spelling, except in the quoted newspaper extracts, speeches and correspondence, where the original spelling, and other conventions, e.g. Downing-street, have been retained.

Newspaper titles (which change over time) are given as of the date quoted, albeit omitting subtitles which some papers added as a result of acquisitions.

# Index

After a career as an international economist, scenario planner and strategist, Richard has turned to storytelling through songs and biographical studies. He has written and edited more than a dozen books, including *The End of Geography*, released six albums, and an online study, *The Dinner Puzzle*, on Lady Margaret Rhondda and the pioneering women of the 1930s. He is the grandson of the Rev. J.T. Rhys, the private secretary of Margaret Lloyd George.